THE MEEK AND

THE MEEK
AND THE MIGHTY

*The Emergence of the Evangelical
Movement in Russia*

Hans Brandenburg

MOWBRAYS
LONDON & OXFORD

ISBN 0 264 66349 7

First published in 1976
by A. R. Mowbray & Co. Ltd.
The Alden Press, Osney Mead,
Oxford, OX2 0EG

KESTON BOOK NO. 7

Text set in 12-13 pt Monotype Bembo by Cotswold Typesetting Ltd., Gloucester
and printed in Great Britain by
Lowe & Brydone Printers Limited, Thetford, Norfolk

Contents

Preface

I once made a note of the following statements at a missionary conference:

'The contradiction between Jesus and the world is always bloody.'

'Suffering is necessary because the conflict between the world and the Christian community cannot be softened.'

'Suffering is testimomy to Jesus.'

'I go so far as to say that the decisive thing is not for us to pray: "Take this suffering away from the brethren!" Rather we need to say: "Increase their powers of endurance beneath the sufferings which you lay upon them!" '

'Many believed not in spite of, but because of persecution.'

I heard these words at a Bible conference where Hans Brandenburg was expounding the word of God. Russian labour camps, locked churches and those grave documents now reaching us from the Soviet Union, suddenly withdrew into the background. We were confronted by the exciting fact that Christians really have cause to open their mouths. In fact it is the words they speak that cause this commotion. If Jesus, who was dead, now lives – then new values come into operation.

We recognized the danger of misunderstanding the quiet path of suffering in the registered congregations in Russia and of crudely misinterpreting it simply because they do not shout their suffering from the housetops, because they only use open doors and tell others what Jesus is doing today.

This kind of approach has a long tradition among the Evangelical Christians in Russia. Hatred from the world in a history going back more than a hundred years ensured that a dedicated readiness for suffering became second nature. And yet quietly, in the shadow of power, people still talked of Jesus in such a way that the community of the faithful grew and spread, even though world christendom passed by without heed.

At that missionary conference we took note that we must make a much deeper study of Stundism.* Only by looking at their heritage can we rightly understand current events in the evangelical churches of Russia. This led to an urgent request to Hans Brandenburg to undertake this task. More than fifty years of vital co-operation in the mission group *Licht im Osten* together with many years as its chairman and overseer have knit him closely to many Russian Christians and their path of testimony to Jesus.

I hope that many people will get to know something of how God is working in Russia, as I did some years ago when Hans Brandenburg kindled that interest in me.

WINRICH SCHEFFBUCH

---

* 'Stundism' is a term relating to the beginnings of the evangelical movement in Russia. Its significance will become clear as the book develops – tr.

THE RUSSIAN TSARS:

Peter (I) the Great	(1672)	1682–1725
Catherine I	(1684)	1725–1727
Peter II	(1715)	1727–1730
Anna	(1693)	1730–1740
Ivan VI	(1740)	1740–1741
Elizabeth	(1709)	1741–1762
Peter III	(1728)	1762
Catherine II	(1729)	1762–1796
Paul I	(1754)	1796–1801
Alexander I	(1777)	1801–1825
Nicholas I	(1796)	1825–1855
Alexander II	(1818)	1855–1881
Alexander III	(1845)	1881–1894
Nicholas II	(1868)	1894–1917

Introduction

by Michael Bourdeaux

Every new movement of the Spirit of God is untidy to the human mind. It breaks down barriers of all kinds – intellectual, class, denominational. This truth can be seen over and over again in church history, and it is powerfully in evidence again today. The fact that most movements of the Spirit were then trapped in different structures, hedged about with fresh barriers, and encased in new denominations, has been the sad parallel. There are hopeful signs that this is less true today.

The evangelical revival in Russia in the second half of the last century had this non-denominational character. This was also true of earlier movements, linked with names like Golitsyn and Gossner. The author traces elements of the Russian revival far back into church history. The Hussite movement, which pre-dated the Protestant Reformation, became the 'Unity of the Brethren', which is still a major church body in modern Czecho-slovakia. The rich concepts of the Unity of the Brethren were adapted by subsequent revival movements.

The community at Herrnhut (now in East Germany), estab-lished by the Moravian Brethren, and its daughter communities used the name *Brüdergemeine*, which may be loosely translated fellowship or gathering of brethren. The emphasis here is on 'brethren'. This was no strict denominational structure. Rather, it was a gathering of brethren in the faith, who sought to express their common life in Christ in a practical way. Count Zinzendorf of Herrnhut, a fascinating and surprisingly little-known figure in the English-speaking world, used to have fellowship with Catholics as well as Protestants.

Later revival groups within the German state Churches adopted the name *Brüdergemeinde*, which may be translated community or congregation of brethren. The concept is much the same as that of Herrnhut, or even of the original Unity of the Brethren. From

Germany, sparks of revival flew to Russia – so the chain continues.

A characteristic feature of the revival in the Swabian state Church was the *Stunde*, literally 'hour'. This was a gathering for bible study and edification. It was then practised by German settlers in the Ukraine, who were touched by revival through the ministry of Johannes Bonekemper. From there it spread to Ukrainian and Russian neighbours. Hence the designation 'stundism', which the Russian authorities applied to the new movement.

Of the three streams which went to make up the Russian evangelical movement: stundist, Baptist and Evangelical Christian (the latter linked with the name of the Englishman Lord Radstock), only the Baptists had from the beginning a definite denominational character. At first the stundists hoped to remain within the Orthodox Church. This hope was cruelly shattered. Later they joined themselves to the Baptists. The Evangelical Christians were noted for their extreme openness, as exemplified in the genial personality of Ivan Prokhanov. It was only later that the evangelical movement as a whole took on the aspect of a new denomination.

The author of this book was himself born in Russia of German parents. Thus he has a first-hand acquaintance with his subject. He also has a long-standing close connection with the German mission society 'Licht im Osten' (Light in the East). This mission is based in Korntal, a village outside Stuttgart, which itself has an interesting confessional history, and whose name occurs in the book. The mission too finds a place in these pages. It was established just after the First World War, and played a significant role in events at that time.

In a brief final section the author looks at the contemporary evangelical scene in Russia, marked by a split in the movement which has persisted now since the early 1960's. Some might query his numerical assessments here. But his judgments are unquestionably balanced and charitable. In fact, the situation is much too complex to permit tidy reduction to facts and figures. Some further reading on the modern period is suggested at the end of the book.

This book offers a rewarding and personalized glimpse into the history of the Russian evangelical movement. It breaks much new ground for the English-speaking reader. Through these pages move many fascinating personalities – one could wish for a closer acquaintance with a number of them (Gossner, Prokhanov, Martsinkovsky and others). I trust that this book will stimulate many readers to further study. It will certainly deepen their understanding of the Soviet scene immeasurably. Let understanding bring with it compassion and the desire to relate at a much deeper level.

A. In the Beginning

A CHURCH STATE OR A STATE CHURCH?

Those who wish to understand church history in Russia and the Ukraine must first try to forget images from church history in the west. The Church in Eastern Europe inherited its traditions from Byzantium. While the west saw the development of the church state as a political power, and the Bishop of Rome, the Pope, held political sovereignty, in the east there arose the state church. The eastern Church did not know the struggles between pope and emperor, between Church and empire, which characterized the Middle Ages. The court theologians of the east could weave their webs of intrigue, but they remained subject to the emperor.

The eastern Church is very conscious of its name, Orthodox – those with right doctrine. With the great Ecumenical Councils the doctrine of the Church was unalterably established. From that time on the Byzantine Church through its patriarchs and bishops kept careful watch lest anything new or strange be introduced into the Church. The Pope in Rome, in contrast, has authority over church doctrine and even today has the power to announce new dogmas such as the doctrine of the bodily assumption of the Virgin Mary.

The eastern Church is uniquely a liturgical Church. It is not the sermon or the bible which stands at the centre of divine worship, but the celebration of the liturgy. Through the liturgy the Church presents the salvation story to the senses of the worshippers. There are historical reasons for this. The Russian Church is heir to the spiritual life of Greece. Its liturgical service, even its church interior betrays its relationship to Greek drama. Indeed pious Russians describe their liturgy, without any irreverence, as the 'drama of salvation'. In fact, the theatre in ancient Greece was not a place of amusement, but a place of worship.

I

As in the ancient Greek theatre, the church interior is empty. It is closed off by a high partition through which emerge the priest and deacon, like the players in a Greek tragedy. Each liturgy is the presentation of a spiritual drama. There is a dialogue between priest and deacon. And as in ancient Hellas, there must also be a chorus.

The content of the liturgy is the salvation story in Old and New Testaments. On Saturday evening it is the salvation story in the Old Testament; on Sunday there is a liturgy lasting several hours, devoted to the coming and the work of Jesus, the new covenant. It is essential to understand the symbolism of the actions involved here. When the deacon carries a burning light, this represents the coming of the light of the world. On Good Friday a bier is carried through the empty church. The covering, embroidered with a cross (the so-called *plashchanitsa*), symbolizes the body of Jesus. Weeping, the worshippers kiss the tassels of the covering. Whereas the altar usually remains hidden to the congregation behind the closed middle doors of the partition, on Easter night these so-called royal doors are opened, the illuminated altar is visible, and the priest steps on to the threshold repeating the words of the angels: 'Christ is risen' (*Khristos voskrese*). Joyfully the congregation replies: 'He is risen indeed' (*Vo istinu voskrese*).

The west has little comprehension for this dramatic form of Sunday worship. When a Roman bishop in the tenth century experienced the liturgy in St. Sophia, he commented critically that the service resembled a mystery play.

The Greek desires a visual presentation of the truth of God. In this way the 'orthodox' eastern Church stands in complete contrast to the rational approach of the west. Thus they reproach Protestantism, which places the sermon in the central position, with the words: 'You are rationalists. You want to have everything explained. You have no awe before the secret things of God.' These secrets, they say, cannot be grasped by reflection, but only through the five senses, to which they are presented in symbolic form: in the icons on the icon wall – the iconostasis, and in the magnificent priestly robes; in the wonderful singing of the priest and the choir; in the rich smoke of the incense and in the cross held out by the priest. In kissing the cross, the worshipper feels the presence of God.

This is eastern piety. Its worship is the *theatron pneumatikon*, the theatre of the spirit, as one of the Church Fathers called the liturgy.

Another way to approach the secret things of God is through prayer. A Latvian teacher once converted from Lutheranism to Orthodoxy on the grounds that in the Lutheran Church there was a lot of preaching and not much prayer, while in the Orthodox Church there was not much preaching but plenty of prayer, and prayer was more important than preaching! Neither of these reproaches is fair to the real aims of the Reformation. Here too, prayer is a work of faith (thus even here justification by works may creep in). That is why saving faith eludes most people.

For centuries nothing changed in the Orthodox service. There were schisms, but they were rejected by the Church. The numerous Russian sects, to which we shall return, were persecuted by the state. There were theological trends and schools of thought, but their influence was solely upon forms of piety. Thus the history of the eastern Church becomes a history of its devotional life.

That is why up to the time of the forceful Peter the Great, who did not spare the Church and actually imposed a new leadership upon it, the church history of the east is so poor in events, while that of the west is so rich. At the same time the eastern Church took an involuntary part in the manifold political events of the time, since to be a member of the Church is to be a member of the people. A man who is unfaithful to the Church is also unfaithful to his nation. That is why the history of the Russian Church is at the same time the history of the Ukrainian and Russian people. A knowledge of this history, at least in outline, is thus necessary for an understanding of Russian stundism.

RUSSIA BEGINS IN THE UKRAINE

Nationally and linguistically, Russia finds its origins in the Ukraine. The birthplace of the Church as far as the Ukraine is

In the Beginning

concerned is Kiev on the Dniepr, the old capital. The Great Russian kingdom of Muscovy arose centuries later at the time of the Mongol supremacy, after Kiev had been completely laid waste by the Mongols in 1240. That was when the eastern slav tribes began to migrate northwards, where over the next few centuries Moscow grew into the new political and cultural centre. Thus the contemporary Russian language developed as the Slavs moving northwards mingled with the Finno-Ugrian tribes who populated the northern forests. There was also the influence of the Mongols who brought many foreign words into the Russian language, as well as exercising an alien spiritual influence upon the people.

Vladimir (in Ukrainian Volodimir) of Kiev, a prince of Norman descent from the Varangian tribe, ruled from 980–1015 in Kiev. The history of the Russian Church begins with his name. He married a Byzantine princess and in 988/89 he introduced Byzantine Christianity among the slavic tribes whom he had conquered. The whole population was forcibly baptized in the Dniepr.

For several centuries there had been Greek settlements on the north shore of the Black Sea, with which the Slavs had trading links. This development is therefore not a surprising one. The later Chronicle of Nestor (1116) tells that Vladimir also traded with the Muslims, with the Khazars who had turned to Judaism, and with Rome. This trade was hindered in the one case by the ban on wine and in the other by the ban on pork. Neither did Vladimir wish to be subject to the Pope. But when his ambassadors returned from Byzantium-Constantinople, they told him enthusiastic stories about St. Sophia, the cathedral of Justinian the Great, and the service there – 'We thought we were in heaven!' It is said that Vladimir made his decision on this basis.

However legendary this tradition may be, like all legends it has certain parallels in reality. To experience the liturgy as a foretaste of heaven – this is the east! During the terrors of the Mongol era (1237–1590) people found refuge in worship. Here too the serf was later to find calm and peace of soul. However cruelly the Mongols may have treated the people, they never touched the churches and monasteries, and sacrilege bore the death penalty.

Despite this link with the culture of Byzantium, the emerging princedom of Kiev remained in contact with the west. It is true that the Bulgarian alphabet of the Greek monk Cyril (d. 869) was introduced through the Church and that the first bishops and metropolitans were Greeks, but beyond this there does not seem to have been any further Greek influence.

On the other hand, with the founding of the Monastery of the Caves in Kiev (1051) there arose an independent form of monasticism. Although over the centuries there were undoubtedly many abuses, it is impossible to assess the pastoral influence of Russian monasticism on the people too highly. It was the monks who evangelized the people, including the Finnish tribes in the north. They acted as pastors to the people and often had a greater influence on them than the bishops and other spiritual dignitaries, with whom they subsequently even came into occasional conflict. They stood for a doctrine of sanctification which found its highest expression in asceticism. This is still the approach of the pious Orthodox today. Since the Church barely taught sanctification in everyday life, devout churchmanship on the part of the 'laity' often went together with a looseness in secular living. For this reason it is difficult to accuse them of hypocrisy.

Kiev experienced its golden age in culture and therefore also in church life under Prince Yaroslav the Wise (d. 1054). Yaroslav's eldest daughter married Harold of Sweden and his second Henry I of France. It was in his reign that a Russian first occupied the seat of metropolitan.

However in the year that Yaroslav died, the Patriarch of Constantinople, Michael Kerullarios – a member of the imperial family who had been forced to become a monk through a conspiracy – executed the schism with the west by obstructing the recognition of Rome. Mutual excommunication sealed the split between Rome and Byzantium, to which Kiev was subject.

Immediately after Yaroslav's death, the princedom was weakened by interminable internecine struggles. The Mongol invasion in the thirteenth century spelt the final conclusion to this promising new culture. The Mongol yoke lasted about 350 years.

Although this domination had little significance in its final hundred years, now for the first time an iron curtain divided the east from the west. The east now moved towards a national Church, which in turn gave rise to a national Christian culture and learning.

IN THE DEPTHS

The long subjection of the Russian tribes to the Mongols had the most serious consequences both in political and in church life. There is some truth in the Russian claim that they have suffered in a substitutionary way for the whole of West Europe.

The Mongols did not only subjugate the people and violently intermingle with them, unfortunately they also affected their customs and morals. The terrible curses which are often heard in the east and which are difficult to translate are of Mongol origin. Under these influences, the otherwise kindly Russian acquired a tendency to cruelty. But while the people were enslaved and the princes had to curry favour with the Great Khan of Astrakhan, since they only held their lands as feudal tenures from his hand, the Church remained free, even from taxation. While life outside often resembled hell, there was refuge in the churches and monasteries. Sixty years ago people in Moscow still remembered the 'Virgins' Field' (*deviche pole*) which took its name from the Mongol times. Year by year, thousands of young Russian girls were herded together here, to disappear into the Mongol harems. Outside was hell, but in the churches it was 'like heaven'.

Meanwhile Kiev had been destroyed (1240). Moscow began to emerge as a new focal point. In the struggle for self-preservation over against the Mongol conquerors and against Byzantium, Church and state entered into a close alliance. On the other hand, they became more and more isolated from the west. But like individuals, so too nations are formed by God to need each other; isolation leads to peculiarities. The consequences were both good and bad. On the good side was the preservation of originality, but there was lacking the intellectual dialogue with the west which would have prevented a certain stagnation. However, the long time of troubles brought a deepening of religious faith.

Many saw these events as a judgment of God. Countless hermits made their way into the impenetrable forests of the north. New hermitages and monasteries were built, and the people sought consolation from the men of God.

The outstanding name among these holy men is that of St. Sergius of Radonezh (d. 1392). He founded the Trinity Monastery, the so-called *Troitse-Sergieva Lavra* at Zagorsk near Moscow. This monastery became a centre for spiritual revival, not to say national resistance. The people never forgot Sergius' warmhearted pastoral care in the most difficult times.

One of Sergius' contemporaries was Stephen, Bishop of Perm. He was a missionary in the north among the Finno-Ugrian Syryan people. Today they are called 'Komi' after their language, and they form a separate Soviet republic.

MOSCOW – HEIR OF CONSTANTINOPLE

Since Constantinople had fallen to the Turks in 1453, the Orthodox Church of Russia had lost its stay – however weak that may have been – in Byzantium. Church power was now concentrated around Moscow and its prince. The Russian metropolitan had already been resident in Moscow since 1328. In 1589 he took the title of patriarch and from this century onwards people began to speak of Moscow as the third and last Rome. Constantinople had represented the second.

There was a narrow door to the west through the cities of Novgorod and Pskov. These had strong trading links with the Hanse which had a trading office in Novgorod, as in London. In the Middle Ages heretical movements penetrated through this door, such as the *strigolniki* and a judaising sect. However both of these were extinguished.

A momentous controversy arose within monasticism over the matter of fighting heretics. It was carried on by two men, who represented two aspects of Orthodox piety. On the one hand was the strict and rigorous Joseph of Volokolamsk (d. 1515), who had founded a monastery near Volokolamsk in the Moscow region. He stood for the national state Church; this attitude still determined church policy in the nineteenth century. According to this point of view, heretics were to be executed. Because the tsar (this was the Russian title from 1547) was appointed by God himself, he had divine power and must rule strictly. Likewise Orthodoxy must be preserved even by the use of force. People must hold fast to the traditions and writings of the Fathers, which are considered of equal inspiration to the Bible. State and Church belong closely together. The rich possessions of the monasteries, which grew steadily until the time of Peter the Great, were to be preserved and were to serve not merely charity, but also power. Characteristic of Joseph is his statement: 'A man's own opinion is the mother of all passions. Man's own opinion is the second fall.' The fact that Joseph laid great stress on church customs and ceremonies fits well with this portrait of an enthusiast.

The monks in the south, in the Volga region, led by Nil Sorsky (d. 1508), came to quite different conclusions. Nil Sorsky was the abbott of a monastery by the Sora River, a tributary of the Volga. The Volga monks based themselves upon the New Testament, against which all other writings were measured, and according to which they desired to live. Nil stood for the separation of Church and state and for the Church's complete independence. Pastoral gentleness and prayer were the most important things in the struggle against the heretics. Instead of acquiring rich lands, the monasteries should live an exemplary life of poverty and maintain themselves through the labour of the monks. Nil also resisted the many new canonizations of saints and stood for a certain freedom of thought. Freedom and love were more important than outward ceremonies.

The camp of Joseph prevailed, and this point of view characterized the Russian state Church until its collapse in the Bolshevik Revolution. The absolutist state found its most important ally in this Church. Three-hundred and fifty years later, at the time of the autocratic Tsar Nicholas I (d. 1855), one of his ministers of culture was able to say: 'Autocracy, nationalism and Orthodoxy are the stays of the Russian empire.' It was with these principles that tsarist Russia fell.

But even though Nil Sorsky was defeated, his inner piety lived on among monks, priests and lay people. It comes out in the *startsy* (elders), like the *starets* Zosima in Dostoyevsky's novel *The Brothers Karamazov*, and in the 'quiet ones in the land' of whom the much-travelled writer Leskov spoke.

From this inner split came the two faces of Russian Orthodoxy: on the one hand the autocratic state Church, on the other many zealous followers of Jesus. The opinion formed by neighbours and travellers depends on which face they encounter.

THE LEGACY OF YAROSLAV
THE CHURCH IN THE UKRAINE

Through the marriage of the Lithuanian prince Jagello with the Polish heiress to the throne, Jadwiga, in 1386, there had arisen next to the Ukraine a Great Polish kingdom which Jagello now ruled under the Polish name Wladislaw. This Great Poland under the Jagellonians stretched 'from sea to sea', that is from the Baltic to the Black Sea. In this way large areas of the Ukraine such as Galicia, Podolia, Volhynia, Smolensk, Vitebsk, Minsk, Kiev and others came under the control of the Roman Catholic Polish kingdom. The systematic catholicization of these lands led to sharp struggles. A large part of the nobility converted to Catholicism, but the rural population resisted.

This link with Poland now gave the Ukraine too a cultural window on the west, long before that of Peter the Great when he founded his new imperial capital, St. Petersburg, on the swamps of the Neva estuary.

Poland tried to win Orthodoxy over to a union with Rome (1596). This only had a small success. The history of this church union, with its marked political roots, had a tragic course. It was furthered or opposed by governments according to whether they were Catholic or Orthodox. Poland and Austria reinforced the union, the tsars were against it, and in the end it was dissolved by the Bolsheviks. At any rate, this episode awakened in the Ukrainians an inner disposition towards confessional change.

It was here in the Ukraine that stundism later arose among a people who, in the course of the centuries, had grown away from the static nature of their confession and into dynamic movement.

After the battle of the Ugra River (1480) the Western Ukraine, which had barely been affected by the Mongol yoke, was virtually liberated, although for the next hundred years there was still a formal dependence on the Mongol east. The 'Golden Horde', which had had its centre at Astrakhan on the Caspian Sea, decayed through internal struggles. Only a few khanates remained on the Volga (Kazan) and in the Crimea. Ivan IV (1533–84), called 'the Terrible', conquered Kazan in 1552 and through his conquests felt himself justified in turning the title of prince in 1547 into that of tsar. He too saw himself as heir to Byzantium and since the prince had now become tsar and the metropolitan patriarch (1589), Moscow grew steadily as the centre of power.

However, the Rurik dynasty died out with Ivan's son (1598) and the 'time of troubles' began. Usurpers with Polish support carried on fierce struggles lasting decades, which plunged the country into great misery. In times like these, leading church figures acquire influence. Such a man was Patriarch Yermogen, and he was largely responsible for the ending of the troubled times. The *Troitse-Sergieva Lavra*, the monastery at Zagorsk, had developed into a centre of ecclesiastical and national resistance. The Poles who had interfered in the national disputes were forced to abandon the siege of this fortified monastery. When the Polish pretender tried to rule from the Kremlin, Yermogen demanded his conversion to Orthodoxy. Yermogen himself is supposed to have been imprisoned for his resistance and to have starved to death in prison. At this time there grew in the Russian people a fanatical and still prevailing aversion to Roman Catholicism, the religion which Poland exploited in order to increase its influence in the east.

THE CHURCH UNDER THE ROMANOVS

In 1613 Michael Romanov was elected tsar, and his father Filaret, who as Metropolitan of Rostov had been exiled to a monastery by the last tsar, became patriarch. Since Michael was still young and inexperienced, Filaret became regent. He led a decisive struggle against all heresies, and energetically countered the influences of Rome and the union. Never before had a prince of the Church had so much power as Filaret, writes the church historian Bonvech.

It was a different story with Nikon, patriarch from 1652. He became regent for the second tsar of the Romanov dynasty, Alexei, while the latter was occupied by the war against the Swedes and Poles. Nikon attempted a modest reform of the Orthodox Church. Under his rule, the sermon acquired a completely new significance in the service. He founded a school for Greek and Latin, published a book of canon law, the so-called *kormchaya*, and fought for a greater independence of the Church from the tsar. The most momentous reform was his correction of the old liturgies and church books. Through centuries of copying, many mistakes had crept into the service and prayer books. Corrections had already been begun under Nikon's predecessors – not without resistance from priests and laity. Now he began to attack cherished traditions. He used the Greek original texts as an aid, which a large number of the faithful however took very amiss. It is difficult for us to understand that questions like this could lead to a schism which still persists today.

THE GREAT SCHISM

The struggles which preceded this church schism were carried on with extreme passion. The controversy raged around a whole series of externals: whether one should cross oneself with two fingers or three; which direction the procession should go round the altar – from right to left or the other way round; how many hallelujahs should be sung at a certain point in the liturgy – all these questions were rooted in a type of piety which fed on the liturgical.

It is certain that these questions were deliberately inflated, for Nikon was an autocrat and as such had many enemies. He soon created martyrs by exiling protesting priests to Siberia and thus there arose the great schism, the Church of the Old Believers. Because of the severe persecutions from the state Church, there were thousands of self-immolations among the Old Believers. This made a deep impression on the devout, and it is likely that at that time it was not only the conservatives who adhered to the Old Believers, but also many of those who practised a genuine piety. The Old Believers came in for much suffering over the centuries. It is true that a hundred years later Catherine the Great, the empress of the enlightenment, practised tolerance. But her great-grandson, Tsar Nicholas I, in the first half of the nineteenth century again repressed the *raskolniki* (schismatics) and took away their rights. They were treated in a similar fashion to the stundists at a later date.

The liturgical reform was finally completed. However Nikon through his self-assertion, at times obstinacy, had attracted so much hostility – above all that of the tsar – that he was deposed and exiled to a monastery. He died on the way (1681). After him, the Orthodox Church under the tsars had no other patriarch of real significance.

It is interesting that it was precisely from the ranks of the *raskolniki*, the Old Believers, who at first were considered old-fashioned, that there came representatives of reformist political thought. They stood first for tolerance and intellectual freedom on their own account; later, too, they often worked hand in hand with the emerging sects. Experts claim that in the nineteenth century the number of such sects in Russia was greater even than in North America.

The Old Believers often acquired great riches because of their hard work. Thus it was that even revolutionary terrorists drew support from the circle of Old Believer merchants in Moscow. Those who were dissatisfied with church centralization and autocracy gathered together within the schism. This may be seen as a late protest against the influence of the teaching of Joseph of Volokolamsk.

II EARLY EVANGELICAL INFLUENCES

PROTESTANT IMMIGRANTS

Before we turn our attention to the changed situation of the Church and of spiritual culture under Peter the Great, we must investigate early evangelical influences in old Russia.

Anyone who understands ecumenism as a general coming together of the different denominations will not care for the following statements. But anyone for whom ecumenism represents the mutual ministry of brethren in the faith, disciples of Christ, will admit that with all the genuineness and warmth of Orthodox piety, the Church in the east could have learned from the insights of the Reformation. The statement of the teacher who converted to the Orthodox Church: 'Prayer is more important than preaching', which is typical of Orthodox piety, stands in complete contradiction to the words of Paul: 'Faith comes from what is heard' (Rom. 10.17). Of course the Orthodox also had the bible. However the congregations consisted mainly of illiterates, who could not distinguish between the revelation of God in the words of the bible and pious legends. The few sermons which were preached, however good they may have been, only reached a small proportion of the population. It was the Orthodox form of piety which was nurtured and cultivated; without doubt this produced many blooms and also healthy fruit. But the Church limited itself mainly to the liturgy which only had content for those who could comprehend it. The great mass of the people acquired a piety of the emotions. Thus it was that in church 'one felt as if in heaven'; outside was hell, and people lived accordingly. Where belief in justification is missing, there is also lacking a true sanctification. This is abundantly demonstrated in Russian literature. The stories of Leskov – a pious Orthodox believer, who loved his Church – testify to this truth. With time, it was possible to find among the educated – who were slowly growing in number – also a growing number of those who read and loved the bible.

Like all sacerdotal and sacramental Churches, the Orthodox Church too is very open to the danger of putting the pious

'opus operatum' – the mechanical operation of the work of grace –
in the place of devotion to the Lord through faith. Because the
eastern Church does not know the way of salvation in the
Reformation sense, penance can often lead to extreme self-
mortification, but seldom to a break with the old life. One might
say that whereas the Reformation introduced a dynamic piety,
Orthodoxy maintains a static one. The confession 'I am a great
sinner' comes easily from the lips of a pious Orthodox. But the
confession 'I am a forgiven sinner' he would consider unpardon-
able presumption. This is why a sober pietism of the type of
A. H. Francke, Zinzendorf and Bengel could have been of great
benefit here.

Since the time of Ivan the Terrible there had been a small
colony of West Europeans in Moscow, mainly Germans. For
twenty-five years Ivan had waged an unsuccessful war to gain
Livonia.* He had deported many thousands of Germans, Estonians and Latvians and sold many of them into slavery in Asia. A
small number settled, and these settlements formed the beginnings
of the Lutheran communities in Russia.

In the year 1559 Pastor Brakel from Dorpat (now Tartu in
Soviet Estonia) was deported together with Wilhelm von
Fürstenberg, the ruling knight of the *Deutschherren* order. Brakel
later became the first known Lutheran pastor of the congregation
of St. Michael in Moscow, which had acquired its own church
in 1576. Fifty years later a second Lutheran congregation had
already been formed in Moscow, the congregation of St. Peter
and St. Paul, and in 1629 a Reformed church was opened. Soon
Arkhangelsk on the White Sea in the north and Astrakhan at the
mouth of the Volga on the Caspian Sea in the south each had a
Lutheran congregation. But all these congregations were immi-
grant churches and had virtually no contact with Orthodoxy.
Meanwhile professional people were coming from Denmark,
Holland, England and Sweden, at the request of the Russians,
with accompanying letters stipulating that they be permitted to
practise their Protestant faith.

It is true that Ivan held religious discussions with Catholics, and

* A Baltic principality within the old Russian empire.

once with a minister from the Moravian Brethren, but he did not take these discussions seriously. While the Renaissance, humanism and the Reformation were affecting the west, and in particular the Church there, the Tsar of Moscow felt himself to be the protector of Orthodoxy, the heir of Byzantium, a political and religious autocrat.

THE INFLUENCE OF A. H. FRANCKE ON PETER THE GREAT

The first changes in this came with the reforms of Peter the Great (1689–1725). In his impetuous way he opened the country up to western influences, in order to overcome the backwardness in cultural and technical spheres which Russia had inherited through the centuries of the Mongol yoke. This tsar is for us a figure of extreme mystery. Piety does not seem to have been one of his outstanding qualities. Yet at the same time he quickly acquired a deep trust in August Hermann Francke and his works. He was obviously impressed by his work with schools, particularly the emphasis on technical education, which goes back to Francke. Every two years Peter sent a special envoy to Halle. Even the Empress Catherine (I), his wife, once visited the schools incognito. Peter gladly allowed Francke's pupils to come to Russia as educators, teachers and pastors. The first Russian secondary school was a pietist foundation. The first president of the St. Petersburg Academy of Sciences was a friend of August Hermann Francke.

After the Northern War (1710) the Baltic lands of Livonia and Estonia, which had formerly belonged to Sweden, were annexed to Russia. While the Swedish government had passed strict edicts against pietist influences, Peter opened the newly acquired lands to this new form of piety. Many of the Baltic Germans, including a number of his ministers, were of pietist orientation. Arndt's *Books of True Christianity* and many of the writings of Francke were translated into Russian. We know that the tsar himself read them.

Francke's first emissary was Scharschmidt, who came from

Quedlinburg. Although Francke's hope for an ecumenical connection with the Orthodox Church was not realized, nevertheless Scharschmidt fulfilled a valuable ministry. He travelled through the length and breadth of Russia gathering and looking after the scattered evangelical Christians of western origin. The existing Lutheran congregations in Moscow, Arkhangelsk, and soon too in the new capital St. Petersburg, received pietist preachers and teachers. Reval (now Tallinn), the capital of Estonia, became a focal point of pietist movements, and remained so to some extent, with brief interruptions, until the year 1939, the fateful year of the re-settlement of the Balts to Germany on the basis of the catastrophic policy of an unsuspecting Austrian dilettante.

Francke had been made aware of the great tasks to be done in Russia by diplomat and Privy Councillor Ludolf. This gifted linguist and Christian had travelled through Russia and wrote the first Russian grammar for German-speaking people. He prevailed upon August Hermann Francke to found the 'seminarium orientale' in the year 1702. Among the subjects taught there were Russian and Church Slavonic, which resembles modern Macedonian and is still used in the Russian liturgy. Francke himself obviously tried to learn Russian, for his exercise books in that language are still extant.

Peter the Great gave the state Church a new constitution. From the year 1700 he left the office of patriarch vacant. He called the theologian Stepan Yavorsky (d. 1722) from Kiev – a Ukrainian from Lvov in Galicia – and made him patriarchal administrator. It will be seen later how the Ukrainians became to a large extent cultural and also ecclesiastical mediators between east and west. Yavorsky had visited the Jesuit academies in Vilnius and Poznan and was rector of the theological academy in Kiev, founded by Petrus Mogila (d. 1647).

(Petrus Mogila, the son of a Moldavian prince, had defended his homeland against the Turks in 1620. Five years later he entered monastic life and after two years became archimandrite in the Monastery of the Caves at Kiev. At that time Kiev with the western Ukraine belonged to Poland. In 1633 King Wladislaw IV of Poland made him Metropolitan of the Ukraine. Either despite or because of his Jesuit education, Mogila was against the union of the two Catholic Churches. When he extended the school of an Orthodox fraternity in Kiev in 1631 to make it an academy, he did so in order to promote a thorough theological education for the struggle against Catholicism. His 'Confessio fidei orthodoxae' appeared in Latin in 1645, two years before his death. Church historian Bonwetsch says: 'The Kiev school became the instructor of the Moscow Church.')

REFORMS

Now there was a representative of this solidly based theology at the side of the tsar. Although Yavorsky disapproved of the tsar's reforms, Peter named him chairman of the 'Holy Synod', which with the help of his 'spiritual regulation of 1721' he had placed at the head of the state Church – a bureaucratic substitute for the patriarch. It is not impossible that Peter may have found the model for this in the consistorial constitution of the Protestant state Church in Germany. At any rate he replaced the monarchical patriarchate by a collegial body (unlike the royal consistoria of Prussia). The synod included the metropolitans, also some archbishops and bishops, but the chair was taken by an 'Oberprokuror' as representative of the tsar, usually a lawyer, who later acquired more and more political significance and who had the rank of a minister. This development was, as we shall see, fateful for the history of stundism.

It is a testimony to Peter the Great's self-assurance that in the person of Stepan Yavorsky he placed at the head of the state Church a Ukrainian theologian who, with all his loyalty to Orthodoxy, had a Roman Catholic background. For this reason the bishops attempted to shield themselves against Yavorsky's influence. His fellow countryman Feofan Prokopovich (d. 1736), who had only become professor at the Kiev academy in 1704, had a greater influence on the Orthodox Church.

It was Feofan who supported the connection between Peter and August Hermann Francke, so that Francke hoped to exercise a reforming influence on Orthodoxy through him. However

Feofan, like Stepan, was rejected by the Orthodox Church leaders in Moscow, although he genuinely tried to resist the encroachments of the government upon the Church. Among his successors, the Holy Synod remained loyal to the tsars right up to the Revolution.

Peter the Great also saw to it that the enormous lands belonging to the monasteries, which at times are supposed to have amounted to a third of the country, came under state control and use. In fact all church property came under state control. This may have been due to the fact that Peter, remembering bad experiences of his childhood and youth, lived in constant fear of conspiracies and bloody rebellions on the part of the conservative sections of his people, which understandably counted on strong support in the Church and the monasteries.

FRANCKE'S NEW MISSION FIELD: THE SWEDES

After Francke realized that the Orthodox Church was to remain closed to him, he turned his attention to the Swedish officers who had been transported to Siberia together with almost the whole army of Charles XII after the battle of Poltava. In Tobolsk in Siberia, through a voluminous correspondence and large shipments of Bibles and Christian literature, but also through considerable sums of money which Francke collected for the prisoners, there came into being a centre of revival among the Swedes. A school was even established there. These spiritually awakened officers acquired a role in Swedish church history. When they returned home and bore living testimony, the resistance of the Swedish Lutheran Church to pietism broke down. Pietism is still known to have a certain influence on many church circles in Sweden today. Francke also had an indirect influence upon Finland, which was incorporated into the Russian empire a hundred years later and like Estonia remained open to revival for generations.

Francke's writings reached Russia in large quantities. It was in St. Petersburg that 'the strongest concentration of the Protestant element' (Steinwand) was to be found until the collapse of the tsarist empire. However this included very few Russians, but mainly Germans, Dutch, English and Swiss. Around the year 1900 there were still up to a hundred thousand Protestants in St. Petersburg, that is, ten per cent of the population. The Lutherans alone had fifteen congregations here with twelve churches, the Reformed had six churches, and there was also a meeting room of the Herrnhut brethren. These congregations had outstanding primary and secondary schools, hospitals and old people's homes. Although many German families used the Russian language in their everyday life, there was a permanent ban on Russian sermons in these churches, in order to stifle any influence on the Orthodox population. Yet in the south and the east there was to arise an even larger Protestant minority, using the German language, which was to become considerably more significant for the spiritual life of the Russian people.

III   GERMAN PEASANT SETTLEMENTS

At the beginning of the first world war in the summer of 1914, there were an estimated two million German farmers in Russia – from Bessarabia to the Volga valley, across the Crimea and the Don basin to the Caucasus, and in the east deep into Asiatic Siberia. In Russia they were called 'the colonists', to distinguish them from the Baltic Germans and a German diaspora in the cities. They possessed not only considerable land, but also mills and other agricultural and technical concerns and in the course of about 150 years they had accumulated large assets. In the catastrophes of the twentieth century this great national community was deported, scattered and decimated.

How had these great peasant settlements arisen?

Before the German farmer emigrated overseas to the USA, to South America and Australia, he first moved from the narrow confines of the west to the wide expanses of the east. From the eighteenth century, this willingness to 'ride east' was encouraged by politicians. It is known that Prince Eugene of Savoy spread a chain of flourishing German peasant settlements in the south of Austria as a defence against the Turks and their vassals.

Catherine the Great (1762–96), daughter of the Prince of Anhalt-Zerbst, followed the example of her great contemporary. She brought the farmers to the Volga. The empire was constantly harassed at this point by nomadic peoples from the east: Tatars, Kalmyks, Bashkirs, Kirgiz. Catherine gave the German farmers great privileges, and in the Saratov area so many German villages sprang up that the Bolsheviks later established a small Soviet German republic here. The farmers became prosperous through hard work, but only after indescribable hardships at the beginning. The high birth rate enlarged the German element along the Volga. A hundred and four colonies were established here in the years 1764–68.

Catherine's grandson, Tsar Alexander I, followed a similar path. In 1789 the last Turkish fortress of Ochakov fell; after that the Turks disappeared from the north bank of the Black Sea. This extremely fertile land thus came into Russian hands. But it remained almost unexploited because it was thinly populated, and it remained thinly populated because the serfdom of Russian peasants prevented a Russian settlement of the area. The government then tried with immigrants from Persia and Greece, even with Jewish settlers, but without success. During the troubles of the Napoleonic wars, which followed around the turn of the century, the problem remained unsolved. It was only after the victory against Napoleon that the Russian government canvassed for German farmers with the guarantee of tax freedom for a limited period of time, self-administration with respect to churches and schools, and other privileges. Among these farmers, who in the years after 1815 had to struggle with severe harvest failures, they found a ready ear.

EASTERN REFUGE

In Württemberg there was another motive for emigration. Through the peasant Michael Hahn (d. 1819) a new revival movement had arisen among many of the peasantry, also in the towns. This was combatted in many ways by the state Church, which was ruled by rationalism. The experiences of war, as so often in church history, had strengthened the eschatological hope. Had not the great Swabian theologian Johann Albrecht Bengel (d. 1752) in his exposition of Revelation once calculated the date of Jesus' return and indicated the year 1836 as very probable? The exigencies of war, the general inflation and the manifold oppression of believers – all this seemed to many to be a sign of the beginning of the anti-Christian era.

Added to this, Dr. Jung-Stilling, the original and romantic Christian writer, popularized Bengel's expectations and pointed to the east, where the harassed community of the end time was to find a place of refuge (cf. Rev. 12.14). Jung-Stilling even spoke of Samarkand beyond the Caspian Sea. People's minds were aroused; even the Russian emperor was religiously awakened.

Thus alongside adventurers and fortune-hunters, hundreds of German farmers moved to Russia, bible in hand, to religious freedom – although there was a ban on evangelism among the Russians. Sufficient land for each family, complete self-administration, their own churches and schools, tax exemption for ten years, five hundred roubles interest-free loan, even their own courts and police – how could they fail to be attracted by such privileges!

Later they found that promises were not kept and – as so often under the tsars – rights that had been guaranteed were restricted or completely cancelled; the situation of the first settlers was grim. Petty officials refused to help, neighbours were difficult, the climate was strange and the marauding nomads caused trouble and loss. Later, the colonists had a bitter saying: 'The first generation got death, the second got want, only the third got bread.' During the next hundred years there was bread in great abundance, thanks to the ability and the hard work of the settlers. Many became prosperous and bought more land, particularly after the abolition of serfdom under Alexander II in 1861, which caused embarrassment to many Russian landowners. Succeeding generations of Germans, with their large families, in turn became owners of farms and estates, and so the German settlements expanded from one generation to the next. The Russian peasant, who had little land of his own – the land was often the common property of the village and was constantly being re-shared – saw the growing prosperity of his German neighbours and it is not surprising that bitter envy was aroused.

THE MENNONITES

Alongside the Lutherans and the Reformed, the Mennonites form the third Church of the Reformation to have preserved its vitality up to the present, although for a long time it was subject to the most severe persecution – even on the part of its Protestant sister Churches. These are the Anabaptists gathered together by Menno Simons (d. 1559). After long wanderings, many of them found a home in the Netherlands, the first state in Europe to exercise complete religious tolerance. When Frederick the Great won West Prussia, he invited them as settlers and experienced dyke-builders into the flats of the Weichsel and the Nogat. Knowing that they rejected military service on principle, he promised them complete exemption from the army. When Friedrich Wilhelm III, in Prussia's time of great need, withdrew this right from them, they were all the more ready to respond to the invitation to go east, where this privilege was again in force. The first group of Mennonites had already settled in Khortitsa (Yekaterinoslav) in 1789–96 under Catherine the Great. A second group followed in 1803–09 under Alexander I and settled along the Molochna, a small tributary of the Donets.

In economic terms this group, which was incredibly closed in respect of culture and religion, was the most successful. The high birth rate among Mennonite families caused their numbers to double in twenty-five years. From 1860 onwards they began to settle north of the Caucasus and in the Urals, they also crossed into Asiatic Russia and moved through Siberia. Before 1914 there were an estimated 100,000 Mennonites in Russia – a fifth of all Mennonites in the world.

In the middle of the nineteenth century the Mennonites experienced a profound revival through the ministry of Eduard Wüst; this was the origin of the so-called Mennonite Brethren. The particular strength of these congregations lay in their good schools. For reasons of conscience their evangelists did not consider themselves bound by the governmental decree forbidding evangelism among the Russians. Thus the Mennonite Brethren communities later became a secret source of stundism.

Despite their severe losses through the second world war and Stalin's persecution, and despite the considerable emigration overseas, by 1971 there were still an estimated 60,000 Mennonites in the Soviet Union. The figure is probably even larger.

THE INFLUENCE OF HERRNHUT

The contribution of Herrnhut to evangelism in Russia was much more modest. Christian David, who had led the migration of the Moravian Brethren to Bertelsdorf and who founded the community of Herrnhut in 1722, also touched the Baltic lands in his many travels. Count Zinzendorf himself travelled twice to Old Livonia, where he encountered serious danger. There was some evangelism among the Estonians, which is still visible today, also to a lesser extent among the Latvians. It was evident here that the Baltic Germans of Estonia (capital Reval – now Tallinn) were more open to the pietist message than southern Livonia, and certainly than Courland,* which for a long time had been cut off by Polish sovereignty. The hatred of the empress Elizabeth (1741–62), daughter of Peter the Great, was a threat not only to the count, but also to the brethren. A small band of Herrnhut brethren, including Dr. Kriegelstein, languished for decades in the Peter and Paul Fortress. It was the enlightened Catherine II who first treated with Herrnhut about a settlement by the brethren. Thus in the year 1765 there came into being a small colony at the bend of the Volga, roughly where Volgograd (formerly Stalingrad) lies today, at the border with the Kalmyk steppes. The brethren named their colony Sarepta after the small river Sarpa – and with reference to I Kings 17.9 ff. The ground was unsuitable for grain-growing, but there was healthy, even spa water and thus a possibility for market-gardening. The settlers also developed an exemplary activity in the realm of local industries.

* A Baltic principality within the old Russian empire.

Almost all of Russia's mustard came from Sarepta and 'Sarpinka' was the name of the light, gaily-coloured cotton beloved by Russian and Ukrainian peasant girls. Sarpinka could still be bought at fairs throughout Russia at the beginning of this century. The settlers grew tobacco, made candles, founded sugar factories, steam and saw-mills, and demonstrated that the despised pietists knew how to work, as well as to pray.

From here the Herrnhut brethren wanted to evangelize the Kalmyks, but they had small success from their efforts.

After Nicholas I, grandson of Catherine, came to the throne in 1825 – when only one Church, the Orthodox state Church, was permitted to evangelize – the flourishing Herrnhut community like the other German settlements lost its privileges one by one, and in the 1890's Sarepta ceased to be a proper Herrnhut community. Russians, Tatars, Kalmyks and other immigrants came in and Sarepta was eventually swallowed up in the new industrial city of Stalingrad. The civil war against Denikin's army, the terrible famine of 1921–22 and severe epidemics swept through the area like the horsemen of the apocalypse.

However Sarepta found one place in the Russian empire where it could work fruitfully and thus justify its existence as a *Brüdergemeine*: in the German colonies of the Volga. Already in 1764 a Herrnhut brother of Swiss origin, Jean Jannet, had become pastor in one of these colonies. He soon made contact with Sarepta and opened up for them a way into the colonies. The first wave of revival here on the Volga goes back to the Herrnhut brethren. Over a period of fifty-seven years, Sarepta sent eighteen missionaries to the colonies, until denominational narrowness on the part of the Lutheran church leadership in St. Petersburg brought about a ban on their work in 1825. This community work sowed a good seed, which maintained its effectiveness and strength for generations. In fact it was necessary because of the constant shortage of pastors. However the brethren only reached twenty out of the seventy-three colonies (thirty-one were Catholic) with intensive work. They visited a further twenty-three occasionally, another twenty-three only rarely, the rest never.

IV   ALEXANDER I AND HIS TIME (1801–25)

Catherine the Great had called the wife of General von Lieven from Estonia to act as tutor to her many grandchildren; as well as her favourite grandson Alexander there was also Constantine, Nicholas (later emperor Nicholas I) and Michael, and Paul's daughters Catherine, later queen of Württemberg, and Maria, later grand duchess of Saxony-Weimar, whose daughter Auguste married emperor Wilhelm I. The von Lieven family remained close to the imperial court and later became a focal point of the evangelical movement in St. Petersburg.

Alexander probably inherited his uneven character from his sick father Paul who – particularly during his brief reign from 1796–1801 – showed definite signs of mental illness. This was complicated by the fact that Alexander had known of the conspiracy by the officers of the guard against his father, but had thought that the conspirators would merely force the tsar to abdicate. After his father's murder, Alexander could not muster the strength to bring the murderers to trial, because he felt himself party to the crime. This shadow of parricide haunted him all his life. An increasing tendency to deafness, which he would not admit, also made him more suspicious. 'He remained closed all his life, without any lasting affection' writes Pantenius, perhaps rather one-sidedly. His life was further burdened by a premature marriage arranged by his energetic grandmother Catherine. He was barely seventeen years old when he was married to Princess Elisabeth of Baden, who was two years younger than himself. The fact that the marriage was unhappy cannot be blamed solely upon Alexander. In later life he had an unlawful relationship with Maria Naryshkina, the Polish wife of a Russian aristocrat.

Alexander's religious education was soon entrusted to the Swiss teacher La Harpe. The kind of theology represented by this man of the enlightenment can be seen in the following sentence, which he dictated to his pupil one day: 'Jesus is a Jew, from whom the Christian sect gets its name.'

In the year 1812, when Napoleon began his march towards Moscow, the tsar experienced a religious awakening – apparently through his boyhood friend Prince Golitsyn. How far this awakening led towards a biblical conversion we do not know. The historians like to speak of Alexander's 'tendency to mysticism'. But even at that time, this was the general tag used by the early enlightenment to describe the movement of revival in the decades after the Napoleonic wars. The question which interests us here is how far Alexander promoted the influence of the biblical gospel in Russia. We will look at four aspects here.

THE INFLUENCE OF PRINCE GOLITSYN AND HIS FRIENDS

Prince Alexander Nikolayevich Golitsyn (1773–1844) came from an old Russian noble family. One of his ancestors had been tutor to Peter the Great. He himself was brought up in Catherine's page corps. His gifted nature caused him to be made playmate to Catherine's two eldest grandsons, grand princes Alexander and Constantine, sons of Paul. It is said that in his youth Prince Golitsyn, like his frivolous companions, was a child of the world. The date of his turning to the biblical gospel cannot be established. His later piety had that supra-confessional character which is typical of the revival movement. The Orthodox Church had little comprehension for this. Even the great Russian historian Klyuchevsky at the beginning of our century wrote of Golitsyn: 'A kind man, god-fearing to the point of ecstasy, but without any particular belief' (II, 364). The reaction of the Leipzig police was very similar, when Johannes Evangelista Gossner, asked what his faith was, replied: 'I am a Christian.' The official answered: 'That's not enough.' Gossner referred to the bible, but this did not help him much, because by 'faith' the official understood a particular, legally definable denomination.

Thus Alexander's friendship with Golitsyn began in their childhood. When Alexander, still almost a boy, was married, Golitsyn, who was four years older, became his valet. At the age of twenty-three he was already chamberlain. Under Tsar Paul, like many of his contemporaries, he fell into disgrace; he moved to Moscow and read a lot of history and foreign literature.

When Alexander came to the throne in 1801, he called his childhood friend into the state service. In the beginning he only had minor posts. But when the position of Oberprokuror of the Holy Synod became vacant, Alexander quite unexpectedly made his friend chairman, representative of the tsar in the highest Orthodox church body. It appeared that he was following a whim. Golitsyn tried in vain to excuse himself on the basis of his position as a free-thinker and disciple of Voltaire.

But this appointment seems to have led to Golitsyn's awakening. For the first time in his life he immersed himself in the New Testament, withdrew from social pleasures and devoted himself enthusiastically to his new office. He took measures for a better training of the priests and founded three theological academies. In 1810 Golitsyn also became head of the new administration for the affairs of foreign denominations. In this capacity he also had to take care of the interests of the Lutheran and Reformed Churches in Russia. Finally in 1818 he was entrusted with the newly-established Ministry of Religion and Education. He was then released from his duties as Oberprokuror. Officials who worked with him praised his objectivity and honesty. He could even accept contradiction.

Although Golitsyn was fully occupied by his job, it is known that he made sick visits incognito, in order to give quiet assistance. Free of ambition and hard-working, he was one of Alexander I's most respected ministers. He remained single.

It is understandable that Golitsyn's living Christian faith should have deeply impressed the pliable and religiously open tsar, especially in the difficult time of the French invasion. The story is told:

'One day the emperor interrupted his customary stroll along the Fontanka canal and went into Golitsyn's official apartment. On the table in the prince's study lay a bible in old Slavonic. The emperor spoke of the gloomy mood which he could not shake off. He happened to pick up the bible, opened it at random and read the psalm: "He who dwells in the shelter of the Most High, who abides in the shadow of the Almighty, will say to the Lord, 'My refuge and my fortress; my God, in whom I trust.'"

Some time after this he asked the empress, his wife, whether she could lend him a bible. He began to read it and discovered for himself what comfort and encouragement an oppressed heart can draw from the word of God.' This anecdote is to be found in the memoirs of Privy Councillor Peter von Goetze who was a collaborator and contemporary of Golitsyn. He could not be described as a representative of the revival.

THE FOUNDING OF THE RUSSIAN BIBLE SOCIETY

After the establishment of the British and Foreign Bible Society in London on 7 March 1804, there was a growing bible movement in renascent Europe. Bible Societies were founded in almost every Protestant country. Rev. John Paterson, Agent of the BFBS, played a special role in the founding of the Russian Bible Society, the first in an Orthodox area.

It is surely more than a strange coincidence that on 6 December 1812, the day that Napoleon started out by sleigh from Vilnius in order to escape from Russia to Paris as fast as possible, Alexander I in St. Petersburg was signing the decree for the establishment of a Bible Society in his country. During the time of the French pressure, the word of the bible had become his comfort and strength. The ninety-first psalm had opened to him the door to this spring of life.

The first members of the society were some pastors and interested laymen. At their head was Alexander Golitsyn. In 1813 it received imperial patronage and Golitsyn became president. In 1814 the name was changed from St. Petersburg Bible Society to the Russian Bible Society and the Orthodox Church was now represented on the committee by various metropolitans, archbishops and bishops. The committee also included the Armenian Bishop Johanne and the Roman Catholic Bishop Siestriencewicz-Bohusz – the latter with the express subsequent disapproval of his Curia.

The Bible Society was not short of funds since it was supported by Alexander I, and also from London. Editions of the Russian bible in Church Slavonic continued to be printed by the Holy Synod, but the Bible Society sold them at reduced prices.

When Alexander visited London in 1814, he received a delegation from the British and Foreign Bible Society. He told them that 'he regarded the Bible Society as a most beneficial institution and one particularly necessary in Russia' (according to Peter von Goetze). After his return the tsar expressed the wish that alongside the Church Slavonic edition, which was to continue being used in the services of the Orthodox Church, there should be a modern translation, because many Russians could no longer understand the old language and therefore could only read the bible with great effort. This imperial wish later caused offence. However it was all the more understandable as the Patriarch of Constantinople had warmly greeted the translation by the London Bible Society of the New Testament into modern Greek. The Russian Bible Society was already distributing this edition among the numerous Greeks in southern Russia. So the Holy Synod set to work to fulfil the emperor's wish. Archimandrite Filaret, later Metropolitan of Moscow, a personal friend of Golitsyn, belonged to the translation commission.

Branch societies were now formed in many Russian towns and although the Bible Society only existed for some fourteen years, it accomplished much in those relatively few years. It belongs therefore to the most important aspects of evangelism in Russia, and Russian stundism is unthinkable without it. When the Bible Society celebrated its tenth anniversary – marked by an official gathering in the Tauride Palace under Golitsyn's chairmanship – the translation of the New Testament and Psalms into modern Russian was already complete; there were also bibles and bible portions – mostly printed in Russia – in Finnish, Karelian, Estonian (two dialects), Georgian, Armenian, Turkish (two dialects), Samoyed, Cheremiss, Chuvash, Persian, Kalmyk, Buryat, Tatar (three dialects) and modern Bulgarian, altogether seventeen languages. This was a tremendous achievement.

Further work was interrupted when in 1826 Tsar Nicholas I, Alexander's younger brother, closed the society under the specious pretext that enough bibles had now been printed. It was not until

1863 that his son Alexander II permitted the BFBS to take up a large-scale work in Russia again, and during his time the translation of the whole of the Old Testament into modern Russian was completed. The BFBS work in Russia was finally closed down by the revolutionaries in 1917.

Among the friends of Golitsyn who promoted this work was Count Lieven, curator of Dorpat university. He had tried to put men of the German revival movement into the theological faculty there, in order to overcome the rationalism which was also prevailing in the Baltic lands. He was responsible for calling the theologian Ernst Sartorius, who was an opponent of rationalism and later became General Superintendent of East Prussia. We shall meet the name Lieven again for this family was a witness to the biblical gospel in Russia for a hundred years.

It was the weakness of the Russian Bible Society from the beginning that it was carried, not by a national revival movement, as in the west, but by a relatively small circle of spiritually awakened aristocrats. Besides Golitsyn and Lieven one could mention Count Kochubei, Koshelev, Turgenev, Adlerkreutz. Anyone who knew Russia and the Russian state Church will not be surprised that the Bible movement and thus also the Bible Society had to reckon from the very beginning with a strong opposition which cannot be ascribed wholly to ill will. For example there was the concern of Admiral Shishkov, a pious Orthodox. Since almost the whole peasantry, which counted for the majority of the population, consisted of illiterates, he was afraid that the spreading of the bible might encourage a tendency to wild sectarianism which had always been characteristic of Russia. To the pious and conservative educated Russian, Church Slavonic was sacred. The word of God could only be read and heard in that language. All other translations were considered wicked profanations of the sacred. This reaction in the Church against the Bible Society was apparent during Alexander's lifetime, in other words, even before it was closed down by Nicholas I.

This concept need not seem so strange to us, since not so long ago there were strict German Lutherans who declared that even a revision of the old Luther text was impermissible. It is evident that such opposition within a sacerdotal and sacramental Church would be much more numerous. Thus in 1817 Pope Pius VII closed a small Catholic bible work in Regensburg which was distributing the bible translations of Wittmann, van Ess and Gossner, and only a few decades ago the Protestant Bible Societies were anathematized by Pope Leo XIII. The fact that a bible movement is spreading today in that same Catholic Church is an astonishing one, and worthy of considerable attention.

THE INFLUENCE OF BARONESS VON KRUEDENER

In order to understand Alexander I's religious development, it is necessary to describe the influence of an important woman upon him.

Juliane von Vietinghoff was born in 1764 in Riga, daughter of the noble landowner Baron Vietinghoff. On her mother's side she was a granddaughter of field-marshall Münnich, a man famous in his day, an officer of German descent who in the first half of the eighteenth century reformed the Russian army according to the Prussian model. At the age of eighteen Juliane was married against her will to the Russian diplomat Baron Kruedener who was twenty years older than her and already twice divorced. At his side, although often separated from him for long periods because of his many official trips, like her contemporaries she lived a frivolous life in Copenhagen, Venice, Paris and other places. She described this in her novel 'Valerie' which made her world famous. The turning point for her was a conversation with a Herrnhut shoemaker in Riga, who was measuring her for new shoes. It made a deep impression on her that this 'quiet one in the land', living in poverty, could give such joyful testimony to his happiness in life through faith in Jesus Christ. Juliane came to a deep repentance and conversion. With the same decisiveness with which she had formerly given herself to society life, she now dedicated her life to her newly found Lord and sought to serve him in the person of the poor and wretched. Her social work was concentrated on southern Germany (Württemberg-Baden) and Switzerland, as well as her own inherited estate. Her exalted manner and restlessness brought her much criticism, indeed hostility. She lacked understanding of people and so was exploited by dishonest individuals. Nevertheless she was one of the first to point to the great social injustices of her time and fearlessly demanded that the governments introduce aid programmes. She used her own considerable means unstintingly for the benefit of the poor. At a time when governments faced the famines raging after the Napoleonic wars helplessly and often even with apathy, she tried untiringly to awaken the consciences of the rich, so that she was labelled a communist. But her appeals were not heeded. Europe had its answer in 1848 with the Communist Manifesto of Karl Marx and Friedrich Engels, a former member of a young men's association* in pious Wuppertal. She is also reproached by historians for her influence on Alexander I and her collaboration in the so-called Holy Alliance. Today, in this age of international groupings, we are learning to evaluate that alliance with more objectivity.

The first meeting between Tsar Alexander I and Baroness Kruedener took place after the Vienna Congress. Driven, as she believed, by God's command, this energetic woman forced an audience with Alexander in Heilbronn. The tsar was on his way to a new front against Napoleon who had returned from exile on the isle of Elba and landed in France. After their first conversation, she was permitted to accompany Alexander to Heidelberg. Finally she arrived in Paris, which was occupied by the allied troops. There can hardly be any doubt that Juliane had heard the tsar, his conscience still burdened by the attack on his father, make a total confession. She had powerfully pointed him to the saviour of sinners. The idea that those who conquered Napoleon, at that time widely held to be the prototype of the anti-Christ, should form an alliance based on the gospel of Jesus Christ may have been her suggestion. This 'Holy Alliance', the combination of the three great powers Russia, Austria and Prussia, was supposed to prevent wars for ever and to pave the way for Christian love to flourish. It was Alexander who put forward the detailed plan. It is not surprising that the diplomats of 'Realpolitik' rejected this

* *Junglingsverein* – forerunner of the German YMCA.

plan as eccentric. Yet it may after all have been more sober than the peace plan of the eccentric humanist Woodrow Wilson after 1918. Today many church circles are again asking for Christian standards in international politics. The man who distorted the Holy Alliance was undoubtedly Metternich, who found a ready ear in Nicholas I, successor to Alexander. In this way the Holy Alliance became a bastion of reaction.

It is certain that Juliane von Kruedener strengthened Alexander in his Christian faith for years. Later he listened to other influences as well. If his relationship of trust with her cooled, this was not without fault on her part. After all the successes which God granted her, she believed that she had a prophetic gift, and interfered in political matters which were beyond her grasp. Alexander treated her in a gentlemanly fashion to the end. A Russian friend invited her to come to the Crimea, where she hoped to found a Christian colony with friends and followers. It was here that she died at Christmas 1824, soon after her arrival. Before her death she confessed with sadness that in her prophetic statements, she had often been following her own ideas.

Many people wonder whether these eight or nine years in Alexander's life, during which he was under the pastoral influence of this woman, may not have a connection with the mystery that surrounds his death. History relates that Alexander died suddenly in Taganrog in 1825, one year after the death of Juliane. Many months later his coffin was laid to rest in the Peter and Paul Fortress in St. Petersburg. When the Bolsheviks opened Alexander's coffin after the revolution, they found it empty. In the seventh edition of the 1912 Baedeker guide to Russia on page 507 under Tomsk we find the following note: 'The ascetic Fyodor Kuzmich (d. 1861), known for his similarity to Alexander I, lies buried in the Alexeyevsky Monastery, which was founded in 1605 (the cell where he lived is still shown to visitors in Chistyakov House on Monastyrskaya street).' It seems that the imperial family believed that this ascetic was Alexander I. If the emperor did decide to abdicate and to seek peace for his soul in Siberian isolation, he would certainly not have had many accomplices, and these have maintained profound silence, for obvious reasons. It is impossible to investigate here the probabilities of this hypothesis, which has evoked a considerable literature.

JOHANNES EVANGELISTA GOSSNER IN ST. PETERSBURG

During his short reign, Paul I had invited the Catholic Order of the Knights of Malta, which Napoleon had driven out of Malta, to come to St. Petersburg and had built them a church – one of the whims of this strange tsar. When Alexander I, his son, was faced with the necessity of calling a Catholic priest to this church, he wanted to find a man who, despite his affiliation to the Catholic Church, preached an evangelical gospel.

During those years there was a broad wave of revival running through the ranks of the young chaplains in Bavaria. It had been set in motion by Professor Johann Michael Sailer, later a bishop, and by the influence of the priest Martin Boos, who himself had been brought to faith in justification through the blood of Jesus, by means of the testimony of a dying old woman.* From the circle of these awakened Catholic priests, who maintained contact with the awakened Protestants, Alexander in 1818 called Ignaz Lindl (1774–1845) to the Maltese church. Two years later Lindl became provost in Odessa and founded the supra-confessional community Sarata in Bessarabia. He did not fulfil all the expectations which were held of him in Russia, migrated back to Germany and in Wuppertal joined the so-called Nazarene sect, after his hope of obtaining a parish in Korntal near Stuttgart fell through. It was he who recommended as his successor at the Maltese church his friend Johannes Evangelista Gossner who, like him, had come to faith through the testimony of Martin Boos and who may be considered as the most mature fruit of this revival among the priests.

Gossner (1773–1858) is one of the most interesting figures of

---

* There now exists a detailed and objective description of this remarkable movement, which brought the Catholic Church in Bavaria into a crisis; it is written by a Benedictine from Ettal: Hildebrand Dussler OSB, *Johann Michael Feneberg und die Allgäuer Erweckungsbewegung*, Kempten 1959.

nineteenth century church history. This son of a Swabian farmer from the vicinity of Augsburg studied theology under Sailer, later Bishop of Regensburg. As a young chaplain he read Martin Boos's letters from the ecclesiastical prison in Göggingen. Gossner experienced a deep awakening and from then on he became a reformed preacher and pastor in a Catholic cassock. During his time at the Frauenkirche in Munich there was a spiritual movement there which scattered sparks as far as Berlin. From there he was visited by von Thadden-Trieglaff with his friends, the sons of the Berlin court preacher Sack; Schleiermacher also travelled to Munich where Gossner was holding bible studies in private houses.

For a time Gossner replaced Chr. Fr. Spittler as secretary of the Christian Society (*Deutsche Christentums-Gesellschaft*) in Basle. He seriously considered moving over to the Lutheran Church. But the revivalist pastor Schöner in Nürnberg wrote to him: 'Stay where you are, Gossner! The Lutheran devil is just as black as the Catholic one.' This was characteristic of the non-denominational attitude of that time. Ludwig Richter, the German painter, who was himself Catholic by upbringing, wrote in retrospect: 'We lived within a movement where all Christians with real inner life, both Catholics and Protestants, stretched out their hands to each other in friendship across the fence that had been erected, not with cool tolerance, but from a feeling of wholehearted oneness with the One who was the saviour and redeemer of all' (Memoirs p. 225).

Gossner was driven out by Jesuit influence. He became a teacher of religion in Düsseldorf, but here too he soon experienced difficulties. Then in 1819 came a letter from the Russian ambassador in Berlin, announcing his summons to the Maltese church in St. Petersburg. Gossner was only there for four years, but his influence was amazing. It could still be traced in St. Petersburg eighty years later.

'A wide door for the gospel has been opened to me here', Gossner was soon writing to his friends in Germany. Every Sunday after mass he gave an evangelical sermon. Beneath his pulpit gathered representatives of many peoples in the great Russian empire; since the time of Peter the Great it was not uncommon for people in St. Petersburg to speak and understand German. Here too the denominational barriers were broken down. Where there is hunger for the gospel of Jesus, the fences and the walls crumble. Prince Golitsyn himself was an example of this. Gossner was an excellent match for him. Later they would both be overthrown together.

On 30 July 1820 Gossner gave his first sermon. Four or five hundred people filled the little church. He did the same here as in Munich; those who sincerely wanted to become Christians he gathered in his apartment. But soon that was not big enough. So his friends rented him a palace, where more than a thousand people could be seated in the banqueting hall. Here Gossner held his weekly bible study. It is said that the emperor himself contributed to the rent of this house, although he never received Gossner.

Gossner's influence soon reached far beyond the ten thousand Germans who lived in St. Petersburg. It is thought to be demonstrable that the revivals in Finland had one of their springs in his work. His influence is noticeable in Estonia, the nearest of the Baltic provinces. The well-known family of theologians, Harnack, is descended from a member of Gossner's private congregation.

Except for the preacher of the little Herrnhut community, the Lutheran pastors mostly rejected Gossner, as they were still shaped by the enlightenment. The fact that the Catholic Dominicans did not trust him affected him more.

Gossner deliberately withdrew from the lively social life in private homes in St. Petersburg, but he held his bible discussions upon invitation in many private apartments. Soon there were small missionary hours after the 'Basle' model. In later years Gossner received from his old friends on the Neva many donations for the missionary society in Berlin which he founded in his old age and which still exists today.

Twice a week he taught religious classes for young people. Each Monday was devoted to the German almshouse which up to then had been neglected spiritually. On the other hand he completely refrained from conducting individual priestly offices because his fellow priests were unhappy about his influence. Only a few Catholic families formed an exception to this. But then in each case he had to ask for the permission of the Dominicans, for the Maltese church had no parish.

Gossner published here a *Collection of Selected Songs of Redeeming Love*. Later he became a church writer of breadth and power. The well-known closing hymn in the Protestant service: 'Segne und behüte . . .' is supposed to have come from his pen. It was one of the most popular hymns in the Baltic Lutheran Church.

Despite Alexander's reticence, Gossner found an entry into the court. He writes: 'Two weeks ago I was in the emperor's luxury palace at Tsarskoye Selo, where the noblest of the land were gathered – not many of them, it's true – and they were just as humble and hungry as those in wooden cottages. The Lord has many people here. This is my paradise.' And again: 'It is good to be here. A fruitful ground, a great, wide field, indeed a great door virtually giving entry to a whole section of the world.' In his minister's study he saw not only Russians, Ukrainians, Germans and Finns, but also now and then representatives of the Tatar and other Asiatic peoples, who came to St. Petersburg in considerable numbers.

This time of rich blessing did not last long. Before leaving for Russia, Gossner had said to Martin Boos: 'I'm going to fetch a Russian cross.' Before five years were out, it was laid upon him in its full weight. It is said that even the powerful Count Metternich, the chancellor of Austria and evil spirit of reaction in Europe, had a hand in this diplomatic tussle. It did not suit his plans that the spirit of revival should be spreading at the Russian court, among the nobility and the citizens of the capital. But in the country itself, too, the opposition of the Church was growing stronger and at last Metropolitan Serafim gave way to a dramatic scene. During an audience with the emperor he fell to his knees, took his bishop's mitre from his head and begged the emperor to dismiss Golitsyn, to suspend the ministry for religious affairs and to put controls on the 'harmful books'. These were some Bible Society books translated from English and particularly Gossner's exposition of the Gospel of Matthew, in which the church censors found passages which did not agree with Orthodox doctrine.

Given all reservations concerning Alexander's character, it is still surprising that he was so prompt to listen to Serafim's demands. In fact the tsar's last years were darkened by reactionary measures. He clearly walked in fear of a revolutionary overthrow, for he knew of secret associations among the young nobles and officers, which later led to the Decembrist rising. He had long ago sent his liberal advisers into exile, including the gifted minister Speransky; he was now under the influence of Arakcheyev, a dark autocratic man, and was turning the villages into barracks, which led to much bitterness and to some revolts.

With the fall of Golitsyn, Gossner's position too was undermined. On 19 April 1824 he gave his last sermon lasting one and a half hours. He sensed the end of his work in St. Petersburg and gave one final powerful testimony to Jesus and his saving blood. He closed with the words of Luther in Worms: 'Here I stand, God help me, I can do no other. Amen.'

The following Saturday he was forbidden to preach again. On Sunday came the governor-general's order, that he must leave the country by Wednesday at the latest. No pleas from highly-placed friends could help any more. It is said that the tsar offered him his own carriage and a large sum of money for the journey. Gossner refused the use of the carriage.

Among Gossner's most faithful followers was the family of the very wealthy merchant Nottbeck. His daughter relates how as a small child she was lifted by her mother to the window and how her mother said: 'Look there, child! That's how Russia treats her prophets.' She remembers seeing a man go past in an open carriage and many people standing on the roadside, waving to him.

The following Sunday Gossner's church was closed by the police. The Orthodox Church held an *autodafé*, that is, they publicly burned Gossner's picture and his writings. But the 'Gossner congregation' survived for decades and gathered in private houses.

Gossner's busy pen turned out many more writings – often brought secretly over the frontier – to his friends whom he never forgot all the rest of his life. Despite great successes in his later work, Gossner himself regarded the few years in St. Petersburg as a high point in his life. Adolf von Harnack, that great scholar of the time of Wilhelm, whose grandfather had a tailor's shop in St. Petersburg, writes: 'Gossner's services for children remained forever in my father's memory, although he only attended them as a small boy, for Gossner left St. Petersburg again in 1824; but his influence on the piety of the house continued, and my father always counted this unusual man among his spiritual fathers, even after he had developed into a strict Lutheran and thus moved far away from Gossner's undenominational Christianity.' The father was subsequently professor of applied theology in Erlangen and Dorpat.

The time of revival in St. Petersburg was brief – approximately 1812–24. During the thirty year reign of Nicholas I (1825–55), Alexander's younger brother and successor, the Russian Bible Society was banned (1826); this was followed by a ban on all Protestant missionary work which affected the Herrnhut brethren in Sarepta, Scottish missionaries in Astrakhan and missionaries from Basle in the Caucasus. The autocracy of the tsar, Orthodoxy and Russian nationalism – the pillars of his state – ignored the realities of this state which encompassed millions of heterodox and people of foreign origin– Lutheran Finns, Estonians, Latvians and Germans; Catholic Poles and Lithuanians; Buddhist Kalmyks and many Muslims in the Caucasus and the Asiatic provinces. But tyrants have never regarded realities, and thus Nicholas I, who died in 1855 during the Crimean War against France and England, sowed the seed for the great revolution some sixty years after his death. From that point on Russia was like an overheated boiler on which all the safety vents had been sealed up. The explosions followed one after another in the next generations: the history of the revolutionary movement began with the Decembrist rising of the officers of the guard when Nicholas I came to the throne and continued through many famous and little-known conspiracies to the rebellious groups of the nihilists, the *narodniki*, the anarchists, the social revolutionaries and socialists of all hues up to the victory of Lenin and the Bolsheviks in the autumn of 1917.

This hundred years, from the revival to the Bolshevik revolution, are the background to the Russian stundist movement which arose in the second half of the last century.

Although the German peasant settlements lost almost all their privileges, nevertheless they represent something of an exception in this time of troubles. Their churches remained more or less untouched, as long as they stayed quiet, although no-one was permitted to convert from the state Church to a Protestant Church, all children of mixed marriages had to be given over to the state Church, and Protestants were still forbidden to do any missionary work or evangelism outside the bounds of their own congregations.

In the Baltic lands, the screws were turned even more tightly. Estonian and Latvian peasants were promised their own land from the tsar, if they joined the state Church. Those who followed these blandishments waited in vain for their land. But they and their families had now become Orthodox for all time.

Pastors who dared to give communion to those who were dying with a burdened conscience for this reason risked their job and their liberty. Thus it was not long before more than half the pastors had a trial pending against them.

It would be tempting to follow the wider influences of the St. Petersburg movement among the Russian peoples. However we can only recognize a few, although vital ones. It might therefore be asked why we have described this movement here in such detail.

As we shall see later, the Russian *Stunde* had its origins in the Swabian *Stunde*. It was a product of the influence of Swabian peasants in the Ukraine on their Russian environment, and a profound one. It is fascinating, but probably also necessary to see it alongside the development of the St. Petersburg revival, which, under the same changing policies of the different tsars, was so different from the development in the south both in origin and in the course it took. Later we shall see these two dissimilar streams merge into one movement, whose history of suffering we can still follow today. For this reason we may add a few last words on the history of the St. Petersburg revival.

It can only be surmised that the Baltic painter Baron Ludwig von Maydell from Dorpat, through whom Ludwig Richter came to faith on New Year's Eve 1823, was a fruit of Gossner's work. But it can be said with more certainty about the theologian

Brehm, who helped the young sceptic Emil Frommel out of theological difficulties and opened to him the way to Jesus. His word to him: 'Christ for us! Christ in us!' is Gossner's well-known saying, which he had put as an epigraph to his biography of Martin Boos. Brehm came from St. Petersburg and died there as a young man.

One of the most unusual men of this circle was the Polish Count Felician Zaremba (1794–1874). After finishing his studies he came, a child of the enlightenment, to St. Petersburg, full of religious questions. Here the Reformed Pole became acquainted with the bible through his Baltic friend from student days, von Trompowsky, and he experienced a thorough conversion. His life after this reads like a novel. He gave up the diplomatic career, became a Basle missionary, and as such was sent to the Caucasus. In 1821 he returned to St. Petersburg, where he had an audience with Alexander I. He remained here for nine months. It may be assumed with certainty that he heard Gossner preach and came in contact with him. Zaremba was able to work in the Caucasus until 1835, with one long break, until the decree of Nicholas I put an end to the Basle work. The Armenian Lutheran congregation in Shemakha, between Tiflis and Baku, which came into being through Zaremba, still existed in the twentieth century.

V EDUARD WÜST

Apparently unrelated to all this was the fruitful ministry of Eduard Wüst (1818–59). He had a similar spiritual influence in the south of Russia to Gossner's in the north. His activity took place in the reign of Nicholas I, with his fateful slogan: One tsar, one people, one faith. Gossner, who lived in St. Petersburg under the tsar's eye, had had to go. Eduard Wüst, far away in the southern part of the empire, developed a many-sided activity in spite of this anti-evangelical regime.

Wüst was the son of a Swabian banker and innkeeper in Murrhardt, a small county town in the Swabian forest. He was born on 23 February 1818, thus belonging to a later generation than Gossner, but died at the early age of 41, only one year after Gossner who reached the ripe age of 84. Born in a devout home, Wüst lost his father at the age of seven. His family wanted him to become a minister, but he showed little enthusiasm. He failed the entrance examination for the college in Tübingen, which had a generous grant for theological students. As a free student in Tübingen he fell a prey to frivolous living and became a source of concern to his family. He finally passed his examination with great difficulty. In 1844 he became curate in Bad Rietenau near Backnang and here in the *Stunde* of the Hahn Brethren he was awakened to a personal life of faith. Now through his lively sermons and faithful house visitations, which fanned the flame of faith in many households, he came into conflict with other ministers. Members of congregations from neighbouring communities, whose ministers were ill-disposed towards the *Stunde*, came to attend his sermons and bible studies. Their unfounded complaints to the consistorium led to his dismissal; he remained without employment for some time. Wüst was strengthened and confirmed in his faith by Methodist missionary Müller in Winnenden.

After this God gave him his task: the emigrants from Württemberg by the Sea of Azov had thought that they could manage without pastors and make do with lay preachers. But they had discovered their mistake; so now they appealed to Wilhelm Hoffmann, the leader of the Lutheran *Brüdergemeinde* in Korntal near Stuttgart, which he himself had founded, to send them a suitable minister. After discussion with Hoffmann, Wüst was prepared to go. In the summer of 1845 he made the difficult journey east and reached Odessa in four weeks. He soon found fellowship both with the separatists – this is what the pietists who had turned their backs on the Church used to be called – and among the Lutheran settlers. He had his preaching centre in the colony of Neuhoffnung. Wüst laboured here for fourteen years. until he was called home by his Lord in July 1859.

He had the gift of preaching unto repentance. Soon there was revival. Prayer and bible study circles sprang up here and there. There was a successful drive against alcoholism. The people came to their pastor under deep conviction of sin, to confess. This was no shower of blessing, which would quickly disperse, it was a real downpour. Up to 1859 one can distinguish three waves of revival. Everywhere Christian habits and order reappeared. Three times a day the head of the house would read from the bible at table and close with spontaneous prayer. Many adults took part in the Sunday school teaching for children, and on Sunday evenings the *Stunde* would gather, with free discussion of the bible passages. Every month there was a missionary hour. Communion alternated with meditations on the psalms.

Here in the south, as through the Herrnhut brethren of Sarepta, a basis of faith was laid in the Volga colonies which would withstand the trouble that was to come later. Even today under Bolshevik rule, there are still among the deported German colonists in Siberia and Turkestan hundreds of house fellowships for bible study. When at this time epidemics broke out in the neighbouring Russian villages, Wüst saw to it that the Russian children got free milk from their German neighbours. And when in 1852 there was a harvest failure in Württemberg, he organized an aid programme for the mother country. New churches were built. A strict community discipline ensured that for years the state authorities had no crimes to deal with in these colonies. During the Crimean War, Wüst organized help for the poor Jewish villages in the area and provided the necessary seed for the Tatar Muslims in the Crimea. Here again pietism showed that it was aware of social responsibility far beyond the bounds of its own churches and people.

Wüst was also called to the newly established Mennonite communities nearby. Here through his ministry there came that revival which gave birth to the so-called Mennonite Brethren, who for more than a hundred years gathered together the awakened members of the community, both in Europe and overseas. It is probable that this formation was created on the advice of Wüst, who had after all been sent to Russia from the *Brüdergemeinde* in Korntal, which itself was a gathering of awakened members of the Württemberg state Church. The people in Korntal in turn had taken the Herrnhut *Brüdergemeine* as their example in many respects. Thus over the course of the centuries there was a fruitful harvest from the *unio fratrum*, the Unity of the Brethren, which had first arisen in Moravia, and which had its roots in the Hussite movement. In these *Brüdergemeinden* there was less emphasis on large-scale organization than on the fellowship of brethren in faith, prayer and ministry.

Brotherly love drove Wüst in 1849 to St. Petersburg, in order to have fellowship with those who had been touched by the revival there. He travelled further to Reval (Tallinn), where he visited Pastor Huhn at the old Oleviste church, who was labouring here with similar blessing to Wüst in the south of Russia. Huhn's memorable ministry was continued decades later by Traugott Hahn the elder. It is moving to see how the vast distances of Russia did not prevent the brethren from seeking and finding one another. Otherwise Wüst remained in the south; he also travelled through the Crimea, where he preached in Simferopol and organized mutual 'fraternal visits' just as they are still practised in the Württemberg communities today.

Even here Wüst's activity was not without opposition. He had a similar experience to that of the apostle Paul, who wrote to the Corinthians: 'A wide door for effective work has opened to me, and there are many adversaries' (I Cor. 16.9).

When Samuel Keller received his first parish in the south of Russia in 1880 – more than twenty years after Wüst's death – he came upon visible traces of his labours. And later when he was ministering in the Crimea, he got to know two communities in his large parish which he named the 'converted' villages or the 'brethren villages'. These stemmed from Wüst's labours; his picture still hung in many a colonist's home, until all these settlements were destroyed in the second world war.

Here too the question still remains: how far did these movements have an effect beyond the bounds of the German-speaking Protestant communities? The settlers were still forbidden to do any missionary or evangelistic work among the members of the Orthodox state Church, under pain of severe punishment. Keller himself had to flee from Russia because he was threatened with exile to Siberia on account of his successful preaching activity, which had an effect beyond his own congregation.

Clear traces of that early period cannot be proven among the Russians. It is true that there were in the south 'evangelical' Russian sects, that is, those that had certain similarities with the Protestant Church. These included above all the Molokans (milk drinkers), a community which held the bible to be sufficient, but in such an exclusive manner that they cut themselves off from their environment and did no missionary work. This group too was later touched by revival; but not through the Germans, rather through a converted Persian. They do not seem to have had any contact with Wüst. We do not even know whether Eduard Wüst knew Johannes Bonekemper in Rohrbach near Odessa personally, although they were both working at the same time. But Wüst's field of activity lay much further to the east.

B. Stundism up to the Bolshevik Revolution

I THE ROOTS OF RUSSIAN STUNDISM

All the gospel influences described so far only seem to have had a temporary and individual effect in the vastness of Russia. Whether they contributed to the revival among the Russian peasants in the second half of the nineteenth century, and if so how far, it is impossible to establish at this time. However, they do form the background for the developments about to be described, and one must be familiar with them in order to understand the subsequent events.

Under the general name of 'stundism' we are speaking of the great movement among Ukrainians and Russians (and to some extent among neighbouring peoples also) in the second half of the last century. The contemporary heirs of this movement in the Soviet Union today are the 'All-Union Council of Evangelical Christians-Baptists'. Stundism in the narrower sense is a revival movement which arose in the Russian Ukraine among Ukrainians and Russians, with direct roots in the so-called *Stunde* of German peasants in southern Russia, who had been awakened through a new spiritual movement. This movement began in Rohrbach and reached its peak there during the years 1835–46. From this fellowship hour (in German: *Stunde*) came the name, which may originally have been a term of mockery, and which was taken into Russian as a foreign word.

This irruption of the biblical, reformed gospel into that part of the Ukraine which belonged to the tsarist empire took place with such dynamism that it seemed to many like a miracle. Despite strong opposition, the movement spread with astonishing speed from the district between the Dniepr and the eastern frontier of Bessarabia to the north and east. Seldom has a revival moved so quickly.

The Orthodox Church had not been able to satisfy the religious hunger among Russians and Ukrainians. This was the reason for the innumerable sects which had come into being; these were of the most varied kind: mystical and rationalist, ecstatic and political, moralistic and eccentric. On top of this was the unhappy connection between faith and politics, religion and nationalism. The state Church was the constant advocate of the tsar's state policies: this was the Byzantine heritage. The Church had become the bailiff of the state and the state police were the executive organ of the Church.

The new stundist movement had much to suffer under these conditions. The old *raskolniki* (schismatics) at the time of Nikon in the seventeenth century had been subject to the same things. Now it was an evangelical movement, which at first did not aim to be anything but a pietist movement within the Church, which had to tread the same path. (The Protestant state Churches, which arose out of the provincial Churches of the Reformation, were undoubtedly wrong developments too. But the rights they possessed can scarcely be compared to the ruling prerogative of the tsarist Church. We must keep this fact in mind if we are to understand, at least to some degree, the martyrdom of the stundists under Alexander III and Nicholas II at the time of Konstantin Petrovich Pobedonostsev, Oberprokuror of the Holy Synod.)

The bible movement stemming from Rohrbach was one of the three sources from which sprang the great evangelical bible movement that forms the broad stream of the Evangelical Christians-Baptists in the Soviet Union today.

The second source was the German Baptist movement: Johann Gerhard Oncken (1800–84), founder of the German Baptist congregations and preacher in Hamburg, sent Baptist artisans to Russia, who were to be effective through their testimony, since the law forbade any other kind of evangelism. Oncken himself had travelled to Russia a few times, and his messenger Kalweit had founded the first slavic Baptist congregation in Tiflis, which had a strong influence far to the north. This will be described in more detail on pp. 98–102 ff.

The third source was the second revival in St. Petersburg which had arisen through the salon bible studies of the English Lord Radstock (1833–1913). The evangelist Radstock belonged to the so-called Open Brethren, as did the famous George Müller of Bristol and also Dr. Baedeker, a friend of Radstock who had been converted in one of his evangelistic campaigns, and who later became such a significant figure for Russia. As in the years 1812–24, it was again a small circle of nobility, high officials and court society who gathered together and who disposed of considerable means which they gladly invested in the cause of Christ.

These three sources are certainly not exhaustive. One must also mention the missionary zeal of the communities of Mennonite Brethren, which had come into being through the activity of Eduard Wüst. We shall also mention a few individuals through whom God furthered this movement. To these must be added the many unnamed, unknown persons who played a decisive role in this work of God.

THE STUNDE IN ROHRBACH

Pastor Hermann Dalton, minister of the German Reformed congregation in St. Petersburg from 1858–88, as a part of his duties also had to oversee a few Reformed congregations in the colonies in southern Russia, including the community of Rohrbach, north of Odessa. Dalton himself stood by the stundists with brotherly love, one of the few who openly defended them in their time of greatest suffering. From him we have a report on Russian stundism which is one of the best sources dealing with this early period, and which forms the basis of this section, with some additions from other sources.

God's chosen tools in Rohrbach were the two pastors Johannes Bonekemper and his son Karl. Johannes, the father, was born in 1795 in Nümbrecht in the Oberbergischer Kreis of the Rhineland. He came from a poor family and lost both parents early in life. Since he had to fend for himself even as a small boy, he only had a minimal schooling. He became apprentice to a master blacksmith in Elberfeld. At that time there was revival in this area, but as Bonekemper admitted later, he hated the religious people. And then the young blacksmith's apprentice was won for Jesus, actually through a woman he wanted to make fun of because of her faith. He writes: 'Our Lord wanted to use her as a tool on my immortal soul.' After his military service, he became a member of Pastor Döring's young men's association. Here he heard about the German emigrants to southern Russia, and here too he heard his Lord's call to the ministry. Bonekemper applied to go to Basle, where the mission school had been opened five years previously (1816). From there he was sent for three months to Pestalozzi in Ifferten, who was to check his suitability. Pestalozzi realized that Bonekemper had quite considerable gifts; he undertook to complete the large gaps in his education quickly. In October 1821 he was accepted into the mission school in Basle, where he studied intensively for two and a half years, one of his subjects being the English language. He was ordained in Lörrach in 1824, and the very next day he was on his way to Rohrbach near Odessa, to which he had been called.

His parish included some two thousand five hundred community members. Besides the village of Rohrbach, where the minister lived, there were the settlements of Worms, Johannesthal, Friedrichsthal, Waterloo, Stuttgart and Julienfeld – all between one and a half and two and a half hours journey away. There were also a few scattered German Protestants in the three nearest towns: Voznesensk, which was eight hours away, Nikolayev 75 kilometres away, and the provincial capital of Kherson, which was 150 kilometres journey. It was a huge task for a beginner. Johannes Bonekemper laboured here for twenty-four years – until 1848. The condition of the community was very bad. It was in complete disarray, alcoholism and immorality were widespread, and the school was in a state of neglect. But God used Bonekemper's hard work – he began with the young people and soon introduced community bible studies as well – to bring revival. This reached its peak in the years 1835–46.

Johannes Bonekemper was a key figure in the stundist revival, and for a decade Rohrbach was cited by the authorities and by the Orthodox Church as the place where it started. It was here that the spiritually awakened Ukrainians gained their first teaching,

and also advice in their early needs and difficulties. We are indebted to a subsequent pastor in Rohrbach, Heinrich Roemmich,
for giving a history of the Rohrbach community, making use of
Johannes Bonekemper's diaries.

Rohrbach had been founded in 1810 together with the colony
of Worms by immigrants from Alsace, Palatinate, Baden and
some from Württemberg. Reformed and Lutheran believers had
joined to form a 'Protestant congregation', one of the oldest
German communities near Odessa.

Pastor Hübner had held office here from 1812–14 and had
lamented the poor moral condition of the community, which had
been without a minister in its early years. Poverty, bad harvests
and the wholly inadequate cottages made of earth (the so-called
zemlyanki) bred degeneracy. Hübner writes: 'Despite the many
calamities, the profligacy continued. There were very few who
paid attention to God's hand chastening them for their own good.
Anyone who excelled in lavish spending while under the influence
of strong drink, could count on enjoying the applause of his
brethren, who wasted their energies in the shadow of the public
houses, without a thought for the well-being of their offspring . . .
The young people grew up accustomed to dissipation. Most of
them scarcely learned to read.'

When Johannes Bonekemper came to Rohrbach in 1824, ten
years later, the picture had not changed. And despite the young
pastor's many efforts, still nothing changed in the first four years.
There were small gatherings for edification in a few houses,
particularly after new settlers arrived from Württemberg in 1817.
Bonekemper writes in his diary:

'No-one knows better than God and I that my wish and
desire has been to see not only one or two, but all saved. But
again, no-one knows better than God and I that so far I have not
seen this wish fulfilled, but rather that I have had to observe almost
all of them grow daily worse, and how much unease, anxiety and
care this has caused my heart.'

In the fifth year of his ministry the Spirit of God began to blow.
On 10 March 1829, Bonekemper was able to write in his diary:

'Over the last three months, the attendance at our normal

Sunday and festival services has been unusually observant and numerous, also the weekly catechismal sermons, which have been introduced here over this time, have been listened to by many, with reverence, beyond our expectations. But even more in demand are the private gatherings for edification ... Over the last fortnight I have been visited by various people either by day or by night (or rather, in the evening, like Nicodemus for fear of the Jews). During these visits, people tell me of their fear, their need, and the danger in which their souls stand, and beg me to tell them what they must do to be saved.'

It is interesting from the church historical point of view that the same things were being reported, in almost the same words, in Berlin and in Pomerania, in Württemberg and Wuppertal, in Hamburg and Bremen, at the same time as here. The Spirit of God, who awakens the consciences of men, was blowing throughout Europe – a phenomenon which cannot be explained rationally. Bonekemper gave detailed descriptions of these pastoral conversations in his diary. Here are a few typical ones:

During a funeral service, a woman hears the words from Isaiah 26.2: 'Open the gates, that the righteous nation which keeps faith may enter in.' Terror-struck, she recognizes that she does not belong to the righteous nation, because she has not kept the faith. The very next day comes her husband, saying that he can no longer endure this disturbance of soul! He had already been on his way to the pastor several times, but had always turned back again. Soon after this comes a man who has been earnestly reading the bible with another who had been a soldier for eight years, a rough, godless man. He had heard the sermon about the fourfold field, and was afraid that he belonged to the bad ground, he said. Soon after that comes his companion, and confesses that he has been struggling for years with the flesh, the world and the devil. But now along with many other visitors, he is reading Arndt's *True Christianity* and singing and praying with them! A lad who had just been confirmed thought he had committed perjury because he did not keep his confirmation vow. Now he is grieved at his 'hardness of heart' during the teaching.

The opposition was not long in appearing. At a funeral service,

Bonekemper spoke of walking in the light and walking in darkness. He also mentioned those who sat in public houses. At this, the publican broke out in abuse against Bonekemper. But this man too was caught up in the revival. The doors of the pastor's house were open both day and night to those seeking salvation.

On 29 March 1829 Bonekemper wrote in his diary:

'Despite the fact that there are many unpleasant aspects to these private visits, on the whole it brings me great joy and pleasure, for people's hearts are being touched.'

Other Protestant pastors came from neighbouring places to talk with Bonekemper. One of them, who suffered from severe depressions, and who was his guest for several days, stated that he had not spent such peaceful days and nights for ten years as he did in Bonekemper's house! On 24 April 1829, Bonekemper wrote in his diary:

'Oh God, save his poor soul out of all violence and danger, for the sake of the sacred blood that was shed and for the sake of your promise, to your praise and glory. Amen.'

In his pastoral ministry, Bonekemper always pointed to a right relationship with Jesus and the necessity of the new birth. Even those who only passed through his home as guests heard about the one thing that was necessary. Many were impressed by his faith and testimony, and by his pastoral experience.

In order to protect the growing movement from the sects that were widespread in southern Russia, he moved the meetings into the schoolhouse, chose a council of brethren, eight men, and together with them worked out an ordinance for the *Stunden*. Three men were elected as leaders. After an address to the large gathering on Heb. 10.19–25, the ordinance was read out and within a week it was signed by the participants. There were about a hundred members. The pastor found great support in a Christian teacher, Eberhard, from the settlement of Worms, who led the *Stunde* there.

In 1832 the confessional situation was changed by Nicholas I, who was an autocrat in these matters too. The church ordinance of the Lutheran Church in Livonia was extended to the colonist communities as well, although the colonists from Württemberg, for example, were unfamiliar with the liturgical form of service. Brenz, Luther's close friend and reformer of Württemberg, unlike Luther had not taken over the Sunday mass with certain variations, but the simple weekday service. That is why the Church in Württemberg, despite its Lutheran creed, still has a form of service today which is more like the Reformed one in Switzerland. Now even Reformed believers in Rohrbach were asked to accept the Lutheran form, but they refused. Provost Fletnitzer in Odessa, however, was enthusiastic for the Lutheran way. He found no support from Bonekemper for this and thus became a sharp opponent of his; he made life very difficult for him. It was not until 1836 that a solution was reached: both Reformed and Lutherans retained their own form of service. The unity which had stood the test for so long was now threatened, although there was still one pastor who now had to change the form of service every week. It was a nonsensical decision, but neither of the two sides wanted to give up their beloved pastor.

In the winter of 1837–38, the wave of revival rose once again. In the colony of Waterloo sometimes half of the whole community attended the *Stunde*. The young people were particularly gripped by the Spirit of God. On 10 February 1838 Bonekemper wrote:

'Again our faithful Lord and Saviour does not leave himself without witnesses in Worms, Johannesthal, Waterloo and Güldendorf, just as here in Rohrbach. According to reports, the same is true in Odessa. In Nikolayev too it seems that he wants to bring joy to my dear brother Doll, in that there too since this New Year a small group has begun to form.'

In 1846 there were 'turbulent revivals', but they were all directed into the structured meetings. Thus any splits were avoided.

As might be expected, Fletnitzer used every opportunity to criticise. But Bonekemper reacted calmly. He wrote to a friend:

'Even Jesus and his apostles brought unrest into the world, as one can read in the New Testament.'

The reproach of causing unrest in the Church is an almost

classic expression of anxiety on the part of church authorities in the face of growing revival movements.

Bonekemper was now invited to preach in the surrounding communities – with the exception of Fletnitzer's congregation. In 1838 he accompanied his provost on a tour of visitation through Bessarabia. Both in Tarutino and in Sarata, Ignaz Lindl's former congregation, he was asked to remain as pastor. But Bonekemper remained faithful to Rohrbach until 1848. It was only then that he was forced through evil gossip originating from Odessa to take a congregation in Dobrudja, which at that time still belonged to Turkey.

After his departure, the teacher in Rohrbach wrote:

'A new era began for us with the year 1824. God had mercy on us in every sense, and according to his wise intention he sent us our first gospel preacher, Johannes Bonekemper, who laboured with great blessing . . . the blessing that he left behind through his twenty-four years' ministry will remain in our memory for a long time.'

When Hermann Dalton visited the Reformed congregation in Rohrbach fifty years later, he wrote: 'Although almost half a century has now passed since the noble missionary scholar from Basle laid down the post which he had held for a quarter of a century, the devout, noble Bonekemper the elder is still remembered and honoured today in many circles' (*op. cit.* p. 7).

Pastor Heinrich Roemmich, to whom we owe these facts, also writes that his parents in Worms, where he was born in south Russia, spoke of Bonekemper and his revival sermons with great respect. The *Stunde* in Rohrbach remained intact until the Bolshevik era. We present these testimonies boldly, because attempts have been made to tarnish Bonekemper's reputation.

He was laid to rest in his native Nümbrecht in the Oberbergischer Kreis. On his tombstone is inscribed the name 'father of stundism'. There may be a certain confusion here with his son Karl, who knew the Russian language; while he was pastor in Rohrbach, he held the *Stunde* in Russian for the Russian harvesters. These *Stunden* were undoubtedly the basis for the awakening of several men who later became leaders in Russian stundism.

Nevertheless, the description 'father of stundism' is in a sense justified for Johannes Bonekemper. It was as a result of the profound revival in Rohrbach, which God granted during his ministry, that some ten years after his departure from Rohrbach the spark of revival spread to the Ukrainian peasants.

It is painful to recall the alienation between this revival community and the church authorities. Here too there is great need for understanding. Most of the Lutheran pastors in southern Russia came from the Baltic. Württemberg pietism was completely unknown there, and the *Stunde* may have been looked upon as fanatical. Fletnitzer may also have been moved by personal reasons in his struggles against Bonekemper. When Bonekemper's first wife, the daughter of an official of German origin, died, he married a simple member of his congregation, which led to evil gossip about him in Odessa. It is impossible to establish whether this was the true reason for his resignation. His son and later successor wrote that his father's health was 'gradually undermined by his zealous preaching'. The father laboured for a few more years, until 1853, in the German settlement of Atmagea. At the outbreak of the Crimean War, the Turks left the Dobrudja region. Bonekemper then returned to his native Rhineland, and died in 1857 at the age of sixty-one.

Bonekemper's successor was the Swiss pastor Uhlinger who had previously worked in the German Reformed orphanage in St. Petersburg. He was followed soon after by Bonekemper's eldest son Karl. Karl Bonekemper had attended the Russian schools in Kiev and Odessa and then, after a brief period as tutor in Constantinople, emigrated to America. It is said that his personal conversion to Jesus took place during a severe storm on the ocean. He became a Presbyterian minister in the USA and later taught for eight years at St. Chrischona, the bible school of the pilgrim mission founded by Spittler. From there he visited his native Rohrbach near Odessa, and during this visit he was elected pastor of the community. When the tsarist struggle against stundism reached its peak, state pressure forced Karl's transfer from Rohrbach to Moldavia, because his influence upon the Ukrainian peasants was well known. He later emigrated to

America again, and ended his life there. He was the one who gave the *Stunde* to the Ukrainian peasants.

THE UKRAINIANS

It was undoubtedly God's provision that the important stundist revival began among the Ukrainian peasants who in their history and their mentality are so different from the Great Russians in the north that there is today a strong nationalist movement among Ukrainians.

The emancipation movement among the peasants after the abolition of serfdom in 1861 by Alexander II (1855–81) was particularly strong in the Ukraine, because the peasants here had been subjected to serfdom relatively late – only some eighty years previously, under Catherine II, who was in many other respects proud of her enlightened attitude. She extended this harsh law to the Ukraine after parts of the Ukraine, which had belonged to Poland, had been annexed to the tsarist empire. Because the empress used favouritism so much, she found herself forced to give some reward to those whom she regarded as having rendered a service. Since serfdom had been in force throughout Russia for a considerable time, and Catherine would not risk suspending this inhuman system because of the economic upheaval that would be associated with it, the Ukrainian peasants too were now available as serfs.

The abolition of serfdom took place under conditions which were so unfavourable to the peasants that they found economic survival difficult. However in the Ukraine the peasants had the privileged German peasant colonies as neighbours. There they saw how agriculture could be carried on profitably, and they learned from their German neighbours not merely better methods, but also the value of hard work and thrift, insofar as the revival among the Germans had brought moral renewal, after the apathy of the difficult years. The observant Ukrainian peasant recognized the connection between faith, family and village life, and success in work. They saw that those who had been touched by revival knew their bible. In order to get to know the bible one had to learn to read and write. Thus the Protestant faith promoted more education than the Russian peasant needed to listen to his liturgy and to follow the prescribed rituals.

At the same time it is true that of all the slavic peoples the Ukrainians are particularly open to education. This is a result of their history, as we have seen.

After the annexation of the Ukraine to the Great Polish-Lithuanian empire (1320), Ukrainians were already studying at West European universities. Here, and also through Reformed Poles and Lithuanians, they came in contact with the Reformation. A large part of Poland had been won for Reformed teaching through the work of Johannes a Lasco, and only through the Jesuit counter-reformation was it again brought almost completely under Roman influence. In these struggles, Orthodox Ukrainians stood alongside the Reformed and the Moravian Brethren in a united front.

When after the Council of Florence in 1489 an attempt was made to force the Union upon the Ukrainians, in order to defend themselves against Catholicism they formed lay brotherhoods, a lay activity which is otherwise foreign to Orthodoxy.

We have already mentioned Petrus Mogila and his famous theological school in Kiev which was established according to the pattern of the Jesuit schools, thus influenced from the west, although its work was wholly anti-Catholic. The collegium of this school maintained close links with the University of Königsberg (now Kaliningrad), which again strengthened Protestant influences.

All these things over the course of the centuries kept the Ukraine ahead of Moscow. This became evident when the Ukraine again came under Muscovite rule – the eastern part under Peter the Great, and the western part under Catherine the Great, in whose reign a new time of suffering began for the Ukraine through the imposition of serfdom. While Alexander II liberated the peasants again, at the same time he systematically destroyed the independence of the Ukraine. The Ukrainians were given the name of Little Russians (*malorossy*). The name Ukraine could no longer be used in public life. According to an imperial decree of 1876, the Ukrainian language was also banned from schools and churches. The printing of Ukrainian literature was forbidden; the Ukrainian language was considered a peasant dialect, devoid of any cultural significance.

When Poland was divided into three under Catherine the Great (1772, 1793 and 1795), Austria had acquired a considerable part: Galicia and Bukovina. The Ukrainians here were now strongly encouraged in their national and literary development. This was characteristic of the tension between the monarchy on the Danube and the tsarist empire. The Austrian government did everything possible to persuade those on the other side of the frontier of its liberality. In so doing it strengthened the desire of the Russian Ukrainians for the west.

It is also important to note that not only St. Petersburg, but also the Ukraine maintained relations with Halle, the town of August Hermann Francke. Pietism was not wholly foreign to the Ukrainians. Their popular religious philosopher and poet Grigori Skovoroda (1722–94) is supposed to have studied in Halle from 1751–53. It is true that August Hermann Francke was long dead by that time, but his son and son-in-law Freijlinghausen were caring for his spiritual heritage. After his return, the eccentric Skovoroda wandered about the country with his bible, attacking both the monasteries and rationalism. He had certain similarities with his contemporary Johann Georg Hamann, the wise man of the north, and he exemplifies the spiritual openness of the Ukrainians. One of Skovoroda's sayings: 'The world tried to seize me, but it could not hold me,' characterizes his pietism. Taras Shevchenko, national poet of the new Ukraine, who was a powerful influence upon Ukrainian national feeling, also liked to quote the bible. The New Testament was translated into Ukrainian at that time by the Ukrainian Panteleimon Kulich, but the Holy Synod forbade the printing of the book.

However, since the language in the schools was Russian and not Ukrainian, it was of no little significance for the revival in the Ukraine that in 1875 for the first time there appeared a complete bible in popular Russian – not old Church Slavonic. The New Testament and Psalms had already been completed in the 1820's, done by the Russian Bible Society.

TWO FORERUNNERS

John Melville was a Scot and a strict Calvinist puritan. He had dedicated himself to colportage early in life and at the age of about twenty, he arrived in the south of Russia. Until 1848 he worked independently, then he was accepted into the service of the British and Foreign Bible Society. For sixty years he was a colporteur far into the Caucasus. He laboured under Alexander I, under Nicholas I when evangelistic work was very difficult, under the liberal Alexander II and during the time of reaction under Alexander III. Melville died in 1886. Dalton writes of him (*op. cit.* p. 13): 'I met this dear, humble Christian on my first journey to the south of Russia . . . For decades he travelled the south of Russia, the Crimea, the Caucasus and Armenia as far as the Persian frontier.' Everybody knew and esteemed Ivan Vasilievich, as he was called in Russian: Ukrainians and Germans, especially the Mennonites in the Donets area, the Karaites (a Jewish sect), Armenians, Tatars, Turks. Everywhere he distributed the word of God – if not complete bibles, at least the New Testament or even gospels or tracts in their own language. Those who were hungry for the truth of God he would gather in some back room to explain the word of God to them very simply. The 'omniscient' police in old Russia did not seem to notice anything; at any rate they did not hinder his work. 'Even after his death, I came across his traces in the Caucasus,' writes Dalton. It is impossible to measure how far this faithful sowing by Melville first prepared the way for and then strengthened the subsequent stundist movement. The only figure which has become available concerning his work testifies to the growth of the hunger for bibles: in 1869 there were 2,323 bibles distributed from Odessa, where Melville had his bible depot – three years later (1872) the figure was 69,346 bibles or bible portions.

Many anecdotes have been preserved about Ivan Vasilievich (John Melville) which are trustworthy insofar as they stem from firsthand sources. Remaining unmarried, and travelling about incessantly, this man must have had a constitution of iron. He exploited every possible opportunity for witness. At the same time he was not what one might call a lovable personality. His Scottish inflexibility was linked with a puritan legalism. Even during the liveliest conversation, at precisely ten o'clock in the evening he would stand up and bid his companions goodnight. In the middle of one missionary's report, when the clock struck ten, he stood up and took his leave. 'Decent people go home at ten o'clock,' he said and disappeared. On another occasion he was invited by a believer to Sunday dinner. His host hurried to pick some cherries, which had just ripened. Melville declared: 'Do you think I would eat cherries that have been picked on a Sunday? I would never touch such a thing.' His puritanical concept of the sabbath was like that of the Pharisees.

He was as strict in his personal principles as he was unbending in his faith in Jesus and the truth of God's word. One must know something of Russia to understand what that means to a Russian. Here in their midst was one who was quite different from them. Even though one might be offended by him, it was impossible not to be impressed by his consistency. He did not aim to make propaganda for any Church or denomination. He brought nothing other than the bible and quoted only from that – never a human testimony! Usually he did not even read the passage himself, but simply quoted the reference, leaving it to his companion to look it up and to draw the consequences. If he was a witness to arguments – for example, concerning baptism or doctrines of the last things – he could close his eyes, as if it had nothing to do with him. At the end of the argument he would then indicate the relevant bible passage and add with a smile: 'But haven't you read this? It's quite clear!' If anyone contradicted what the bible said, again he would close his eyes, and remain silent. The word of the bible was enough for him. The fact that stundism and also the Baptist movement have remained so close to the bible right up to the present has much to do with Melville. The evangelical movement in Russia was and still is today a bible movement.

A later friend of Melville tells how one day in his school, the district school in one of the most outlying towns of Russia, the school inspector came into the classroom with a tall man, a

Britisher, who was distributing bibles and New Testaments. This visit was not without result: later the inspector himself read to the pupils from the New Testament. It was here that the present author heard the story of the prodigal son for the first time. Later he too became a brother in Christ.

Not many of the hidden witnesses to the truth of Christ, who had a part in the approaching revival, can be portrayed so clearly as John Melville. But there is one other who should be mentioned: Yakov Delyakovich Delyakov, called Kasha Yagub – Jacob the priest. By birth he was a Nestorian from Persia; he had been awakened and brought to faith through the American Presbyterian missionaries. It appears that the Presbyterian missionaries gave large numbers of such men training in their bible schools, and then sent them out in the various countries as independent workers. There were too many of them to use them all as evangelists in the relatively small work in Persia. And not all of them stood the test so well as Kasha Yagub. The latter had a brother named Simon, who had also gone out into the world, but had now disappeared. Delyakov looked for him in Russia, and found him in Rostov-on-Don, married to a Russian woman, but unfortunately gripped by alcohol.

On his journey Delyakov noted with surprise how willing the people he met were to talk about religious questions. He soon learned enough Russian to make himself understood. And now he realized what a great mission field lay before him, calling out for labourers. He sent a written report to the headquarters of the Presbyterian mission in Urmia, and after his return, too, he spoke about these open doors. The mission recognized Kasha Yagub's calling, gave him money to return to Russia and at the same time guaranteed him a small monthly allowance of about ten pounds. This was at the beginning of the sixties, when the revival was beginning among the Ukrainian peasants. It is a testimony to Yagub's thrift, but also his practical bent, that he carried on his missionary work for thirty years on this extremely small support. He travelled as far as Siberia, visited the deportees on Sakhalin Island, and is even supposed to have worked in Manchuria. He too married a Russian girl, by whom he had several children. He spent his final days in the USA. This is a rough outline of his life in externals.

Many stories are told of Delyakov's ministry. He also found an entry into the Molokan community, the 'milk-drinkers' previously mentioned, who like the Quakers reject the sacraments and recognize neither minister nor preacher, where every member of the congregation has the right to preach and the focal point is the reading and exposition of the bible. In 1805 they had obtained religious freedom from Alexander I and were able to settle along the lower Volga around Saratov and Astrakhan. They were looked upon as hard-working, clean, sober separatists, who rejected all worldliness, theatre-going and pleasure-seeking. Through their spiritual in-breeding they had moved into sterile legalism and narrowness. Through his testimony, Delyakov brought about the renewal of several settlements. This was the origin of the New Molokans, who later joined the stundist movement. From here there came a number of important leaders of the revival movement, such as Prokhanov and Pavlov, about whom more will be said later.

It is said that Delyakov often travelled about as a pedlar in order – like the Waldensians in the Middle Ages – not to attract attention from the authorities. Thus he moved from settlement to settlement, from village to village. As well as the various haberdashery items which he sold to the peasants, he also offered bibles. Wherever he found open doors, he held a meeting and spread the word of God. His lack of pretention recommended him to the simple Russians, and his poverty was certainly a key to their trust. An old Russian describes his acquaintance with Kasha Yagub thus:

'My family consisted of more than twenty-five persons, most of them adults. I liked to welcome this traveller, who always talked about the gospel, I myself loved to talk with him about the faith. I investigated what he said, compared it with the word of God, and I often allowed him to talk about the Holy Scriptures and to expound the word of God to the whole family, which they enjoyed, and also neighbours and friends who came specially. But one day I had to forbid him to come any more, because I noticed

that his visits caused not only various disputes, but even real splits
in my formerly peaceful family. But he looked at me gravely and
said: "Would you forbid a servant of God, who preaches to your
children concerning the gospel of Jesus and conversion, to enter
your house? Think about it!" And I gave in, so that he was able
to visit my house just as before. But in the end I could not bear
these endless disputes and discussions any longer, and I told the
man – even though I was in agreement with all his ideas, no
matter how many times he came – to stay away. But when he
went out of the big room, I could be sure that he had gone through
the kitchen into another room, to talk there with some of my
people who liked to listen to him about spiritual things, and to
pray. He knew that I was not against him in my heart; for he
only spoke what could be proved in the word of God; so he kept
on coming to my house, and despite my reluctance, we would
always get into the most lively discussion, in which my children
usually took part. The man wanted to see me, as the head of the
house, won for the gospel – and he made no secret of this fact.
Well, it happened, and now, when he favours us with a visit, he
is our most welcome guest.'

This simple account by one believer is an example of how
Delyakov and a great host of others who have remained anony-
mous bore the good news of Jesus Christ to the peoples of Russia.
God had many other instruments. Because of the opposition of the
state Church, they sought to remain unknown and anonymous.
We shall see later how much they still had to suffer.

Wandering monks, pilgrims and eccentric saints had been
travelling through Russia for centuries. The Russian writers –
Dostoyevsky in his novel *The Devils*, Leskov and others – speak
about them. There can be no doubt that they included some
dishonest figures. We knew one beggar who year in and year out
begged money for his journey to Jerusalem, but probably never
got there. But many of them were genuine seekers after God.
They were in search of *pravda*, that is, the truth of God, according
to which we must shape our lives. (It was a sly trick on the part
of the Bolsheviks that they named their main official newspaper
Pravda, too.)

II   THE BEGINNINGS OF UKRAINIAN STUNDISM (1860)

THE FIRST REACTIONS OF THE ORTHODOX CHURCH AGAINST THE *STUNDE*

It is possible to gain a reasonable picture of the first stundist villages, where Ukrainian peasants gathered around the bible as in the *Stunden* in Swabia. The picture comes in fact from sources hostile to stundism.

Ukrainian doctor of theology Michael Klimenko shows in his dissertation of 1957 how the Russian Orthodox Church in the Ukraine reacted to the rise of the *Stunde*. One of his sources was the archive of the late Professor D. Steinwand in Erlangen, who himself had been a pastor in south Russia and kept a collection of Russian literature on stundism. Since these accounts come from Orthodox priests and theologians, and are not sympathetic to stundism, they give an objective picture. What they say about the attitude of the Orthodox Church and of the government will therefore not be exaggerated either. Some of these sources are official reports by state and church authorities, which were little known until now. Michael Klimenko deals with the period 1860–84, in other words, before the persecution of stundism which set in under Pobedonostsev, Oberprokuror of the Holy Synod. These were the first two and a half decades during which stundism followed a relatively peaceful development. Relative, that is, in comparison with the terrible persecution that came later.*

THE FIRST *STUNDE* IN THE VILLAGE OF OSNOVA

Although it was not until 1866 that the press in St. Petersburg began to wite about the 'new sect' of stundists in south Russia, Dalton had a brief encounter four years previously with the men who may be regarded as the founders of the *Stunde*. As a Reformed

---

* In the following description we have also used the accounts by Hermann Dalton, contemporary of the first *Stunde*, and Pastor Roemmich, the last pastor in Rohrbach.

minister, he visited the German Reformed congregations in the
south of Russia, which were under his consistorium, including the
Rohrbach community. Here in Rohrbach, where at the time of
Johannes Bonekemper there were Reformed and Lutheran
services side by side, he attended a *Stunde* of the German congregation which Pastor Karl Bonekemper was holding in the Russian
language. Here he noticed two Ukrainians who he thinks may
have been Ratushny and Onishchenko, who then began their own
Stunde in the neighbouring village of Osnova.

Their village bordered on the fields of the Rohrbach community, twelve kilometres away; it had no Orthodox church of its
own. For services the inhabitants of the village had to go to the
church in Ryasnopole, seven kilometres away. In 1887, twenty-
five years later, Osnova had eighty farmsteads with some 220
male inhabitants. It was probably not much smaller in 1862. Since
the *Stunde* was already functioning in Osnova in 1862, it may be
assumed to have begun in the year 1860/1. (In 1960 the All-Union
Council of Evangelical Christians-Baptists celebrated the centenary of stundism.)

We shall try to follow more closely the struggle of this small
community, about which a fair amount is known.

The first official report dates from the year 1865, from Orthodox
rural dean Kiryakov to Archbishop Dmitri of Odessa about the
'reformed sect in Osnova'. The dean was not yet able to say a
great deal; only that he had instructed the priest in Ryasnopole,
where the villagers of Osnova attended church, to watch the
'suspicious ones'. It was not yet known what type of sect it was.
It was suspected that the Reformed congregation in Rohrbach
was behind it, and that the group was tending towards the
Reformed faith. It must be remembered that the small group of
those who had been spiritually awakened had no intention of
becoming disloyal to their own Orthodox Church. They hoped
for a similar relationship to the Church as they had seen between
the pietist fellowships and the Protestant Church. It is part of the
tragedy of these early stundists that they did not realize that a
sacerdotal Church is never able to endure such a maturity and
inner independence among its members, as an established

Protestant Church can. It took years of conflict and suffering before both sides realized that they could not walk together.

On 10 February 1865 Stoikov, the priest in Ryasnopole, asked the local authorities (*volost*) in Osnova how many people took part in the *Stunde*, whether German pastors were also present, and whether the icons were hidden during the meetings. The state authorities and the Church worked together from the very beginning. Anything else was unthinkable in old Russia. The concern for icons reveals the true Orthodox priest.

The official reply came back within a week. The meetings had been taking place in the home of Michael Ratushny for four years (!) No German pastors attended. The number of those attending was given as seventeen men and three women. This small band was thus God's mustard seed, from which grew a great tree that overspreads millions of believers today. It is clear that the civil authorities had known about the *Stunde* for some time, but did not consider it as a sect dangerous to the Church.

In April Stoikov wrote to the rural dean to say that there was nothing special to report. In their meetings they read the gospel and sang 'hymns', church chorales. He appended a few texts. But by this time there were already thirty-two persons – twenty-four men and six women, also one citizen from Odessa and another from Voznesensk. So visitors were occasionally coming from outside. The *Stunde* in Osnova had become known, and may already have had parallels in other places.

There was peace until autumn. In October the rural dean complained that the stundists in Osnova had been inviting people from the next village. He asked the priest to establish whether the persons under suspicion still had icons in their homes and whether they really venerated them. Surprisingly, Stoikov was able to set the dean's mind at rest on this point. It is clear that the conflict concerning icons, which was to play such a large role in the subsequent interrogations, had not yet broken out. But the conscientious priest went on to say that he had forbidden the peasants to read the holy scriptures. This ban was illegal, and was not observed. But he also offered to give them a bible exposition on Sunday afternoons. This offer was not taken up.

Soon the justice of the peace was asking for the first time for information about the 'sect of the reformists'. He said he had heard that they also read things in German there, and that their Russian writings and prayer books had been printed abroad! These rumours, and the secular concern behind them, are extremely characteristic of old Russia. Anything printed was subject to censorship – even a death announcement. At the same time, as already mentioned, the Ukrainian language was forbidden in print. Nevertheless, Ukrainian writings were secretly brought in from Austria. For this reason all foreign books were automatically suspect. Also, Russian was the language of the Orthodox Christian faith.

It appears that the whole thing had now become a burden to Stoikov. His reports to his superiors obviously tried to make the whole thing appear harmless, so that he would be left in peace. For in February 1866 he reported that the stundists (although this name was not yet in use at that time) came to church regularly, took part in confession and communion, and had stopped the house meeting. However they did not attend the bible exposition in church, and on holy days (Wednesdays and Fridays) they drank milk. This is what he reported.

All these reports moved along the official channels. The activities of a few dozen people reading the bible engaged the attention first of the priest, then the rural dean, then the Archbishop of Odessa, and finally a High Consistorium. The reply which came back to the local priest from above was very non-committal: he was to handle everything 'with the necessary pastoral caution and wisdom'. This was after all normal for a minister.

THE MOVEMENT SPREADS

Quite apart from the *Stunde*, Ratushny obviously had considerable influence in Osnova as a former community leader; people respected him. The situation in the neighbouring village of Ignatovka was different. Here there was opposition among the inhabitants. On 30 December 1866 it was reported from Ignatovka that three families were to be evicted from the village and driven away because of their apostasy from the Orthodox Church and their conversion to the 'Reformed law' (!) The exact words of the village elder were as follows: 'We as a village community took decisive measures to bring the sectarians to their senses. But all our measures and our pleas were in vain. The sectarians reproach our community with having forgotten the true faith and say that we are lost. They also abuse the holy icons and the statutes of the Orthodox Church. We have taken ultimate measures in order to prevent this religion they have chosen from spreading any further among our people.'

This violent step was not a successful one. The new *Stunde* continued in Ignatovka, although one landowner reported that two founders of the sect had been sent into the army. This was one way of settling a religious controversy!

From the beginning of 1866 the ecclesiastical and secular authorities were combatting the spread of stundism independently of one another. The reports of the justice of the peace (*mirovoi posrednik*) to the governor in Odessa included the following statements:

'A sect has formed in the village of Osnova. It has twenty members. They meet at night (!) and sing hymns from Russian and German books . . .'. 'Many peasants from Osnova have been employed by Germans in Rohrbach for years, they have learnt German there and are accepting their doctrine . . .'. 'The Reformed colonists also meet at night, sing their hymns and read holy books.' 'Michael Ratushny was agricultural foreman in Rohrbach for a long time.' 'Seven peasants from Ignatovka and Ryasnopole have converted to the sect at the same time.'

Two weeks after this last report, the governor demanded from the police 'detailed information about the new sect'. The first police report among the documents dates from February 1867:

'The sect is indeed offensive, because it has a schismatic character similar to the Reformation.' According to the police investigations there were fifteen persons in Ignatovka, five families in the church village Ryasnopole, and fourteen families in Osnova. But these figures only appear to be estimates. It goes on: 'They meet in homes, read books in Church Slavonic' (this is doubtful – otherwise it would be a sign of their Orthodoxy), 'which they interpret for themselves, sometimes under the leadership of other Reformed schismatics from Rohrbach. As a result of this, the peasants who have adhered to the schism have developed a stubborn attitude, according to which they no longer attend the Orthodox Church, or venerate the icons, or observe the customs of the Orthodox faith. The priest here was a Greek' (Stoikov?), 'he could not speak Russian well and thus was unable to talk them round. The group is said to have formed in the year 1862.'

It is noticeable in this report how difficult it must have been for a police official to get a true picture of this movement. At the same time there is an interesting point here: since Karl Bonekemper, who could speak Russian well, did not come to Rohrbach until 1865, the *Stunde* in Osnova was thus in existence before his arrival. In that case the accusation that he brought the *Stunde* into being in Osnova is not wholly accurate. It may have been simple pietist farmers from Rohrbach or from somewhere else who started it. Nevertheless the Reformed believers in Rohrbach are said to be the guilty ones!

According to Archbishop Alexi, who in 1908 published a collection of materials on the history of stundism, the governor had a good opinion of Karl Bonekemper. He called him a 'remarkable man' (*zamechatelny chelovek*). This sounds positive. Nevertheless Bonekemper was later transferred to Bessarabia. The Lutheran church leadership in Odessa was not sympathetic towards the pietist movement in Rohrbach. It was also policy with the German Protestant Church in Russia to avoid conflicts with the government as far as possible, especially since they themselves were only one of the 'tolerated' confessions in the tsarist empire.

Since the press was now printing new articles on stundism from time to time, the authorities were forced to take a stand. In February 1867 there was an inquiry from Governor-General von Kotzebue to the Governor of Odessa. These governor-general figures, appointed by the tsar, ruled supreme over a number of provinces; they had special powers: for example, they could declare a state of war in their area, or a state of siege, as actually

happened in the Baltic provinces of Estonia, Livonia and Courland in the revolutionary year 1905. Kotzebue's territory, New
Russia, consisted of the southern provinces by the Black Sea. He
had read an article in the Odessa daily newspaper *Odessa Herald*
about stundism, and wanted to know more about it. We can see
how the interest in what was happening was escalating from the
village itself to the highest authorities. Even newspapers in the
capital St. Petersburg were reporting on the new 'sect'.

This may be the reason why in March of that year we find
rural dean Kiryakov himself in Osnova, Ryasnopole and Ignatovka, the places affected by the movement. He wanted to form
his own picture of the 'apostates' by talking with them. He
concluded that there was not yet any question of a sect having
formed. It was true that some people had fallen under the influence of Lutheranism (!), that they had attended some German
services out of curiosity, and that they sang their songs to
German tunes, but the books they were reading were 'Orthodox
in character'. He found no foreign books. It must be remembered
that the bible was printed with the *imprimatur* of the Holy Synod.

Thus Bishop Alexi of Odessa was able to report to his superiors
that it was merely pietist circles for mutual edification, such as
could be found in a number of places since the abolition of serfdom. This assessment, that it was a question of people seeking
fellowship within the Orthodox Church, was probably fair on
the basis of the investigations. Who knows what might have
happened, had the Church been sufficiently tolerant to embrace
such circles! On the other hand it must be realized that to have
permitted the continuation within its membership of a piety
determined solely by the bible, would have been a self-contradic-
tion on the part of Orthodoxy, which has such a firmly established dogmatic and liturgy. The contradiction would have
erupted sooner or later over the question of icons and veneration
of the saints. A community which found its revelation in the
bible alone, and not in church tradition, could not be contained
within the state Church.

The gradually increasing interest of the secular authorities may
have had another cause. It was in the 1860's and even more so the

1870's that the secret revolutionary movement of the *narodniki*, later the social revolutionaries, was growing, which finally led to the assassination of Alexander II in 1881. This movement tried – albeit with very little success – to get support from the peasants. In 1874 (there are specific data on this) thousands of revolutionary students went 'to the people'; they tried to whip up the peasants, who were dissatisfied with the completely inadequate land distribution after the emancipation of the serfs, against the government, and to stage revolts. This was particularly true in the Volga provinces which in former times had seen the uprisings of Stenka Razin and Pugachov, and still preserved their memory. But the students also worked in the so-called New Russian provinces in the south. The governors were instructed to practise special vigilance. The *narodniki* tried repeatedly – as they admitted themselves – to find allies among the sects which were so numerous in Russia. But despite repeated attempts, they had no success here.

A movement similar to that in Osnova took place in 1867, in this case 120 kilometres north-west of Odessa. However it does not seem to have lasted. The circle in Osnova had nothing to do with this. The local police chief for the Ananev area reported to the Governor of Kherson that a citizen from Ananev had begun a *Stunde* in the farming settlement (*khutor*) Nikolayevsky. (The name *Stunde* now seems to have become usual for any such phenomenon.) The person involved here was a Polish Catholic, Adam Foisarovsky. When the homes in this small settlement were searched, they found in each one a New Testament in the synodal edition, that is, approved by the Church. 'They do not recognize the holy relics, and thereby blaspheme against God. They abuse the saints, despise the icons, and deny the cross.' It was reported that a soldier called Lev Popov was instructing four boys and two girls 'in a spirit contradictory to Orthodoxy'. There were fifteen families – thirty-five persons, including children – on the list. The police chief arrested the soldier Popov, and confiscated the books. The participants came not only from Nikolayevsky, but also from Odessa, Nikolayev and even Bendery (Bessarabia). Catholics and Orthodox sat side by side.

This account shows what happened when the church authorities called on police help. The provincial administration in Kherson in this case forbade the police to take court action. The books had to be given back. Nothing more is heard of this group. It may be that this 'ecumenical' fellowship was suppressed. But this little episode is interesting as a symptom. Who knows how many similar things may have happened in other places, without it becoming widely known!

FURTHER DEVELOPMENTS IN OSNOVA AND ENVIRONS

In July 1867 the examining magistrate (!) had handed over to the Archbishop of Odessa his papers with the results of his investigations. Now the latter appointed a particular priest to take care of the 'apostates'. The report of the examining magistrate reveals a similarly excessive character to that of the police, mentioned above. Besides the abandonment of church rituals (such as making the sign of the cross), of fasting, of the veneration of icons, and of the saints, the charges stated that the apostates had fallen away from the Orthodox faith and instead accepted 'Protestant doctrine and the apostolic epistles!' It had obviously come to the attention of the examining official that during their meetings they also read the letters of the apostles in the New Testament. These may have been unfamiliar to the official, who was probably Orthodox.

Now the rural dean Kiryakov himself took over the dialogue with those who attended the meetings. He too seems to have been rather balanced and to have played down the contradictions. The efforts of a number of subordinate church bodies to effect a peaceful solution should be noted in view of the subsequent fanaticism of the struggle under Pobedonostsev. They were probably also confused by the novelty of the phenomenon, particularly since they would have appreciated the stundists' lack of pretension and their real courage as Christian witnesses. A mere three weeks later, the rural dean reported that nothing new had emerged.

Nevertheless, the archbishop came to the conclusion that the sect was dangerous, because it rejected the sacraments, the priest-hood, the icons and veneration of the saints. From the viewpoint of the Orthodox Church, this was a reasonable assessment. The rural dean and the local priest were censured. The (Greek?) priest was removed. He was replaced by a young man, Nogayevsky, fresh from seminary.

Soon after this, the rural dean reported that the stundists 'affirmed with tears that they had not abandoned their faith, that they recognized no new doctrine and therefore could not name any instigator. They did not feel guilty because they met to read the bible and to sing. They would be happy even to speak with the archbishop.'

It must be noted that the Orthodox Church has never known any ban on the use of the bible, and it is well known that the Russian bibles were printed in the text approved by the Holy Synod.

At the ordination of the new priest, the rural dean had fresh talks with the stundists, and reported that they had complained of being arrested without cause. 'We shall be ruined if we are forcibly kept from our work.' Unfortunately it cannot be established with certainty who had been arrested, and for how long. Ratushny is one possibility. This is the first report of a police intervention. Unfortunately this was only the beginning of fresh troubles.

At the end of 1867 there is another interesting document from a different source, containing some surprising information. A landowner by the name of Znachko-Yavorsky, who is otherwise unknown, appealed directly to Governor-General von Kotzebue in a letter. This appears to have been a formal memorandum, showing that stundism – this name had now become common usage – was much more widely spread than might have been supposed by looking at Osnova and its environs. The writer headed his memorandum: *The Stundist Community in Southern Russia*. He emphasized the firm organization of the movement, which he said already had its own customs. In the village of Kulikovka (Odessa region) it was being suppressed by the energetic action of the priest. The writer even suspected the stundists of 'communist principles' – a dangerous charge in a time of growing revolutionary activity throughout the tsarist empire.

This memorandum seems to have passed without any action being taken. However, it did find a place in the daily newspapers. These even mentioned a figure of about 300 adherents, which cannot be verified. The governor of Kherson made a reassuring statement that it was a purely religious movement, without any dubious background. In this way he hoped to ward off political suspicion. It was simply a group of people, he said, who liked to read the bible in their homes. Since John Melville from Odessa, the messenger of the British and Foreign Bible Society, was occupied quite officially with the distribution of bibles, he went on, there was no cause for alarm. However in January 1869 for the first time there came a query from the Minister of the Interior in St. Petersburg regarding the *stundovtsy* (a new form of the name, but one which never gained currency). It is not known what kind of answer the minister received. However it may be supposed that in replying to higher officialdom, everything was made to appear as harmless as possible.

Meanwhile the newly-appointed and enthusiatic priest, Nogayevsky, had also reported to the archbishop that the *Stunde* was not declining! They try to prove that they are true Christians, he stated. Instead of going to the public house on Sundays, they go to their meetings. Outsiders were sympathetic towards them. The Germans had taken these simple people under their wing and were trying to help through reading and expounding the gospel. 'For otherwise the people live like animals.' It was the Germans who were responsible for stundism! He himself was trying to win the trust of the stundists. Something which brought about a new order of things in the countryside should not be suppressed.

We know that revolutionary propaganda was having a strong influence upon the seminaries. Here were men who had been given some training to think for themselves, and who as priests could soon have considerable influence upon the peasants. It is well known that Joseph Dzhugashvili, later to be called Stalin, also passed through a seminary, where he became familiar with revolutionary writings.

The young Nogayevsky could see that there were undoubtedly moral influences at work here. While the poor peasant tried to drown his sorrows in alcohol, and spent Sunday playing cards in the public house, the stundists were reading the bible, praying and singing. It was clear that they had overcome a problem which had so far defeated the Orthodox Church. Where had these people learned to act like this? From the neighbouring colonists, where such meetings were quite normal!

Behind all this lay a serious social problem. Although the peasants were no longer slaves, they still had to pay for the land on which they were working and which barely gave them a living. The big landowners had used their influence to water down the law. They were to pay dearly for this later. Prime Minister Stolypin, who was murdered before the first world war, was the first to recognize the importance for Russia of a free and economically strong peasantry. But by then it was too late.

In May 1868 came a report from the Archbishop of Odessa to the governor-general: The persons under suspicion were not sectarians, nevertheless he requested the governor to consider what measures should be taken against them. Should the Germans perhaps be forbidden to hold meetings together with the Russian peasants? Should Ratushny not be removed from Osnova as a leader and trouble-maker?

The fact that Church and state stood as equals confused the demarcation of responsibility. At the same time, it is clear that the individual had absolutely no rights. Admittedly he could not be accused under the law (not even as a sectarian), but even without a trial he could be expelled from his home. We in Western Europe ought to study conditions under the tsarist empire more closely. We would then be less surprised at the measures taken by the new rulers in the Kremlin. This is how it used to be, and this is how it has remained. The governor-general had the power to exile a man in Siberia 'by administrative methods', that is, quite arbitrarily, without having to give account for his action. The Russian people had grown accustomed over the course of centuries to this legal anarchy. Even Alexander II's welcome reform had not effected any real change in this state of affairs.

In 1868 the archbishop also reported to his supreme church authority, the Holy Synod in St. Petersburg: Since the new sect (sic!) was distinguishing itself by zealous proselytism – in other words, it was attracting a good number of people – the archbishop hoped that the civil authorities would take action. Evidently he had no spiritual resources to hand.

On 8 July 1868 the stundists made their first self-defence before the higher authorities. The appeal to Governor-General von Kotzebue bore four signatures: Ratushny, Kapustyan, Balaban and Osadsky. Here we come across some new names of church-historical importance. Unfortunately, here too we do not know the details and the events which preceded the appeal, and can only draw conclusions from the complaint itself. The signatories ask for legal protection against the clergy whose harassments they can no longer endure. 'The civil authorities take the part of the clergy and inflict numerous penalties upon us, although we are completely innocent', they write. They mention an arrest which took place on 6 January 1867, carried out by the village elder at the instigation of the village priest. It is not revealed who had been arrested at that time – possibly Ratushny? It seems that the person in question was held without trial until 18 September 1868, when he was released in Odessa.

The complaint goes on: 'They are tormenting us because we read the gospel . . . We want to live as Christians, and they want to make us stop this. But we will not reject Christianity, we want to live according to the gospel, as it is written. And for this they harass us.'

This complaint in its simplicity reveals the essence of stundism – a bible movement which is not concerned with questions of church organization or theological problems. This movement is concerned rather with living faith and practical Christianity.

A police report on Ratushny stated that: 'His economic situation is good; in respect of morals, he is peaceable; but his doctrine is bringing unrest to the population. He holds stubbornly to the *Stunde* and tries to disseminate it further.'

A few months later (in the autumn of 1868) another police report stated that Ratushny, Balaban and Kapustyan were reading from the Church Slavonic bible (that is, the traditional church text) in the Sunday meetings. They were imitating the German colonists in their behaviour and their clothing. For example, they wore heavy, high boots, which they had copied from their neighbours.

It also said that Ratushny was complaining that his farm had been ruined by the persecution (evidently he was the one who had been sentenced for the long period, perhaps with interruptions?) He also complained that the inhabitants of the village called him a heretic, even an anti-christ.

Unfortunately the sources say nothing about the success or otherwise of the stundists' appeal. But it does seem that a local police official, the *ispravnik* (police superintendent) took steps on his own initiative, while the governor considered the whole affair unimportant. At the beginning of 1869 the police superintendent placed Ratushny 'under strictest police supervision'. What did that mean? Was Ratushny no longer able to leave the village? Did he have to report regularly to the police-station? Was this a case of a small village policeman wanting to demonstrate his efficiency? At the end of the year, the same superintendent reported that the *Stunde* had made no further gains. At that, the provincial administration declared that the affair was now settled and the file was to be closed.

A year later, it was opened again. In 1870, barely ten years after the birth of the *Stunde* in Osnova, the struggle became more severe.

In March the *volost* authorities, which encompassed several villages, decided that the stundists must be removed. In practice this decision did not mean a great deal, but it reveals the mood of the neighbours, who may also have been envious of the stundists' economic prosperity. The resolution was not carried out because, it was stated, it was 'only the decision of a few officials in the administration'.

The same month, the Governor of Kherson reported to the Ministry of the Interior in St. Petersburg that the *Stunde* was not concerned with questions of dogma or doctrine. He saw the cause of the movement rather in the poor quality of the priests. They did not, he suggested, have the qualities 'which they ought to have on the basis of the holy scriptures'. This was where the criticisms of the stundists began. There was a need, he said, for educated, experienced priests, but the diocese of Kherson did not have any.

It is evident from this assessment that the governor had a certain sympathy for the stundists and that his opinion of the village priests was not exactly high. Priests with a certain education were sent to the towns, for they were to take up recognized positions in society; the villages and the simple illiterates of the rural proletariat had to make do with a priest who could cope with the liturgy and the sacred customs; there was no need here for theological education. This corresponded to the two forms of training offered by the Orthodox Church: the spiritual academy, which was something like our theological faculties, was attended only by the cream of those with talent. The rest received a seminary training, but this was unable to prepare them for the kind of problems which they met as priests when confronted by those who had been spiritually awakened. These village priests were mostly poorly paid, and thus they are frequently portrayed in Russian literature with a fatal tendency towards alcohol. They were ill-prepared to minister to the peasants who were ruled by alcohol.

The *Stunde* meetings continued to grow. At the beginning of the year forty persons were counted in Ignatovka, even a hundred in the church village of Ryasnopole! It is also emphasized that these are mainly young people. In one place it is even stated that the majority of the peasants in the Ryasnopole district belonged to the *Stunde*, which was probably an exaggeration. But there must have been some truth behind this statement. It is understandable that the old people held more firmly to tradition, while the younger ones welcomed something new.

During this year, 1870, the connection between the stundists and the Church began to be severed. One report stated that the priest no longer attended the *Stunde* because he met with disrespect there: when the priest approached the house, the peasants disappeared through the back door.

It may be that the arrest of Ratushny at the instigation of the priest led to the break with the Church. During this year for the first time the stundists carried out a funeral service without the help of a priest, which they no longer considered necessary. This must have been taken as a declaration of war. In May 1870 the stundists began to bring their icons to the home of the priest, and to leave them there. They said this was because they were so often accused of disrespect for icons.

In September the Archbishop of Odessa had a personal interview with Ratushny. But since even his words had no effect, he now asked the Governor of Kherson for a 'legal penalty against the heretic'.

The figure for members of the *Stunde* in Osnova is given in June as 219. Of fifty-four families in the village, only seven are said to have remained Orthodox. A third of the population of Ignatovka are said to be stundist.

Who were the leaders of this movement? Let us try to portray three of these men, as far as this is possible after a lapse of a hundred years.

Michael Ratushny was undoubtedly a born leader. In the year 1886 he is said to have been only fifty-six, thus he was born in 1830, and in 1870 he would have been in his prime. He had a large farm, lived in a house built with stone, and owned horses and draught oxen. Before his conversion he was the village elder (community leader), in other words the leading farmer in Osnova. The governor was personally acquainted with him and had a good opinion of his character and talents. He had advised him to return to the Orthodox fold and to become a priest himself. Evidently Ratushny seemed to him better suited to this job than the actual priest in Osnova.

In earlier life, Ratushny had been poor. He had actually trained to be a shoemaker. He would have learned his agricultural skills in Rohrbach, where he worked for the colonists. Like many peasants of that day, he had not learned to read and write until adulthood, and he then acquired a good knowledge of the bible. He is typical of many Ukrainians who show an amazing ability to grasp things quickly, and a natural intelligence. In order to take the gospel to the neighbouring villages, he often travelled about as a pedlar, like Kasha Yagub. In this way it was easy to move from house to house.

Gerasim Balaban (also called Vitinkov), born around 1832, was Ratushny's zealous helper and a stundist evangelist. He came from the village of Chaplinka in the Kiev province. It was not until 1867 that he came to Osnova as a seasonal labourer. Through his sobriety and hard work he became a prosperous farmer, owning eighteen horses and numerous cattle. This was a sign that with the right moral pre-conditions, a farmer could do well. He was considered to have a special gift for preaching.

Before the systematic persecution of the stundists began under Alexander III, these stundists worked themselves up to the top of their village communities in economic terms. They had learned the skills of agriculture thoroughly from their German neighbours. They avoided the public house and card-playing. Thrift and hard work and a Christian sense of responsibility became evident on all sides.

Onishchenko helped to found the *Stunde* in Osnova, but he does not really appear in the foreground. He is never named in the police reports. For a time he was a migrant worker and evidently lived with the German farmers in the Nikolayev region. He was a quiet mystic, who soon began to avoid Orthodox services, and often attended the German Protestant churches. He lived apart from his wife and grown-up son, probably because they did not share his religious views. He cooked for himself and even made his own clothes. He is reckoned to have been unusually hard-working. It would appear that he was converted to a biblical faith before the other two men. Ratushny liked to take advice from Onishchenko. 'God gave me light, and to Michael (Ratushny) He gave understanding,' Onishchenko is supposed to have said. He was an unusual individual, such as one sometimes finds in western revivals too. On one occasion only – in 1870 – did his name appear on a list of stundists whom the *starosta* (village elder) wanted to remove from the village. But his name was the last one.

THE *STUNDE* IN KARLOVKA AND LYUBOMIRKA

Konstantinovka, a village very near to Osnova, on the other side of the river Bug, is also named as a place where a *Stunde* began. We do not know any more of its history. At the same time, however, there was also a movement in the two villages of Karlovka and Lyubomirka in the Yelizavetgrad (now Kirovograd) district; this was clearly quite independent of Osnova. Let us look at the leaders in these two villages, and at their communities, as being representative of many others.

In Karlovka the movement had from the beginning a Baptist character. Infant baptism was rejected and the baptism of believers recognized as the only way shown in the bible. This came about through the influence of the German colonist Ephraim Pritzkau in the neighbouring village of Alt-Danzig. A revival had been in progress here since the 1860's, which was Baptist in orientation and had broken with Orthodoxy from the very beginning. Ten peasants joined together to form a Ukrainian Baptist congregation, led by the two Ukrainian peasants Trifon Khlystev and Yefim Tsymbal. Their numbers were augmented by Feodor Golumbovsky and Grigori Voronov, who came from other places. The latter was a citizen of the district capital, Yelizavetgrad. More than half of this small congregation let themselves be persuaded to return to Orthodoxy for a time. But when four of the peasants stood firm, and rejected the veneration of icons by appealing to Is. 44, the others returned to the Baptist congregation again. The reference must have been to Is. 44.10–20, where the folly of serving images is bluntly censured. It is very doubtful whether this group had any connection with Osnova, since the question of baptism had not yet arisen there.

It may have been as much as a year earlier that a *Stunde* began in the neighbouring village of Lyubomirka, without any connection to the congregation in Karlovka, this *Stunde* having more the Osnova character. The leading peasants here were Maxim Kravchenko and Ivan Ryaboshapka. The latter was to become an important figure in the history of stundism.

Ivan Ryaboshapka was born around 1832. It is said that he came to Lyubomirka in 1857 as a shepherd. Two years later he entered the service of a German master miller, possibly Martin Hübner. Through his employer, who was clearly a believer, he acquired his first impression of the gospel. At the age of twenty-seven, he bought himself a Russian New Testament at a market – this may have been the work of the Scottish bible messenger John Melville. The story is told of how the miller saw the book among his possessions, and asked him whether he understood it. Ryaboshakpa, who had here learned to read Russian and to speak German for the first time, is supposed to have replied: 'If I were to follow this book, I would have to change my whole life.' Upon which the miller responded: 'Ivan, either this book becomes the basis of your life, or else you perish because of it.' This story is supposed to have come from Ryaboshapka himself.

In any case, the book did become the basis of his life. He found a companion in early years, married and settled in Lyubomirka. In 1886 – about twenty-five years later – Ryaboshapka was a prosperous man with a large farm, two smiths, a threshing-machine, three horses and some cattle. It may be assumed that in the confined conditions of a village, those who had not done so well must have been envious. This was often a factor in the subsequent persecution.

Ryaboshapka became one of the most successful evangelists of the first generation of stundists. This new *Stunde* soon comprised twenty men who were ready for the trials to come. These were not slow to follow. Already in 1867 Ryaboshapka was arrested for the first time, after an unsuccessful interrogation, but soon released again. In 1868 he was arrested a second time – 'for a longer period'; it is not disclosed how long. However it is said that the justice of the peace in Yelizavetgrad had 'set him to do penal labour in other colonies'. Under the old tsarist empire, anything was possible. This deportation cannot have lasted very long. An attempt to expel him and Kravchenko from the village community failed when the Governor-General of New Russia protested against it. The men were 'neither harmful nor vicious', he said. We have already observed how the higher authorities had a better opinion of these sober workers. However, when Ryaboshapka complained to the senate in St. Petersburg, the highest court of appeal, and demanded that the justice of the peace be penalized for treating him unjustly – which the senate agreed! – the same governor-general then requested the senate to ignore this; it must not seem as if the stundists were being encouraged, he said. This was painful to the Church and made a bad impression. Possibly the archbishop had called on the governor-general in the meantime.

By the year 1870 *Stunden* had begun in eleven villages through the work of Ryaboshapka. Fines and occasional arrests only served to draw the brethren closer together. Mutual aid was given. Here too one can observe a certain confusion on the part of the authorities. The Church was waiting for the state to intervene, while the state said: this is a church matter!

On 11 July 1870 it became known that the stundists of Lyubomirka and the surrounding area were taking their icons out of their living rooms and putting them in the attic. At this time, the *Stunde* in Lyubomirka was being attended by 65 men and 75 women. (Here the women were in the majority, unlike Osnova). There were supposed to be 224 stundists in the whole district of Yelizavetgrad. The same year the *Stunde* in Lyubomirka broke with the Orthodox Church by accepting believers' baptism, probably under the influence of Karlovka.

THE *STUNDE* IN CHAPLINKA

The *Stunde* was also beginning to spread in the province of Kiev. The peasants were accustomed to hire themselves out as seasonal and harvest labourers. Because of the size of Russia, with its varying climate, the harvest does not all ripen at the same time. Since harvesting machines were not yet available, every possible work force was in demand at harvest time. This movement of workers also promoted the exchange of ideas, and opened avenues for spiritual influence too.

In the district of Tarashcha, in Kiev province, there was a village called Ploskoye. Already in 1868 some peasants, who had been in Kherson province as harvest labourers, were gathering together to read the bible. The peasant Pavel Tsybulsky put his home at their disposal. It was not until a year later that the priest noticed this, and reported it to the rural dean. When discussions with Tsybulsky and another stundist by the name of Tyshkevich proved fruitless, they were put in prison. For they declared publicly that the crosses and icons, the relics and Mary Mother of God were 'of no avail'. They even stated that drunkenness was a sin! It is true that an official statement declared that the two men later returned to the Church. But it must be remembered that subordinates liked to report to their superiors that the desired result had been achieved.

A meeting also started in the village of Roshki. This caused the spiritual authorities to exhort the priests to greater watchfulness. But at the same time they were to look for ways of meeting the demand for spiritual food. They were to combat drunkenness and other vices and promote moral living. However commendable all this may have been, it could never be more than patching up and 'good works' as long as it did not include the proclamation of the biblical way of faith, which these stundists had found.

The stundist Balaban from Osnova, Ratushny's faithful comrade-in-arms, had turned up in the village of Chaplinka, where we know more about the course of events. Balaban had been born in Chaplinka, and had been instructed by the police to return here to have a passport made out. Since the matter was delayed, and Balaban had to remain in Chaplinka until it was settled, he made use of the opportunity to found a *Stunde* here as well. He was summoned to Kiev and imprisoned for a short time, but after his release he worked with even greater effect. He held meetings three times a week; this soon spread to neighbouring villages as well.

Balaban was arrested with several others in January 1872, but meanwhile there was no shortage of preachers. It is characteristic of both Ukrainians and Russians that when they come to a new conviction, they are able to pass it on very successfully. This was also exploited by the revolutionary movement of those decades.

Nowhere was there any difficulty in finding an *udarnik*, a propagandist. The same was true of the awakened Christians. As soon as they received their basic experience, they were already true evangelists. This natural gift on the part of the Slavs proved of great benefit to the stundist movement for more than a hundred years. Preachers who had studied or even had a seminary training were always in the minority. Of course this is still true today. For the Evangelical Christian-Baptist movement in the Soviet Union today still has no bible school, not to mention a seminary for preachers. And yet the word moves rapidly through this great eastern land.

It is true that at this time, many people first had to learn to read. Their textbook was the bible, for whose word they had such a great hunger. It must be borne in mind that with the abolition of serfdom, there began an emancipation movement, especially among the young peasants, who had a particular thirst after education. The priests of their own Church often had no answers to their questions.

Here in Chaplinka, too, it began as a pietistic movement within the church. It was not until the priest stepped in, with police assistance, that an independent community began to form. When the church consistorium formed a commission to talk with the apostates, a police official had to be present at every discussion. Obviously this display of crude force was supposed to intimidate them.

The fact that it was to be a question of crude force soon became apparent. The local policeman was called Popov. He was the *stanovoi pristav*, the district police superintendent. When he found a house without icons, he took a whip and tried to restore church order by whipping both parents and children! Although it may not have been the consistorium's choice, nevertheless this direct method, which was not a unique occurrence, was certainly not unfamiliar to the church authorities. It was a throwback to the time before the abolition of serfdom, which had not yet disappeared from the minds of subordinate officials. Meanwhile, the brethren had to suffer. One Orthodox, Lukyanov, in making his report had to admit that: 'This approach was not helping the matter!'* One cannot help remembering the scene described in Acts 5.40 ff.

Orthodox priest Rozhdestvensky describes Popov thus: 'He was almost continually drunk, intellectually backward, coarse and malevolent and open to bribery. He was soon to demonstrate his heroism. Known as the "patriarch of the stundists", he persecuted them wherever he could, dispersed the meetings, beat the participants and imprisoned them according to his own whim. The consequence was that the stundist meetings were held with greater secrecy and caution.'†

This was the report of an Orthodox observer, who was certainly objective. Anyone who does not understand this mentality in the old tsarist authorities, will also fail to grasp the methods of the Bolsheviks.

Before this commission of the consistorium, with the help of police officer Popov, began its 'exhortations', the local priest was replaced. However, the efforts of the church authorities came to nothing. At the same time, the fifty participants in the Chaplinka meeting had absolutely no wish to be stundists, branded with the name of sectarians. They were nothing more than 'true Christians', they declared, basing themselves on the New Testament. They rejected any other doctrinal books.

In November 1872 the stundists brought all their icons to the local church and deposited them in the bell-tower. When a fresh official warning at the beginning of December 1872 again had no results, the rural dean sent a report to the Metropolitan of Kiev and suggested that all the stundists be removed from the village and deported to another province. This drastic measure seems to have proved impractical.

In the same month Balaban was brought to trial: on the grounds of enticing Orthodox Christians into stundism, and for blasphemy (probably the contempt of icons), he was sentenced to a

---

* Lukyanov, Grigori: 'Two or three words from the history of southern Russian stundism'. From the weekly newspaper *New Times*, volume three, August 1879 (in Russian).

† Rozhdestvensky, Fr. Arseni: *Southern Russian Stundism*, St. Petersburg, 1889 (in Russian).

year's imprisonment, which included his pre-trial detention. All the other defendants were acquitted. Here too one can find parallels with modern trials in the Soviet Union.

When Balaban was released in May the following year (1873), he immediately returned to his former activity. He was soon arrested again and in October of that year sent to Odessa, where a new trial was set in motion against him and some other brethren from Osnova. The outcome of this case is not known.

Even when the Kiev consistorium sent to Chaplinka the priest-monk Vladimir Terletsky, a former Catholic, who was well suited to this task, this too turned out to be fruitless. He soon returned to his monastery, although he left behind a recommendation for dealing with stundism. He too could suggest nothing better than:

Exiling the instigators of the *Stunde* to distant regions;

Banning house meetings, using billeted soldiers (compare the notorious dragoons used to combat the Hugenots under Louis XIV);

Banning the coming and going of 'suspicious' persons;

Police supervision of itinerant pedlars;

Severe penalties against all 'blasphemy';

Appointment of strictly Orthodox teachers and officials.

He also proposed:

Convocation of village clergy to discuss the situation in their congregations;

Homiletical and catechetical instruction;

Establishment of Orthodox lay fraternities to 'strengthen morality';

Sunday bible groups.

Terletsky presented all these suggestions in person to the church authorities and to the provincial administration. Apart from the final, positive suggestions, much of his advice is painfully reminiscent of the subsequent *cheka* methods, or of the Inquisition by the Roman Church, from which he came. Any means is valid, as long as people come into line. It is well known how much the Orthodox Church had to suffer in the years of revolution through the same methods of repression. Terletsky's positive suggestions would have been worth implementing, but the spiritual resources that would have been needed for this were largely lacking.

The governor-general made a report to the Minister of the Interior in St. Petersburg along similar lines to these. But the minister rejected any suggestion of exile. The liberal tsar, Alexander II, was still on the throne. Under his son, Alexander III, however, not only exile but much more terrible forms of repression would be put into practice. This 'liberal' minister (in the tsarist empire of that time, this expression should be understood in a relative sense) wrote that they should avoid creating martyrs. Apart from that, people who were sent into exile would only spread their doctrine more widely, he said, and the whole thing would become worse.

However the consequence of this was that the church authorities, feeling that the minister had left them in the lurch, made all the more use of the local police. One of the stundists – his name is not given – was sent to a monastery 'for instruction'; the conditions there were unbelievable. All this was reported by the above-mentioned Orthodox priest Rozhdestvensky, who remarked that these measures were in fact achieving the opposite effect.

The stundists for their part now began to seek protection from the imperial government. Thus in 1873 Ratushny travelled to St. Petersburg to present a petition from the stundists to the tsar. Unfortunately it cannot be established whether this brought any success. He appended to the petition a list containing 61 names from Chaplinka, 18 from Ploskoye, 15 from Kuchkovka and 12 from Kosyakova (thus there were now other villages affected). The petition stated that at that time there were thirty-five people in prison for their adherence to stundism.

It is clear from this incident that Ratushny felt himself called, beyond the confines of his work in Osnova (which was not even mentioned in the appeal), to be a spokesman and defender of the brethren. It may also be noted that imprisonment for reasons of religious conviction was not introduced by the Bolsheviks, but was an old tsarist tradition.

HOW STUNDISM FOUND A NEW CHURCH FORM

IN THE BACKGROUND

How did it come about that this movement, which had sprung from the Orthodox Church and which saw itself as a fellowship within that body, led to the formation of a Baptist Church? Since the Union of Evangelical Christians-Baptists in the Soviet Union today represents a significant section of the world Baptist community, the decision taken by those simple Ukrainian peasants when they founded the Russian Baptist Union in 1884 may be described as an event of church-historical importance.

It has been shown that the Orthodox Church expelled the stundists from its fold. Although the outward symptoms, such as the stundists' refusal to venerate icons, may seem to lay the initiative for the separation at their door, nevertheless it is abundantly clear that the Orthodox Church, based upon its own tradition and church canons, was unable to bear these mature believers. The stundists had found a way of faith that was independent of the priest and the sacraments. They did not want any support other than the bible. The fact that they had thereby become 'Protestants' in the true sense of the word only later became clear to them.

At the same time, it was impossible for them to go over to the Protestant Church, Lutheran or Reformed, because a Russian-language Protestant Church was forbidden by law. Thus the stundists were left without a Church to which they could belong.

It might be asked why no visible help was forthcoming for the stundists from the German Lutheran Church. The reproach has been levelled at the Russian German and Baltic Lutheran Church, which was by no means a small community, that it did not help the stundist movement because of its own fundamental loyalty to the state. However, anyone who reads the history of the Lutheran Church in the Baltic lands will be amazed at the courage and readiness for suffering on the part of the congregations and the pastors, as they stood against the intolerance of the tsarist government. Under Nicholas I there began the long chain

of trials against pastors, so many of whom followed their conscience rather than the commands of the government. Many of
them were dismissed from office, others exiled to the central
parts of Russia, and many put in prison. Thus it is not true to say
that the Lutherans obeyed Caesar rather than God, even though
they sought to remain loyal to the last possible point. We know
from the troubles of more recent times, too, that the definition
of that point may be partly subjective.

The fact that the Free Church circles of Baptists and Mennonites
ventured further in supporting the stundists will always be
reckoned highly in their favour. It was somewhat easier for them,
inasmuch as it was in the course of these conflicts that the German
Baptist movement first received official recognition. Up to that
time, the German-speaking Baptists had received as little recognition as the stundists. Thus they shared the same fate, and this
was a uniting factor.

Believers' baptism as the act of initiation into an organized
congregation was understandable to the stundists. The ritual of
their former church community did not give them what they
hungered after. Thus the question arose: what did we get through
infant baptism? They did not receive a biblical answer from Orthodoxy which, like western Catholicism, recognizes seven sacraments, although according to Reformed assessment, these have no
basis in the scriptures. How easy it was to say to these new converts: the new church affiliation should begin with a new baptism.
Undoubtedly clever theological and dogmatic objections can be
made to this. But these are 'unrealistic', as politicians say today.
For these young bible Christians had no complicated theology.
Yet the Baptists were prepared to suffer with the stundists, and
to dare with them. It is not surprising, then, that the stundists in
their search for new church forms pricked up their ears!

It is also true that the first German Baptist congregations,
founded by Oncken, Lehmann, Köbner and others, were opposed by the German state Churches of the day as 'harmful sects'.
It was to be some time – and a time of much suffering for the
Baptists – before there arose the ecumenical relations which broke
the monopoly of the established Churches. Even if we hold to

infant baptism, we should be objective and brotherly in our judgment here. The historical viewpoint is always helpful to this end.

One last thought might be mentioned. The Orthodox Church, as we have already attempted to show, gave its members a ritual that appealed to the senses. However decisively the stundists may have rejected the veneration of icons, which for Protestants is the most difficult phenomenon in Orthodoxy to understand, nevertheless the Ukrainians and Russians were still influenced by this upbringing. Thus they too wanted a visible, experiential sign of the mercy and presence of God, in which they could know that he accepted them. Baptism by actual immersion in a river or in the sea, later in a baptismal pool in a prayer house, was a memorable and tangible experience. It made up for the loss of incense, candles and golden priestly garments. We western Christians think too abstractly, and we need to make an effort to comprehend our slavic brethren. At the same time, baptism by immersion was natural for Orthodox Christians, for even the priest immersed an infant three times in the deep waters of the font.

Before stundism became Baptist, the question of baptism had already led to controversy among the German colonists. The Mennonites of Yekaterinoslav and the Molochna colony in the Donets region had been aware of this from the beginning. They only baptized those who had been awakened to a conscious faith. But the revival at the time of Eduard Wüst led to a new baptismal form among the Mennonite Brethren – the blessing of infants, and believer's baptism at a later date. This led to a serious conflict between the older Mennonites and the Mennonite Brethren.

In 1863 the Mennonite Brethren received recognition from the government in St. Petersburg, but the Mennonites with their longer history did not want to be allied with the Baptists. Apart from other differences, they held firmly to their privilege of refusing armed service, while the Baptists were more tolerant in this matter; nor did the Baptists ban the use of tobacco, like the Mennonites.

The first Baptist believer's baptism was carried out on 10 May 1864 in the German colony of Alt-Danzig. Oncken himself came to Alt-Danzig in that year, and was even imprisoned here for a short time. The colonist J. Pritzkau was the first German Baptist elder.

It was not until fifteen years later, in 1879, that state recognition was given to the German Baptists in Russia. As long as it was a German matter, the state was prepared to do it. At times it even seemed that the government was glad of a church split among the Germans, in order to weaken the unity of the Lutheran Church, according to the principle: *divide et impera* – 'divide and rule'.

BELIEVERS' BAPTISM AMONG THE UKRAINIANS

The transition from stundism to a Baptist movement took place gradually. Heated debates continued among the stundists for decades between those who baptized infants and those who baptized believers. Dr. Johannes Lepsius, the only German missionary who took an active part in helping the stundists, tells how he experienced such a fraternal conflict at a conference. When tea was served in the interval, the young man, according to Russian custom, first put some black tea extract into Lepsius's glass, and then filled it with boiling water from the samovar. Lepsius asked him whether it would not have been possible to pour the water in first, and to add the tea extract afterwards. The young Russian replied: 'Nichevo! (It doesn't matter!) As long as the two come together.' It seemed to Lepsius that this was the best solution to the question of baptism. Whether the faith came first and then the water of baptism, or whether the water came first and then the faith – as long as the two came together!

Jakob Kroeker has told the story of a similar stormy conference, which ended in dispersal by the police. The two leading representatives, one for infant baptism and one for believers' baptism, were arrested and put into the same prison cell. First a moving reconciliation took place, sealed by many brotherly kisses. Then the two men lay down on the cold flagstones, using one man's coat as their mattress and the other for a cover! Kroeker added: 'Thus the secular police often have to stir up flagging brotherly love.'

The Mennonite Gerhard Wieler from the Molochna colony also encouraged believers' baptism among the Ukrainian stundists. He and a few of his brethren carried out the next baptisms among them. For this, Wieler was imprisoned for a short time in 1865. The Mennonite movement should thus be seen as an important factor in the development of stundism into a Baptist community.

Tsymbal, who has been mentioned previously, was one of about thirty German colonists who became Baptists. In 1870 he in turn baptized Ivan Ryaboshapka from Lyubomirka and two other stundists. The following year Ryaboshapka baptized Ratushny.

At first Ratushny's friend Balaban protested against the new rite. His desire for a purely spiritual movement was understandable in contrast to the legally prescribed customs of Orthodoxy. Thus in the beginning Balaban had a large number of like-minded friends. But in the end all of them, too, saw the need for a new organization and church form, which cannot exist without common rules.

At the beginning of the 1880's stundism had spread even further, not only in the southern and south-western provinces: Bessarabia, Kherson, Yekaterinoslav, Kiev, Podolia, Volhynia, Minsk, Mogilev, Chernigov, Poltava; it had also penetrated to northern Russian areas, as far as Oryol and Tver (now Kalinin). It was also spreading along the Don as far as the Caucasus.

It was obvious that they should try to model their congregational organization on that of the early Church. At the head of each local congregation stood an elder and a deacon. Since this form of organization had no state recognition, everything depended on the strong internal bond of genuine brotherly love. This was natural to the slavic people. But since it now demanded sacrifices, the selection of men was good.

Old Russia did not have any state registry offices; all family documents were kept by the church. So now the brethren drew up their own membership lists, although these were not recognized by the authorities. Marriages among the stundists were not recognized, thus they were considered as cohabitation and the children as illegitimate. This led to painful conflicts.

The first independent conference of Russian Baptists took place on 30 April 1884. The leader of the conference was the German Mennonite Johannes Wieler, another member of the large Wieler family.

LEGAL REPRISALS

As we have seen, the state was rather uncertain of itself in the first years of the struggle against the stundists. There was no clearly-defined legal basis for such cases. However this was not a serious problem in old Russia. As already mentioned, the authorities had the power to act in an 'administrative' fashion, that is, as they thought best, even without legal precedent. Nevertheless the stundists met with considerable sympathy at all levels. They were good workers and farmers, they were sober and thrifty, and therefore good tax-payers. Thus there were places which welcomed them for very worldly reasons. At the same time their genuine piety impressed many devout Orthodox. Even Leskov, who had nothing but mockery for the pietists of the St. Petersburg salons, found warm words of recognition for the stundists, who brought their children up well and lived exemplary family lives.

It was against the law to go into schism, like the old *raskol* (the Old Believers), or to become a sect; at the same time, according to the law it was only the instigator who could be punished, not those who had been led astray. Even some judges wondered why the Old Believer schism was now tolerated, but stundism was not. Some prosecutors refused to move charges against the stundists. Even their evening meetings for bible study could not be forbidden. Thus in order to take proper action against the stundists, new laws had to be introduced, but this took time. Meanwhile things moved relentlessly on.

The public prosecutor for the Odessa district court wrote, with considerable insight: Stundism is a reaction against deep religious and moral uncertainty among the people. There is no leadership in spiritual matters, or teaching in the truths of the Christian faith. The liturgy is not properly interpreted and understood. Individual offices are celebrated for payment. Many priests give a bad example by their life. There is no spiritual influence on people's consciences.

This represents a bitter reproach to the Orthodox Church from within its own ranks. It would be small excuse to say that the Church did not reckon on the sudden emancipation of the peasants after their liberation, since it is the Church's essential task to promote the knowledge of God through acquaintance with the bible, which implies reading and reflection. It is true that up to that time the rural population had been uncritical and conservative in outlook. But now people were learning to read and to think for themselves, and their own Church was giving them no lead. On the contrary, it was waging a defensive struggle and relying on administrative state measures in the process. The liberal press on the other hand, which opposed the government and the state Church in any case, took an active interest in the stundists.

In 1878 Ratushny, Balaban, Kapustyan and others from Osnova were brought to trial, but were acquitted and released by the court of assizes. This happened several times. Ratushny and also Ryaboshapka appealed a number of times, too, to the 'supreme name' – the tsar. It is not known whether this was ever successful.

In 1879 there appeared a new law recognizing the Baptists, and permitting them to hold services according to their own form. The stundists hoped that this law would apply to them as well. Unfortunately, however, it soon became clear that only the German Baptists were included. The Russian and Ukrainian Baptists were excluded on the grounds that they were apostates from the Orthodox Church. Thus the stundists had no choice but to tread the dangerous path of illegality.

Another law passed in 1883, which brought further relief to the *raskolniki* (Old Believers) and other older sects, such as the freedom to celebrate services in private homes, did not apply to the stundists either.

Nevertheless it must be said that in the 1870's and even later, the state representatives were more reserved in the struggle against the stundists than the Church, which of course was more directly affected. At the same time, the priest could still call on the local police. In many places, those who attended stundist meetings were liable to detention or fines, or blows from the knout. It sometimes happened that those in the meetings had all their books taken away, even Orthodox ones. All this was a customary expression of private justice, in which non-stundist citizens were often incited to participate as well. However one village elder who tolerated, or even instigated some acts of violence against the stundists was dismissed by the governor. One public prosecutor protested when at the beginning of the seventies the governor subjected the participants in a stundist meeting to fines. Yet stundist funerals without the priest, who refused to take part, were disrupted by the police. Many other such incidents could be enumerated, showing that the treatment of the stundists was somewhat arbitrary.

This led to a considerable confusion in people's minds – this is exemplified by the priest in Lyubomirka who drew up a memorandum on the 'Immorality and Perniciousness' of the stundists; this he tried to prove by reporting on the Mormons in the USA, whom he had confused with the stundists. The new Bishop of Odessa, Leonti, went so far as to ask the Oberprokuror of the Holy Synod, Count Tolstoy, to ban the German bible groups in Rohrbach as well, because they were a dangerous influence. (This is reminiscent of the Soviet ban on bibles: anyone who sends a bible to the Soviet Union today receives it back with the stamp: *zapreshcheno*! – forbidden!).

Until the time of Pobedonostsev, the secular authorities continued to be more reserved; however there was less moderation in public criticism of the Church. Official bodies emphasized that the priest in Lyubomirka was inciting the Orthodox to acts of violence, instead of calming them down; but that nothing was to be achieved with violence.

In 1881 the Governor of Kherson reported to the minister that the movement was continuing to grow. Thus after twenty years, it was evident that all counter-measures had been in vain.

Two years later, the senior priest in Ryasnopole wrote that the stundists were bold, independent and resolute, while the Orthodox were indecisive and lacking in courage. The stundists practised open propaganda, he said, and were supported by the Germans and the 'socialists' (!)

From the point of view of the Orthodox state Church, this odd terminology may have had a certain justification, since according to its concept, only the Orthodox Christian was a true Russian. However the charge that they were supported by the socialists, who at that time were considered nihilists and rebels, was venomous and untrue.

The only defence the stundists had against the evil accusation that they were a pernicious secret society was openness and courageous testimony. It is certainly true that they had connections with their brethren in the faith as far away as the Caucasus, and that they had frequent visits from strangers. These were then described as 'sinister individuals', since it was not normal for peasants to look beyond their own immediate community. (The accusation of being involved in secret conspiracies or suspicious secret societies was also a favourite one at the time of the old pietist movement in Germany.)

Nevertheless in 1882, at a faith conference of the Mennonite Brethren in the Molochna colony (Donets region), Ryaboshapka was able to report that after years of severe harassment, they had had two years of rest and were able to hold their meetings without fear. The stundists had even been able to build a prayer house in the village of Einlage. This was a new turning-point in the formation of the Church. At the same time it must be borne in mind that, since there was no legal guarantee, it was always a question of local conditions.

The fact that the Orthodox Church now became more active in a spiritual sense, as well, was a pleasant by-product of stundism. The Church began to combat illiteracy among the peasants, sermons were to become normal practice, bible groups were started here and there, or at least they were recommended. The Church even began to distribute bibles. Archbishop Dmitri's only regret was that the village priests were not qualified to hold discussions with the stundists.

In the year 1880 an Orthodox lay fraternity was established, as recommended by the monk Terletsky, the former Catholic. It placed itself under the protection of St. Andrew, the patron saint of the Ukraine and of the Russian Orthodox Church. The aim of this fraternity was to combat stundism – unfortunately a mainly negative goal. Yet its methods were fairly positive: the preservation and spreading of sound Orthodox doctrine, also the founding of a publishing house to distribute books, brochures, tracts and sermons. Later, the fraternity sent out missionaries – evangelists, as we would say today – to speak against the stundists. But even the bishops had to admit that all these well-intended measures did not hinder the further spread of stundism. The Church could no longer influence those who had been awakened.

In 1881, after Alexander II's terrible death from the bombs of the social revolutionaries, his son Alexander III came to the throne. The new tsar took the path of relentless reaction, like his grandfather Nicholas I. Those who knew him well have described him as peace-loving, chivalrous, irreproachable in his family life. One must grasp the psychological reasons why – after his father had been hunted down like an animal by his political opponents – he lent his ear to the politicians who told him: You see where your father's liberal policies brought him. Russia must be governed with an iron fist! Thus the liberal ministers were dismissed; from now on, internal policy was determined by Pobedonostsev, Alexander's former tutor, for whom he had a deep love and respect, and whom he created Oberprokuror of the Holy Synod. Pobedonostsev became Alexander's *eminence grise*.

Pobedonostsev declared that stundism in the Kiev region had a socialist character – with these words, an irreversible sentence had been passed on the stundist brethren. Now their long path of suffering and crucifixion was to begin. When Alexander III came to the throne, the first Russian Baptist congregation was thirteen years old.

III   THE BAPTIST MOVEMENT IN THE CAUCASUS – THE
      SECOND SOURCE

The Baptist movement took root in Europe through the work of Johann Gerhard Oncken, the energetic organizer of Baptist congregations.* The first Baptist congregation in Denmark was founded in 1839 by the Hebrew Christian Julius Köbner, who had been baptized by Oncken. In 1845 Köbner baptized Dr. Feisser, a Dutch Reformed minister, who began a Baptist work in Holland. Sweden followed in 1848, Switzerland in 1849, Poland in 1850. It is believed that the first baptism in the Baltic lands took place in 1860, when a Latvian believer was baptized in Memel (now Klaipeda in Soviet Lithuania). This was followed by a strong Latvian Baptist movement. This was the entry into the tsarist empire. There were numerous baptisms in Courland.

The Ukrainian Baptist revival movement began with the congregation in Tiflis in the Caucasus. This took place independently of the events in the Kherson province, and led the way for the many peoples of the Caucasus, where one generation previously, the *Baseler Mission* had been working through Zaremba and others.

Among the Molokans who had been spiritually awakened through the work of Kasha Yagub, Father Jacob, was a merchant called Nikita Voronin in Tiflis, the capital of Georgia, now called Tbilisi. Because the Molokans, in reaction to Orthodox sacramental piety, did not recognize any sacraments, even baptism, Voronin had never been baptized either. After his spiritual awakening, he read the bible avidly, and as a result of this he wanted to be baptized. At this time he met an interesting person – the East Prussian-Lithuanian artisan Martin Kalweit.

Born in Jokschen in Eastern Prussia, Kalweit moved to Kowno, later to become the capital of the Lithuanian republic (now called Vilnius). In 1863 he moved on into the Caucasus, and settled near Tiflis. In this he was evidently following Oncken's commission. Like Spittler with his pilgrim mission at St. Chrischona near Basle, Oncken too looked for artisans to send out as missionaries who would support themselves in the new environment by their trade, and would spread the gospel by their life and testimony. Thus Kalweit became a link in the chain of the great Russian revival. For he brought Nikita Voronin into the Baptist movement. and the latter in turn (1868) founded the first Russian Baptist

* W. Gutsche, *op. cit.*, p. 51.

congregation in Tiflis. From here came a number of men who gave themselves completely to the revival movement. Vasili Gurevich Pavlov (1854–1924) and Vasili Vasilievich Ivanov-Klyshnikov (1846–1919) were both baptized in Tiflis in 1871. Both these men became leaders in the Russian Baptist movement.

If we compare the dates of birth of these early Russian Baptists with those of the first Ukrainian stundists, we see what an able generation this was in the spiritual struggle for the biblical gospel message. In 1876 the congregation in Tiflis had forty members. Kalweit himself was exiled for his missionary activity, which in the tsarist empire was permissible only for the. state Church – first to Gerusi, later to Ararat, the mountain where the three lands of Russia, Persia and Turkey met.

Vasili G. Pavlov became the recognized leader of the Russian Baptist movement. He came from a Molokan family in Vorontsovka in Georgia, and was born in 1854. Under Nicholas I his family together with other Molokans had been exiled as sectarians to the border areas, which were partly unsubdued, and had settled there. At that time Transcaucasia was still largely a land of brigands, where the Kurds made periodic raids, or Azerbaidzhanis persecuted the Armenians. Anyone who lived there was in constant peril. Vasili Pavlov was the eldest child in the family. The devout father dedicated the child to the Lord even before it was born. The mother, an officer's daughter, was a talented instructress. At the age of five years, Vasili was reading the bible in Church Slavonic in the meetings. In fact this gifted youngster read widely. At the age of fifteen he found assurance of faith through a small booklet that he had bought at the market. The importance of the distribution of tracts can be seen in this revival movement. We do not know where this pamphlet came from, or what it was called. This was in 1870, when the *Stunden* in Osnova and Lyubomirka were fighting for their existence.

At the age of sixteen the young Pavlov joined the merchant Nikita Voronin as an apprentice. He was baptized the same year. This was not easy for his parents, who were still Molokans. The young Pavlov was to continue all his life as a definite supporter of those who practise baptism – by immersion – only for those who have already come to faith. He was able to develop his gift for languages in the Caucasus, the land of innumerable languages. As well as Russian he spoke Georgian and Tatar, probably also Armenian and Persian (Azerbaidzhani). Pavlov also learned German and studied Hebrew, so that later he is said to have known about twenty-five languages. When he was twenty-one, the congregation sent him to Oncken in Hamburg, where he became Oncken's faithful pupil. Oncken ordained the young brother in 1876, and sent him back to Russia. In the Ukraine Pavlov took up contact with the leading stundists, whose path into the Baptist movement has already been described. *Thus the stundist and Baptist movements flowed into one another at this point.* In Tiflis Pavlov worked with Voronin chiefly among the Molokans. This may have been the reason why, unlike the Ukrainian stundists, he remained unhindered by the state Church and the police. Evidently these bodies considered his work a Molokan affair. Also, Tiflis was a long way from St. Petersburg, where they had learned to be cautious in handling the Caucasian peoples – the conquest of the Caucasus had after all cost almost a hundred years of bloody struggles. In 1880 Pavlov took the office of preacher in the Tiflis Baptist congregation. Here too he published the Baptist hymnbook *Voice of Faith* (*Golos very*). His influence soon grew among the Orthodox Russians, too, with whom he came in contact on his many travels.

Meanwhile, however, Pobedonostsev had come to power. It is said that the latter personally requested the tsar for Pavlov's arrest and banishment. The Armenian scholar Amir Khanyants was arrested with Pavlov and Voronin, and exiled to the Orenburg province in the Urals. (Khanyants worked for the British and Foreign Bible Society, translating the bible into Eastern Armenian and Azerbaidzhan-Turkish.) Pavlov spent four years here near Orenburg. His family was permitted to follow him. After completing his sentence, he returned to Tiflis where he was asked to give written assurance that he would not preach again. Since he refused to do this, he was again arrested and put in prison. The authorities tried to bring him to the station secretly. But the news had spread through the town, and there was a great crowd of people at the station, waiting to greet him. This time Pavlov was exiled to the Kirgiz steppes and transported there in chains via one prison after another. He was soon in great need, since he had no work and nothing to eat. Yet even here he testified for his Lord, and in 1891 he wrote that he had been able to baptize seven believers. His family followed him even to this lonely spot. But then came the cholera, and carried off his wife and three of the children. Another son drowned in the Aral river. He only had one son left. Pavlov took all this suffering as a sign that he was not to have any further aim in life but evangelism. Later he married a woman of German origin from St. Petersburg. It was a real 'fighting match', as Zinzendorf called couples who lived for nothing else but the spreading of the gospel. When the second exile came to an end in 1895, there was a Baptist congregation of 150 members in the Orenburg province, and this doubled in two years.

When Pavlov was threatened by a third exile, after he had turned down a good government job, he escaped to Tulcea in Rumania. This town was only twenty-five kilometres from the Russian border, and harboured a good number of Russian refugees. Here Pavlov became preacher in a stundist refugee congregation and organized a large relief work for the starving families of exiled stundists and Baptists, with the help of believers in the west.

We have now gone ahead of events. We shall meet Pavlov, who returned to Tiflis in 1901, at a later stage. But first we must deal with the third source of revival.

IV   LORD RADSTOCK IN ST. PETERSBURG

St. Petersburg had already been the scene of a great revival, linked with the names of Golitsyn and Gossner, in the time of Alexander I. In the last twenty-five years of the nineteenth century, it experienced a fresh spiritual movement. Fifty years had gone by since the people of St. Petersburg had waved farewell to Gossner. The land had been stamped by thirty years of intolerance under Nicholas I. Thus it is difficult to trace any direct connection

between that and the revival to be described below. The name
Lieven might seem to indicate a degree of continuity, however
the Prince Lieven whose house was to become a centre of the
revival for some decades was not a direct descendant of Count
Lieven at the time of Alexander I.

Nevertheless, the spiritual preparation for this revival movement
may have been very similar. In the aristocratic circles of St.
Petersburg there had always been men and women with a hunger
for God. The German Protestants who formed a relatively high
proportion of the capital's population (around ten per cent) did
not play a large role in the awakening at the time of Alexander I,
since the Protestant Church in St. Petersburg was then gripped
by an arid rationalism. But this had changed in the course of the
century. Like the Lutheran Church in Germany, the Russian
Lutherans had moved on to confessional theology. Teaching at
the theological faculty in Dorpat were men who represented a
positive and vital Lutheranism. Theodosius Harnack taught
applied theology here; he was in Dorpat from 1844-75, apart
from his time in Erlangen from 1853-66. We have already noted
his son Adolf's statement that his father came from Gossner's
congregation. His colleagues in the faculty were the Lutheran-
Orthodox Philippi, a baptized Jew, who was in Dorpat 1842-51;
Old Testament scholar Keil 1833-58; later von Oettingen 1853-90
and von Engelhardt 1853-81. All these men influenced more than
one generation of German pastors who went on to serve in the
Baltic and throughout Russia. Court society in St. Petersburg had
considerable contact with Protestants because the tsars always
invited many members of the Baltic nobility to come there.
There were also many marriages between Baltic and Russian
nobility. An intellectual and spiritual exchange could not be
avoided, although Protestant sermons in the Russian language were
still forbidden.

The Lieven princes, who were Protestant, were considered one
of the oldest noble families of the Baltic, since according to
tradition they were descended from Kaupo, from the Cremon
region, the first Livonian chief to be baptized – soon after 1200.
From the time of Catherine II and particularly from that of

Alexander I, members of the Lieven family were being summoned to positions of responsibility in the court of St. Petersburg. Thus they became a kind of traditional link for Protestant influence in St. Petersburg.

The new movement that was about to take place in the city was to be a bible movement stemming from the salons of the St. Petersburg nobility.

Even under the intolerant Nicholas I (1825–55), the translation of the Old Testament into modern Russian continued, although Nicholas had dissolved the Russian Bible Society. The work was successfully carried on by Professor Pavsky and by Archimandrite Makari, who have both been described as friends of the Bible. Under Alexander II the whole work was revised by Professor A. Khvolson, and finally published under the auspices of the Holy Synod in 1875 – a date that still holds significance for the evangelical movement today, for it has always been a bible movement. In 1863 Alexander II permitted the British and Foreign Bible Society to take up work in Russia again, which continued until the Bolshevik Revolution in 1917.

Up to that time bible distribution among the vast Russian people and the other nationalities was carried on by numerous bible couriers. Thus for example Baron Hendrik Wrede from Finland, brother of Mathilde Wrede, who was famous for her work among prisoners, was active in bible distribution in Siberia. Even before that Count Modest Modestovich Korf, later chamberlain to the tsar, had distributed Russian gospels in St. Petersburg on behalf of the British and Foreign Bible Society. This took place in 1870 at the first trade exhibition, where no less than 62,000 gospels were distributed free of charge at a bible kiosk erected at the expense of the Holy Synod. On each gospel was printed the words: 'Believe in the Lord Jesus, and you will be saved, you and your household' (Acts 16.31). Count Korf later became a very active member of the St. Petersburg revival.

The revival in St. Petersburg came about not through Protestant Germans, as in the Ukraine and the Caucasus, but through British influence. In the 1860's there had been a movement of faith among the English aristocracy. Among those who were spiritually awakened was Granville Augustus William Waldgrave (1833–1913), who after the death of his father inherited the title of Lord Radstock. This young nobleman became mortally ill during the Crimean War, in 1855, and this was his spiritual turning-point. He recovered and became an extremely enthusiastic witness to his Lord. He soon conceived the desire to carry the gospel of Christ to the land against which he had once fought: to Russia. For ten years he prayed that God would open the door for him to go to Russia. At the end of those ten years he found himself in Paris again for testimony meetings. Since high-class Russian society liked to visit the metropolis on the Seine, it was here that he met the first Russians. Here too he met a Russian Grand Princess, who had actually wanted to avoid such a meeting, because she was prejudiced against him. But Lord Radstock had been feeling unwell and against his normal custom had taken a cab; thus he arrived earlier than the princess expected. This unexpected meeting allayed her misgivings and in the end she invited him to St. Petersburg. She wanted to put her house at his disposal. The other Russians who were present agreed enthusiastically, and this was the answer to Radstock's prayer.

He travelled to St. Petersburg in the winter of 1874. He did not even allow himself to be deflected by the news that his mother was dying, so strongly did he feel himself commanded by the Lord to go.

Despite his aristocratic origins, Radstock had an unfeigned modesty and humility and it was certainly these qualities which gave him such an opening among the Russians of St. Petersburg; for he had no gift for oratory. But the Russians are particularly sensitive to genuineness, and they had long held humility to be the chief Christian virtue. Radstock did not seek respect and did not promote his own personality among his listeners. He had a simple way of developing the main Christian concepts by using the bible, to which he constantly referred his hearers. He belonged to the so-called Open Brethren, as did two men of German origin: George Müller, the father of orphans in Bristol, and Dr. Baedeker, who later followed Radstock's footsteps to Russia. We shall return to Baedeker's influence later.

Radstock began in the little English-American church on Post Office Street in St. Petersburg. Many of his hearers came with a desire for clarity and certainty, for the Spirit of God had already been at work, preparing their hearts. Count Korf, chamberlain to the tsar, distributed bibles; Princess Lieven, who was still quite young (born Countess von der Pahlen, wife of Alexander II's senior master of ceremonies) had already had a glimpse of the life of a spiritually awakened English lord in the home of the former Transport Minister, Blackwood, and had found assurance of forgiveness. 'The whole fullness, the responsibility connected with being a Christian,' writes her daughter, Princess Sophie Lieven, 'she did not realize until later' – through Radstock.

A surprise for everyone involved was the change in the life of Vasili Alexandrovich Pashkov, aide-de-camp to the emperor, and captain of the cavalry (d. 1902). He too had a deep mistrust for Radstock, and tried to avoid him. But when he met him unexpectedly at a coffee gathering, and the two men finally had a private talk, the conversation ended with them kneeling in prayer. This fabulously rich Russian handed his life and his wealth over to Jesus Christ. Pashkov then became the leading personality in the movement, so that official reports described its members as *pashkovtsy* – Pashkovites. Pashkov's palace became the meeting-place for the believers. Count Bobrinsky, then Minister of Transport, also became a willing and outspoken member of this circle. At first he too emphatically rejected Radstock's message, particularly since the latter never referred to anything but the bible. Bobrinsky undertook to prove to Radstock that the bible was full of contradictions. He took great pains to write out the relevant passages. But in conversation with Radstock – as he is supposed to have related later – all the bible references which he had cited were turned into sharp darts against him.

The women were no less active. It must be emphasized that among those who have been spiritually awakened in Russia, even today, to be a Christian is to be a missionary. Princess Lieven's sister, Countess Gagarin, whose palace was next to that of the Lievens, joined herself to them very decisively. She too, happily married and a charming personality, used her considerable wealth for the work of Christ and for the poor. She explained how Radstock's exposition of the Creator's question to Adam: 'Where are you?' opened her eyes to the condition of her heart. When Radstock ventured at the end of the meeting to ask those who wanted to give their life to the Lord to stand, Countess Gagarin stood up and declared that she had grasped the saving hand of Christ in faith.

Alongside the young Countess Gagarin we must mention Madame Chertkov, the widow of a general, whose name became famous through her son Vladimir Grigorievich, long-standing secretary and companion to the poet-philosopher Count Leo Tolstoy.

(Tolstoy, whose religion was limited to a moral exposition of Jesus's sermon on the mount, certainly knew the revival in St. Petersburg, but had nothing but contempt for it, and caricatured it in his novel 'Resurrection'. Although a religious man, Tolstoy rejected the biblical gospel of the forgiveness of sins, and all his life he remained an opponent of the stundist movement. An anarchist in sociological terms, he could not tolerate any lasting bond, which had tragic consequences for his marriage. It was the misfortune of this great and courageous man that he disdained the biblical and realist judgment of the human heart, and made out of Christianity a dry moral doctrine. Thus he and his disciples unintentionally paved the way for the Bolshevik revolution.)

Madame Chertkov, a sister of Countess Pashkov, had gone through deep suffering. She had lost her husband early in life, and two of her sons died young. She met Radstock abroad and there she found the path to life with Christ. In St. Petersburg she belonged to a ladies' committee which had existed for quite some time, the aim of which was to visit the prisons. In Russia the prisoner – even the criminal – is called *neschastny*, the unfortunate one. It may have been due to the severe sentences, also the many unjust condemnations, that the pity felt for prisoners was so great, even those who were genuinely guilty. Among the upper classes, this led to a readiness to undertake social assistance and prison visiting. This sympathy was increased by the fact that in the tsarist empire, with its many internal conflicts, 'prisoners of conscience' often had to suffer severely, and in the period we are describing, this applied particularly to the stundists who were persecuted for their faith.

Thus Madame Chertkov like Mathilde Wrede was a 'ministering angel' in the prisons. Princess Sophie Lieven in her book *Spiritual Revival in Russia* (Korntal 1967) describes a number of moving experiences which this general's widow had in her prison work.

Another active member of this small household community in the Lieven palace was Alexandra von Peucker, who had been converted through the famous American evangelist Moody, while on a visit to England. She was German by origin, but like many Germans in St. Petersburg, she was accustomed to speak Russian. She originally wanted to train for the opera. Now she placed her beautiful voice completely at the service of the gospel. At the same time she displayed a great energy for organization in the believers' social work. Together with a number of young girls, including the Lieven daughters, the Pashkov daughters, three daughters of Konstantin von der Pahlen, the Minister of Justice, and two Golitsyn princesses, she formed a women's choir. One Countess Shuvalov and two Koslyaninov sisters also took part.

The fact that names can be given shows that in the beginning this was a small circle, before the movement spread beyond the nobility and court society. After that, it reached such a large number of St. Petersburg citizens, that two congregations formed in the capital, and from here the message spread to the estates and villages of the north.

After Lord Radstock's first visit, which only lasted six months, he returned to St. Petersburg one or two years later, bringing his family with him, and this time he remained for one and a half years. His second stay was of particular importance, for his meetings virtually represented a bible school. Knowledge of the bible was also the distinguishing feature of stundism in the south; here in the north, thanks to the higher intellectual level of the core members of the community, there developed a thorough, general bible training, which was to prove a great support in face of the reaction from the state Church which was soon to follow. Deep grounding in the bible strengthened understanding and tireless labour strengthened love.

This whole movement was undenominational – as so often with such spontaneous revivals. Radstock came from the Open Brethren, who themselves strove for a Christianity without organization and official positions. Old Prince Lieven, who died soon after Tsar Alexander II's violent death, was a Lutheran. When his wife, who belonged to the Orthodox Church, permitted the meetings to be held in her home, he drew her attention to the consequences; for these people with education could see sooner than the peasants in the Ukraine that this path would lead them out of Orthodoxy. But she was not afraid, so he allowed her to continue and himself took part in the meetings and prayer gatherings until his death (1881).

He was not the only Lutheran among the people of the revival. When a committee was formed for the welfare work, its secretary and treasurer was Dr. Mayer, head of the Lutheran hospital, which had an excellent reputation in the city. His daughter Jenny de Mayer worked in the Midnight Mission in Moscow, later among the convicts on Sakhalin Island, and finally found her life's work in the Bible Mission among the Muslims of Turkestan. As a nurse, she accompanied the pilgrims bound for Mecca across the Black Sea to the Arab port on the Red Sea. Her life story reads like an adventure novel.* Whereas the parents had been persecuted by the tsars, the daughter was hounded by the Bolsheviks; she spent years in Soviet prisons.

Count Zinzendorf had called the first generation of his people at Herrnhut *gens aeterna* – the eternal people. The same might be said here.

The fact that the St. Petersburg revival was no eccentric movement can be seen in that conversions were immediately followed by deeds of sacrificial and ministering love. Pashkov himself visited hospitals and prisons, where he had constant access as a

---

* *Eine Zeugin Jesu Christi im alten und neuen Russland. Erlebnisse und Erfahrungen einer Schwester des Russischen Roten Kreuzes.* Basle.

high official. Some incidents took place which are reminiscent of the apostolic era. Princess Sophie Lieven, who was only six months old when her father died, found among the Pashkov daughters notes going back to the year 1887, when Pashkov was already in exile in Paris. Here were recorded events which had never been made public before, such as the healing of a possessed woman, who later became an active member of the congregation. Through her testimony, her husband was set free from alcoholism. Thus they found happiness, and a good position on one of Pashkov's estates, where they became tireless witnesses to Jesus Christ. In the Pashkov archive in Paris is the note: 'The last thing we know of Anne K.'s husband is that he was sentenced in 1887 to exile in Siberia for his gospel sermons.' What striking life-stories we encounter here!

Although we may not dwell on these stories too long, one more name must be mentioned: Gorenovich, the former anarchist. He was the son of a Ukrainian village priest; while at high school, he became a member of the 'nihilists', as the anarchist revolutionaries called themselves at that time. He was put in prison, where he heard the joyful singing of some stundists in the next cell, and thus gained a first impression of the power of the gospel. He gave in to the pleas of his aged parents, and betrayed the names of his fellow conspirators. After his release, he experienced their frightful vengeance: they invited him to go for a walk, then they struck him down and, probably thinking he was dead, poured sulphuric acid over him. His eyes, his nose, one ear and part of his mouth were destroyed. He was found and taken to hospital and his life was saved. His right arm remained paralyzed and his appearance was so dreadful, that he could only go into company wearing a black mask. He lived in a hospital for incurables in St. Petersburg, twenty-two years of age. Pashkov heard of his terrible fate and visited him, but found his will to live totally destroyed. He had already asked the doctors for poison to put an end to this terrible existence, but in vain. Thus he also violently rejected Pashkov's consolation. However he could not stop Pashkov speaking and reading the word of God to the other patients, and praying with them. In this way one seed after another of God's truth also dropped into him. A few days later, the head nurse asked Pashkov to visit Gorenovich again. She thought that she could see some effect from the visit in his behaviour. Pashkov continued his efforts, which ended with this unfortunate young man sincerely giving himself to Jesus, who saved and renewed his life. Count Bobrinsky took him on to his estate. Then followed a miracle: a young Christian girl decided to become his wife. Together they started a home for blind children, paid for by Pashkov. When his 'murderers' were brought to court, Gorenovich had to appear as a witness. Publicly before the court he testified to his faith, declared forgiveness to those who had injured him, and expressed his heartfelt desire that they too might one day be as happy as he was!

This information is based not only on Pashkov's papers, but also on autobiographical material by Gorenovich.

The social work which had been started under Pashkov's leadership was taken up with particular love. Count Korf visited the no-alcohol tea-rooms for cab-drivers (*izvozchiki*). He talked with the customers, distributed tracts and bible portions, and gave short evangelistic addresses. Pashkov did the same. In one of his houses in the Vyborg region of the city he set up a canteen, originally intended only for the students, who often had no money at all, where for a ridiculous price of a few kopecks they could get a good meal. Lunch was served for ten kopecks (about five pence). For one kopeck there was a plate of soup, or porridge with butter. Later it was opened to other poor people as well. The remaining costs were paid by Pashkov and other brethren. Pashkov's favourite text was: 'God is love' (*Bog yest lyubov*) – a text which is prominent on the walls of most churches and prayer houses of the Evangelical Christians-Baptists today.

Strangely, these social undertakings were soon restricted by the authorities. It was also forbidden to hang texts on the walls.

Sewing rooms for poor women had existed in various parts of St. Petersburg for some time. When the person who started them left the city, she handed the work over to Mrs Pashkov who took it on together with her sister, Madame Chertkov, and Countess Gagarin. Young girls learned to sew here, and women who worked at home received commissions. The material they needed was given to them. The women were visited in their poor dwellings, and pastoral work carried out in this way. Two Koslyaninov sisters helped Countess Gagarin, and the Lieven princesses also participated. Sophie Lieven has declared how significant this glimpse into social need was for all of them. They gathered a circle of young girls for bible study – a work that flourished for several decades. This circle later joined the Young Women's Christian Association.

In the year 1884 – three years after the murder of Alexander II – a frost fell upon this spring bud of genuine evangelical revival. Pashkov had sent out invitations to a conference in St. Petersburg. He knew of the revival centres in the Ukraine and the Caucasus, and the renewal among the Mennonite Brethren, and he desired a fraternal link on the basis of an alliance, that is, without denominational uniformity. This Christian conference was intended to strengthen the brethren in the faith, to deepen their understanding of the bible and to emphasize brotherly fellowship. To these groups Pashkov sent a letter requesting them to send representatives to St. Petersburg.

On 1 April 1884 more than seventy participants arrived for the conference. Pashkov bore all the costs of the travelling and the hospitality. Social differences were unimportant. At one meeting in the Lieven palace a converted cab-driver led the bible study. Unfortunately a joint communion service proved impossible, because the Baptists held firmly to Oncken's rule that shared communion was possible only with those who had been baptized as believers, by immersion. In the St. Petersburg group, however, the question of baptism was left open to the individual conscience.

Almost every young Christian is threatened by two childhood diseases: legalism and over-enthusiasm. It is understandable that the Russian converts were not spared these problems. They had no historical experience to go by, and even their theological understanding in the beginning was small. In this way a narrow legalism often crept in. Thus even today smoking is considered a serious sin; likewise the use of alcohol. At the same time the slavic nature is pre-disposed towards emotionalism. Thus it is hardly surprising that later the so-called Pentecostal movement also gained influence.

However all these problems could have been solved. This time shipwreck came from an external source. On the third day of the conference Princess Lieven prepared a meal for about a hundred persons in her palace, but she waited in vain for the visitors. It was not until evening that an Armenian brother arrived, very upset, and reported that all the visiting participants had been arrested early that morning, issued with a strong warning that they could be punished as vagrants, and given return tickets with strict orders to leave St. Petersburg immediately, and not to let themselves be seen there again. This Armenian brother had got out at the first station and returned on foot to report what had happened, particularly since the police had warned them not to appeal to Pashkov, since he had fallen into disfavour in high circles.

Soon after this Pashkov and Korf, who because of their high positions at court were considered the leaders of the movement, were called to account. Count Korf writes:

'I was supposed to sign an undertaking not to preach any more, not to organize any more meetings, not to engage in free prayer and to give up all relations with the stundists and other religious communities.'

Pashkov was asked to sign a similar undertaking. Since both men refused on conscientious grounds, they were condemned to exile. Pashkov went to Paris, followed by his family. He carried on an active and zealous ministry in France and other countries for several decades and died in Rome in 1902. He was buried in the non-Catholic cemetery near the Cestius pyramid. Only once did he receive permission to return to Russia for a few weeks, when his son lay dangerously ill with typhus.

Korf went to Germany (Baden), later to Switzerland and survived until November 1933, when he died peacefully of a weak heart in a car on the way to Basle hospital. He was ninety-one years old. He was known and loved among the Russian Christians.

The widowed Princess Lieven was also threatened with exile. Alexander III sent his adjutant to her to convey his wish that the meetings in her home should stop. A long conversation ensued.

Finally the princess said: 'Ask His Majesty whom I have to obey – God or the emperor.' It was rumoured that her bold confession was to be punished with exile. But the tsar is supposed to have said: 'She is a widow. Leave her in peace!'

And so the palace at Great Morskaya 43, which later housed the Italian embassy, became the focus for the converts in the imperial capital until the year 1917, the year of revolution. It is true that it was under police supervision. But there were no interventions. Princess Lieven once told us with a laugh that on one occasion the police officer told her mother that he was very satisfied with her behaviour. All sensation was cleverly avoided. Professor Karl Heim, who was in St. Petersburg at the beginning of this century and attended a meeting at the Lieven home, relates in his memoirs how surprised he was that at the end of the meeting those who had been present were asked to leave the house in small groups, not all together. This Swabian German, accustomed to German conditions, was almost alarmed at this security measure. He could not know how watchful was Pobedonostsev's eye.

V   POBEDONOSTSEV AND HIS POLICIES

Konstantin Petrovich Pobedonostsev (1827–1907) took upon himself responsibility for the fate of many thousands of people. Anyone who experienced the terrible years of enforced russification of the Baltic provinces knows with what horror that name was mentioned. It is easy to prove Pobedonostsev responsible for the suffering and misfortune of so many people. It is hard to be fair to him and to portray him objectively. There is no doubt that he was a fanatic, and fanaticism always leads to catastrophes. Yet his biographer, Dr. Friedrich Steinmann, says, probably with justification, that even for this, Pobedonostsev may not be called a Grand Inquisitor. He was a religious man. But it was not religious intolerance which really motivated his policies and actions, rather a blind and reactionary nationalism of the most dangerous kind.

Count Witte, a liberal politician, himself Orthodox and a monarchist, who despite his German name was a pure Russian, a successful Minister of Finance and later Prime Minister under Alexander III and Nicholas II, in his memoirs writes the following about Pobedonostsev:

'A man of outstanding education and culture, totally honest in his intentions and personal ambitions, a very clever statesman, with an intellectual tendency to nihilism, a negative critic, an enemy of every creative impulse, in practice a devotee of police measures, since every other approach demanded changes which he accepted with his mind, but feared with his heart because of his critical and negative spirit. For this reason he strengthened the police regime in the Orthodox Church to the ultimate ... The history of Russia could have taken a different turn, in which case we would probably not have to experience the most base and senseless revolution and anarchy today.'

Witte died on 13 March 1915; he wrote his memoirs in the years 1907–12. What interested him most about Pobedonostsev was his passionate defence of the tsarist autocracy, and his opposition to the slightest hint of a constitution. At the same time his judgment of Pobedonostsev betrays no hatred or malice, while he often slayed other statesmen who were his opponents. For this reason Witte's judgment here is of particular weight.

Hermann Dalton, who has been mentioned a number of times already, was friendly with Pobedonostsev while he was Reformed pastor in St. Petersburg. He wrote his memoirs in 1906, in other words in old age, far away from the banks of the Neva. But since he waged a sharp struggle against Pobedonostsev and his policies, and was thus his explicit opponent and adversary, his judgment too, weighed carefully and written with a deliberate objectivity, is of great importance.

Dalton admired his opponent Pobedonostsev for the fact that he was far above average in intellect, that he never 'allowed himself to be swayed by selfish motives, by his own advantage'. 'Always and everywhere he showed himself unselfish and unaffected by the opinion of the crowd. He did not curry their favour, nor did he fear their disfavour. He kept his eyes steadfastly on the goal which he, the advocate of the ruling state Church, saw as salutory for Russia. As far as I had opportunity to observe his efforts and his actions, he never desired anything for himself, but always served the cause which he had espoused. He served it with the versatility of an outstanding mind, with tenacious energy, with the acumen which the study of law lends to its best pupils, with cleverness and a highly developed temperament' (Dalton, _Lebenserinnerungen_, Vol. III, pp. 96–7).

According to Dalton, Pobedonostsev was 'completely convinced that only in this way could he achieve the goal which alone would bring happiness and prosperity to the empire and its state Church. The goal seemed to him, a statesman trained in law, more than worth even the unchristian oppression of a small portion of the great Russian population.' He describes him 'walking along the street, simple, almost unsightly in his outward appearance, undisturbed in the midst of the noisy crowd, deep in thought, not unlike an unkempt, unworldly ascetic; at home, in the company of men who were not his subordinates, with whom he had no official business and whom he respected, he was extremely pleasant, in lively conversation he was full of spirit, captivating and charming, a cultured and knowledgeable man of the world, who spoke three or four foreign languages fluently and showed himself astoundingly familiar with the thought treasures of West European culture . . . This lean, pale man with the sunken cheeks, the horn-rimmed spectacles on a prominent nose, the drawn-in mouth, simple and modest even in his clothing, looked as if he must be a German professor who had grown grey over books and parchments . . . But sometimes, too, people who happened to know us both would stop in amazement and wonder how the Oberprokuror of the Holy Synod could have got into such a lively conversation with a Protestant pastor' (_op. cit._ pp. 97–8).

Pobedonostsev's complete honesty is admired by Dalton many times, even though he reproaches him of 'legal tricks' or 'Jesuit morality'. At the same time however he testifies to Pobedonostsev's obliging manner. Dalton's last visit to Pobedonostsev, when he informed him about his public pamphlet, the so-called 'Open Letter', ended after a long and frank exchange with a warm handshake. Pobedonostsev even handed him 'his photograph, which was a good likeness'.

Pobedonostsev was born in Moscow on 18 November 1827, the youngest son of a large family. His father, the son of a priest – parish priests in the Orthodox Church must be married – was professor of Russian literature at Moscow University, after having himself received priestly training in early life. The boy was educated by his father at home until he was fourteen years old. There was no compulsory education in tsarist Russia. After that he was placed in the famous law school in St. Petersburg, which was really intended only for pupils from the nobility, and which had a very good reputation because it trained the future diplomats and high officials. It was to this school, as well as to his own lively interest and great talent, that Pobedonostsev owed his superior legal training. Here he learned to speak German, French and English perfectly. He was always first at school, and even among his fellow-pupils from the nobility, he had a leading position. He also acquired a social polish here, which gave him his subsequent assurance in society. At the age of nineteen he returned to Moscow. Ten years later, as a senate official, he became prominent among his faculty colleagues through his wide knowledge. His essays were published. On the basis of his work *On the Reform in Civil Action*, he became professor of civil law at Moscow University in 1859, at the age of thirty-two.

Two years later his life took a decisive turn. On the recommendation of Count von der Pahlen, Protestant Minister of Justice from Courland, he was summoned as tutor to the heir to the throne, Grand Prince Nicholas Alexandrovich. Nicholas died after a long illness, and his brother, Grand Prince Alexander Alexandrovich, took his place. Until that time Alexander had been an officer, and was unprepared for the high office that he was to assume sixteen years later. His education was handed over to Professor Pobedonostsev, who became fatherly friend and adviser to this young man who was straightforward in character, but not very independent in thought. Pobedonostsev moved to St. Petersburg, where he also took on the instruction of Alexander's younger brother, Vladimir Alexandrovich.

At the age of forty-four, Pobedonostsev received the highest award that could be made in the tsarist empire: he became a member of the imperial council, a gathering of high officials which had the confidence of the tsar and which could be called together to advise the autocrat – although their advice was wholly unbinding. This distinction was very unusual and related both to his ability and to his candid character; nevertheless, the decisive factor may have been the influence he exercised over the heir to the throne. Despite his many duties, it was at this period that Pobedonostsev wrote his most important book, the two-volume *Handbook of Civil Law*, which was considered a classic of Russian legal literature. The book appeared in 1868. Just one year later there appeared his translation of the famous medieval book of edification, Thomas a Kempis's *Imitation of Christ*, one of the most widely-read books in the world. It is typical of Pobedonostsev that all his life he was occupied both by public law and by Christian piety. Pobedonostsev's numerous other writings cannot be fully dealt with here. Suffice it to mention that he also translated *On Christian Family Life* by Heinrich Thiersch, son-in-law of the famous Protestant pedagogue Heinrich Zeller-Beuggen. This underlines our assertion that, despite all his contrary qualities, Pobedonostsev was a deeply religious man.

The Grand Prince was a grateful pupil, and with respect to political decisions remained under Pobedonostsev's influence until the closing years of his reign. The relationship is supposed to have cooled towards the end.

Pobedonostsev had no particular concept of foreign policy. His influence upon the course of internal policy was all the more decisive. Like Alexander's grandfather, Nicholas I, he put the empire back on the three pillars: autocracy, nationalism and Orthodoxy, although thirty-five per cent of the population was neither Russian nor Orthodox.

Pobedonostsev's programme could only be implemented with a large police force. On the one hand the government had to cope with strong revolutionary and anarchist movements, and on the other with countless schismatics and sectarians. Pobedonostsev particularly detested any thought of a constitution, a limitation on the autocracy of the tsar. Did this clever man not recognize the anachronism of this? In his letters to Alexander III, also to the last

tsar, Nicholas II, whom he also taught, he warned tirelessly
against any weakening of the tsar's ruling power. 'We do not
need any new freedoms, any new institutions, any new laws,
least of all a constitution; what we do need is a strong state power
and energetic men in the government, who know what they
want.' He had venomous and crude words for all liberal politicians. The tsar at the head of holy Russia, with obedient officials
beneath him, was responsible to God alone for his actions. 'That
the people should trust the government – this is the foundation
of the state!'

With a strange blindness, Pobedonostsev did not see that
virtually everything needed for the realization of this concept
was missing. The tsars – both Alexander III and particularly the
weak-willed Nicholas II – were not strong men. There was
corruption among officialdom, and much mistrust and rejection
of the government among the people. For some reason Pobedonostsev often spoke in his letters and speeches of the 'simple Russian
man' with a blind devotion to his tsar. But where were these
people? In Moscow there was the strong pan-slavist group:
Aksakov, Khomyakov, Samarin and others – skilled journalists
and propagandists. Pobedonostsev felt a link with them, at least
in respect of their nationalism; but he had no time for their
romantic idea that the other slav nations should also be linked to
Russia. It was not only the Poles who emphatically rejected this.
The Slavs in Austria and the Balkans, too, wanted Russia's help
in national liberation, but not the tsarist yoke.

For twenty-five years Pobedonostsev was Oberprokuor of the
Holy Synod, that is, he represented the emperor at the head of the
Orthodox state Church. Thus from 1880 to 1905 he also held the
rank of a minister. The unity of the people in the Orthodox faith
was for him the guarantee of the state and its security. He was a
religious man; but his violent measures against the Lutheran
Churches in the Baltic and the terrible persecution of the stundists
had nothing to do with religion. Rather, they were the consequence of his political convictions. Apostasies from the state
Church weaken the state – thus for the sake of the state, such
conversions must be prevented with the severest police measures.

At the same time Pobedonostsev himself was 'heterodox' in many aspects; he was by no means a model of Orthodox piety, for he had no icons in his rooms, as he demanded of others. Here too one can see the contradictions in his nature.

A few sentences from Pobedonostsev's speech for the ninth centenary of the introduction of Christianity among the Slavs by Vladimir of Kiev illustrate his profound conviction that Russian nationality and Orthodoxy were one. He said among other things:

'It is terrible even to think what would have become of us, had it not been for this Church. She alone, she alone helped us to remain Russians . . . The Russian house of God is the home of the Russian man. It is here that our strength is rooted, here we find the secret treasure-store of our destiny.'

Pobedonostsev determined the internal policies of the empire for more than a decade. Under Nicholas II he had to share influence with a number of sinister personalities, of whom Rasputin was the best known, but not the only dubious figure to affect the imperial family. Another was Dr. Badmayev; he was either a Buryat, in other words a Mongol shaman from Siberia, or a Tibetan lama. Witte called him a filthy swindler. Dr. Philippe, a Frenchman from the Lyon region, a charlatan who had no proper medical training, practised miracle cures together with predictions. Unfortunately this occult trait was characteristic of the court of Nicholas II. Without it, the 'miracle monk' Rasputin could not have gained such an influence over Alexandra Feodorovna and through her, over the tsar. The whole terrible end of the imperial family is bound up with this sinister figure, who even turned those who were well-disposed towards the court against it. At the same time, however, Pobedonostsev's talk of the 'simple Russian people', whom he constantly praised, led here to something which he did not intend. In the person of Rasputin, the 'simple Russian' appeared to have found entry to the court.

It was not until 1905 that Pobedonostsev had to announce his resignation. It is characteristic that Gorchakov, Russian chancellor at the time of Bismarck, honestly declared: 'Nowhere in Europe is there such a broad freedom of conscience as in Russia.' This was also the opinion of Alexander III, and of Pobedonostsev who, when Dalton pilloried the intolerance of the tsarist empire in religious matters, displayed amazement. He did not seem to know of any intolerance. This was probably unfeigned. By freedom of conscience was understood the tolerance of the many religions within the empire. It was only that no Orthodox was permitted to convert to another Church. And if Pobedonostsev had no regard for leading personalities within court society, even the emperor's adjutant-general, if he took such strong measures against the Senior Master of Ceremonies and the Minister of Transport, Bobrinsky and Korf, how much less inhibited was his approach to the stundist peasants who had no connections in high places! He even had the religious philosopher Solovyov, who was known abroad, put under supervision, not to mention Leo Tolstoy, who had been excommunicated by the Orthodox Church. He even affected the visual arts through his censorship. He had realistic oil paintings, such as those of the famous painter Repin, removed from exhibitions. Pobedonostsev's supreme power in the end became wearisome even to the Church leaders.

Pobedonostsev's influence on Nicholas II, the last tsar, was still very great during the first years of his reign. The autocratic speech of the young ruler on 17 January 1895, in which he described all thoughts of a constitution as 'empty dreams', was Pobedonostsev's work. The appointment of Goremykin as the new Minister of the Interior – almost the most important office in the tsarist empire – was also Pobedonostsev's suggestion. Later, Pobedonostsev wrote to Witte concerning Nicholas II: 'During the first two years I gave advice when I was consulted from time to time. But then I stopped being consulted. After that I only did what my office required and concerned myself with nothing outside my own sphere' (Steinmann, p. 89). But Witte himself stated that even in the years of Stolypin's power, in other words long after his retirement, Pobedonostsev still had a major influence on all decisions. It is difficult to believe that Pobedonostsev could allow his tremendous energy to be chained up.

How did Pobedonostsev's influence affect the stundists and other representatives of the biblical revival?

VI   IN THE CRUCIBLE

Pobedonostsev was responsible for the stundists' time of greatest suffering. Paragraph 187 of the penal code was now applied ruthlessly.

This paragraph read: 'For enticing Orthodox Christians into any other confession, the guilty person is condemned to the loss of all particular personal rights, and those adhering to his status, and to exile in Siberia or despatch to the convict corrective labour brigade.'

Then there was Paragraph 155: 'Those who have left the Orthodox faith to go over to another, even a Christian confession, are to be delivered to the spiritual authorities who are to warn them, to bring them to their senses, and to deal with them according to ecclesiastical law.'

These two paragraphs, which probably went back many years, now became the basis for persecuting the stundist movement. But even this was not enough for Pobedonostsev in his zeal. On several occasions he called special church conferences in Moscow. This was in order that church leaders and state representatives might confer on the struggle against the stundist and Baptist movements, which were spreading with surprising speed, and decide on effective means to overcome 'the pernicious sects'.

The year 1888 seems to have brought a worsening of the situation. This was the year when the ninth centenary of the christianization of the slav tribes by Prince Vladimir was celebrated in Kiev. The statue of Vladimir holding the eight-pointed Greek cross still stands high above the Dniepr at Kiev. It was on the occasion of this festival that Pobedonostsev gave the above-mentioned speech, which his biographer describes as his 'historical-political testimony'. In this speech he said for example:

'Fathers and brethren, what is dearer to us, both great and small, than the Church, and what beauty awakens greater response in the Russian heart than the beauty of the Church? The Church is a beloved mother to the Russian man. We are all her children, and if someone strays from her, with God's help he will return to his home and his mother ... It is here that our strength is rooted, here we find the secret treasure-store of our destiny . . . We have become great beneath the banner of absolute power and autocracy; we still stand beneath this banner, here we form a single body with a single will, and here too we see the future guarantee of truth, order and the country's well-being.'

Even from these few sentences of this passionate festival speech it is clear that for Pobedonostsev any deviation from Orthodoxy represented betrayal of national identity, of the Russian empire and of the tsar. If we also recall that he made this speech in the ancient capital of the Ukraine, where almost every village was 'infected' with stundism, it is not surprising that the year 1888 was to be the beginning of the systematic extermination of stundism.

Secret measures against 'sectarianism' must have been decided upon in that year. Three years later there were two conferences in Moscow, the resolutions from which were published in May 1893, and in July 1894 elevated into the 'law against the stundists'. This is how the authority of a dictatorial state came down upon the little groups of simple stundists. One cannot help being reminded of the Roman emperors of the third and early fourth centuries – Decius, Valerian, Diocletian, Galerius and others, who wanted to exterminate the Church through the might of the state. The words of the law show that this is no exaggeration:

'The children of the stundists are to be taken from their parents and put in the charge of relatives who belong to the Orthodox Church; if this is impossible, then they are to be put in the care of the local clergy.'

Henceforth it is forbidden for the stundists to hold services or to establish schools.

The stundists' passports and identity documents are to carry a reference to their adherence to a sect. Any employer who takes a stundist into service is subject to high fines.

The names of the members of this sect are to be sent to the Minister for Roads and Railways, who will have them posted in railway offices, so that they cannot find employment there.

A stundist is forbidden to employ an Orthodox.

Infringements are to be punished by exile to the Caucasus for up to five years.

Stundists are forbidden to buy or lease land. Any stundist who is discovered reading the bible or praying with others is to be imprisoned and immediately sent to Siberia by administrative means (i.e. without trial); all preachers are to be sentenced to forced labour in the mines there.

Stundists are to be buried away from consecrated ground; it is forbidden to hold a funeral service for them.*

In another formulation of this law, we also read the following:

'All sectarians are forbidden to leave their places of residence. They are to be declared legally incapable of transacting financial and trading business.

Preachers and authors of religious writings are to be sentenced to 8–16 months imprisonment, for a second offence to 32–48 months imprisonment in a fortress, on a third occasion to exile.'†

These textual variants show that we do not have the authentic text. Unfortunately we are unable to give the official wording for comparison. However there is no doubt that action was taken according to these regulations. Bearing in mind the size of the tsarist empire, and the frequent lack of proper order, it is quite possible that the individual governors used different wording in their instructions to the police.

Anyone who reads these legal provisions for the first time will be amazed that anything of this kind was possible at the end of the last century. And yet there was a parallel almost half a century later, in Germany, the land of Luther's Reformation: these were the infamous 'Nürnberg laws' concerning martial law for the 'non-Arians'.

The whole thing is a document of inhumanity. It is small comfort that these decrees were often not implemented, since the stundists in many cases enjoyed considerable popularity. On the other hand, however, many who were filled with envy were provoked to express their feelings. We know of some examples of tremendous cruelty, which we prefer not to cite. But we may mention two literary works from that time of persecution.

Samuel Keller, who was himself in southern Russia and the

* Quoted from Gutsche, *op. cit.*, p. 78.
† Warns: *Russland und das Evangelium*, p. 122.

Crimea for some time, wrote a short story called *The Salt of the Earth* (*Das Salz der Erde*), originally under the pseudonym of Ernst Schrill. An English writer, Hesba Stretton, also wrote the widely-read story: *The Way of Great Suffering*. In a subsequent story, *In the Hand of the Lord*, she described the sufferings of the women and children in this time of persecution. Both authors wrote about historical events.

But neither this publicity, nor the protests of believers abroad affected the situation in any way. Oncken, the courageous leader of the German Baptist movement in Hamburg, went right to the government in St. Petersburg to complain about the harsh treatment of the Baptists. The World Evangelical Alliance sent an appeal to the Russian government. This was endorsed by some Swiss ministers, and individual Protestants wrote to Russia and to the government there. But none of the protests and appeals had any effect.

We do not have statistics for those who were sentenced and deported. But it is certain that countless numbers were deported to Siberia and Transcaucasia, often after spending long years in prison. They were brought to their destination in chains like criminals, 'by stages' – i.e. from one prison to another, usually on foot, travelling for weeks on end. The suffering was increased by vermin and lack of hygiene. The 'instigators' and preachers were sentenced to forced labour. We know of some who bore the scars on their wrists to the end of their lives. They were bound with iron chains to the trucks which they had to look after in the mines, and which they did not leave day or night. The women were often transported separately, and they were exposed to the advances of the guards. We do not want to write about the cruel mistreatment and tortures that took place. Shocking descriptions of this can be found in literature. The many who perished on the journey may have looked upon this as a release. Even those who were 'only' sentenced to settle in inhospitable regions often found their lot unbearable. Dalton gives some eye-witness accounts of this. If the stundists were acquitted by the court, which often happened because of the love they enjoyed, then they were simply deported without sentence.

Dalton relates for example: 'During my travels in the Caucasus, once in Yelizavetpol I saw the wretched exiles at the market by the Gandzha. Hungry and idle, they stood around the miserable stalls and baskets where food was being sold – treasures beyond their reach in their total poverty . . . Like criminals, they were dragged off with their families, who held the same beliefs, to the distant Caucasus, to the borders of the empire where wild Kurdish tribes lived, and the strange language formed an insuperable barrier to communication. Into these remote regions they came by the hundred, not to be settled, but simply banished there and left to their own devices, these poor, wretched stundists whose only crime is to believe the holy gospel and to want to live by it. . . .

As these people slowly languish and die in terrible misery in the south of the empire, so too we see more of those persecuted for their faith following the long, hard path to Siberia. In this vast land, broad, barren regions can always be found where the stundists cannot present a threat to any neighbours.'*

Dalton goes on: 'A whole series of incontestable, painful and shocking cases have been documented in an almost official manner, and carefully preserved. Here we find the names of those sent into exile, their place of origin, their sentence, the terrible fate which they and the members of their family met on the way to the distant place of exile, their unutterable misery after arrival, until sooner or later death puts a compassionate end to their lives. Some of this carefully preserved and sifted material has already been made public in a series of English pamphlets, and in Godet's essay (*Persécutions actuelles en Russie*, 2nd ed., Neuchatel 1896) – even this small portion being sufficient to render any claim that such persecutions never took place wholly redundant and ridiculous. I have other documents as well. Behind these loud testimonies, which cry out to heaven, rise up the other pale shadows – who can number them? – who were driven along their path of suffering without a word, who bore their heavy cross silently, and who finally breathed their last, heard by no-one, crushed by the weight of their burden. These were true martyrs

* Dalton, *Der russische Stundismus*, pp. 50–51.

of the nineteenth century, whose sighs and prayers were heard by no-one but the one who once revealed himself to Saul as the one being persecuted in his disciples, and who raises his hand in judgment against those who bring trouble upon the least in his kingdom' (pp. 52–3).

We have given this quotation at such length because it comes from the pen of a contemporary of these events. Dalton was also known as a person of unassailably honest judgment and conscience, who enjoyed the trust of the highest circles in St. Petersburg, and made an honest attempt to be fair to Pobedonostsev's frightening authority. We are not dealing here with Dalton's 'Open Letter to the Oberprokuror of the Holy Synod, Privy Councillor Konstantin Pobedonostsev' of 1889, although it is of great interest; but it is concerned less with the persecutions of the stundists than with the oppression of the Lutheran Church in the Baltic provinces of Livonia, Estonia and Courland.

We will not go into details of shocking individual cases, or describe how, aside from the state persecution of the stundists, there were innumerable acts of violence against the believers on the part of neighbours and enemies executing lynch justice – in other words, purely criminal acts. One cannot help comparing this with the sufferings of the Christians in the Soviet Union. We do not wish to minimize individual fates. Each individual life is precious to God and has its own destiny. But it was not the communists who first invented the concentration camps, the deportations and the oppression of 'dissidents'. The former revolutionaries, who suffered under the tsarist knout, used very much the same methods and made the same demand for their own world-view to reign absolute. They demand the same absolute obedience even in men's opinions, conscience and faith – just as under Pobedonostsev. If anyone at that time completed his five years exile and hoped to be set free, he was given another five years suffering, 'because their first exile period does not seem to have changed them' (cf. Warns, pp. 125–6).

This painful situation continued until the revolution broke out in Russia during the unfortunate Russo-Japanese War (1904–05), in which tiny Japan inflicted serious losses on the giant Russian empire. It would not have taken much for the tsarist throne to be toppled and a republic introduced even that year. Nicholas II summoned his former Finance Minister Sergei Yulievich Witte, who had already been Transport Minister under Alexander III, and who as Finance Minister had brought the rouble on to the gold standard. In 1903 he had fallen into disgrace, but he was called back at this time of need and he succeeded in making the Treaty of Portsmouth (USA) and thereby bringing the war to a conclusion which was tolerable for Russia. Now he came to the head of the government, and he succeeded in convincing Nicholas that the people needed a constitution. Although the powers of the parliament, the imperial duma, were again restricted after Witte's retirement, nevertheless it was a first step. Witte's period of office had good consequences for the stundists, however, for on 16 April 1905 appeared the so-called Tolerance Manifesto, which broke with the principle of state intolerance and proclaimed – albeit limited – freedom of belief. It is true that this was gradually eroded again over the next few years, as unfortunately was so often the case during the reign of this last tsar. But still the concept of religious tolerance had at last been introduced and it brought release and help to countless sufferers, who had survived the time of persecution.

Jakob Kroeker relates as an eye-witness what he experienced at Easter 1905 in the palace of Princess Lieven in St. Petersburg:

'It was in the year 1905. If I remember correctly, there was to be a Christian conference in St. Petersburg over Easter. I too had come from the south of Russia to be there. But we had no idea what a great political event we were to experience there.

Nicholas II had conceived the great and fine plan of giving the great Russian empire complete freedom of belief through a manifesto on the first day of Easter. No-one knew anything about this significant decision. Only a few knew what was about to happen on the approaching Easter morning.

On the eve of the first day of Easter we received a sudden invitation to come to an early prayer meeting the next day in Princess Lieven's palace. We were not told what was to happen, it was only indicated that we were to receive a joyful surprise.

Very early the next day a small invited circle gathered in the palace. Everyone was asking what could be afoot, that they had been called together at such an unusual time. But no-one was able to give an answer. It was only known that the princess was going to read out a manifesto by the tsar.

When all the guests had arrived, one of the big folding doors opened and our beloved princess came into the room, deeply moved, holding a copy of the manifesto in her hand. She could hardly read the glad news for inner excitement and joy. When she had finished, those present joined in thanks and worship to the Lord. Not an eye remained dry and not a mouth dumb. We know how very important this manifesto, which would shortly be read in all the churches in Russia, would be for the many thousands who had had to bear the most severe sufferings because of their faith.

How many families had been torn apart, how many brethren languished in Siberian exile, how many sat in the darkest prison cells! And now all these sufferings and torments were to come to an end!

It was no wonder that in that memorable hour of prayer there was released in our souls a gratitude and a joy which one only rarely experiences. God had answered the pleas of his children which had risen for decades, and granted his suffering people freedom, and to the Russian empire the opportunity to take the path of intellectual re-birth.'*

It was in truth a significant moment for church history. Pobedonostsev retired from his post. His word had no more authority in church policies. The fact that the hopes of Kroeker and many others were not fulfilled was due to the fickle character of the weak-willed tsar. Witte's successor Stolypin, a strong personality who could perhaps have helped the empire politically, was himself the victim of assassination after he had introduced a time of reaction. Through his so-called 'field courts' cruel revenge was taken on the revolutionaries of 1904–5, during which much innocent blood was shed. The bitterness among the people became even stronger. It is true that the beginning of the first

* Kroeker, *Die Sehnsucht des Ostens*, pp. 18 ff.

world war saw a natural wave of national enthusiasm sweep through Russia. Nevertheless the war again revealed the inner weakness of the tsarist system, and it ended in the great catastrophe of the Bolshevik revolution. As is well known, the hopes of freedom raised at that time ended with the tyranny of Stalin.

VII   FROM 1905 TO THE FIRST WORLD WAR

It should have been possible to write above this decade: the golden age of freedom for preaching and Christian life. Unfortunately, however, this hope was fulfilled only to a very limited degree. Certainly there was great rejoicing at first, above all over the return of those who had been banished and imprisoned, although death had caused many a painful rift. And how many scars remained! The Baptist preacher Feodor Kostronin had been in exile for sixteen years and in prison for nine, separated from his family all this time. Vasili Ivanov-Klyshnikov, the chronicler of the Russian Baptist movement, had been twice in exile and thirty-one times in prison. These are only two instances out of countless other cases.

'The Russian Baptist Union,' which was re-established immediately after the tolerance manifesto, now developed an intense activity. In the year 1906 it sent out fifty evangelists through the country. Its first president was Dei Ivanovich Mazayev. He was also the editor of the magazine *The Baptist*. Slower action was taken by Ivan Stepanovich Prokhanov who, together with the circle around the Lieven household, brought together the 'All-Russian Union of Evangelical Christians' in St. Petersburg. But this was not until 1909.

It is not altogether easy to differentiate between these two unions, that of the Baptists and that of the Evangelical Christians. Since the latter also stood for believers' baptism, the two should really have been able to come together even then. But this did not take place until 1944, under Stalin's pressure. The reasons for their separate development are probably to be found chiefly in the personalities of the leaders.

The Baptist brethren had very firm principles, which in most cases went back to Oncken in Hamburg. One of these was the principle that communion could be shared only with those who could prove that they had been baptized as believers. Also, baptism was only considered valid when it was done by immersion (thus excluding baptism by 'sprinkling'). The fact that strong discipline and control were practised in the congregations was due to the nature of the people, who often considered order to be pedantic. But the danger of legalism was ever-present. Nevertheless the leaders – apart from those mentioned above, this also included Vasili Gurevich Pavlov, who had returned to Tiflis – held firmly to their course and governed the Baptist Union in a more centralized fashion than was the case in Germany. There, over the course of the years, the union had developed into an association of independent Baptist congregations.

Ivan Stepanovich Prokhanov (1869–1935) was more tolerant in all these questions. This corresponded to his gifted nature. He was never at an end, he always had fresh plans and was tireless in putting them into practice. It may not always have been easy to work with or under him, but those who got to know him found it difficult to resist his influence. He was without doubt the most important and gifted leader of the Evangelical Christians among the Russians. He was a reformist figure of great and varied talent. Like Pavlov, Prokhanov came from a Molokan community, and was born in Vladikavkaz (North Caucasia). While still at school, he fell prey to deep pessimism, and came near to suicide. He was prevented from taking his life by a little slip of paper which an unknown hand placed on his table. 'Do you love Christ?' were the words written on it. This led him to a spiritual awakening. In Tiflis he came in contact with the Russian Baptist congregation which had formed there. In 1887, at the age of eighteen, he was baptized. He studied in St. Petersburg at the Technical Institute. Here he also came into contact with the converts who were grouped around the Lieven household.

Even at that time, the spiritual leadership of the congregations was in the hands of Johann Kargel (1846–1933). He is said to have been the son of a German father and an Armenian mother. He came from Bulgaria and still had his Turkish passport, dating from

the time of the Turkish occupation there; this protected him from
the Russian police. All who knew Kargel remember him with
deep gratitude. He was a pastor and a preacher of sanctification.
He was concerned to deepen men's faith, to get the believers
rooted and grounded in the word of God, and to lead them into a
life of complete yieldedness to the Lord, believing in the victorious power of the Holy Spirit. Not only the older men, but
also the young ones, especially students and academics, held him
in grateful memory. One of those who owed his inner life to
Kargel was Karev, later Secretary-General of the All-Union
Council of Evangelical Christian-Baptists. He had been spritually
awakened as a very young tutor at Oesel in the home of a Baltic
baron. In St. Petersburg he joined himself to Kargel. When the
latter was banished from Petrograd, as it was called then, after the
Bolshevik revolution, a crowd of young men accompanied him
to the station. Karev approached him with the request: 'Write in
my book a word that will guide my path!' The old man took the
pencil and simply wrote two words: 'Poznai yevo!' – 'Know
him!' Karev later testified before other brethren how much
Kargel's word had strengthened and guided him at all times. In
his high-priestly prayer Jesus says: 'This is eternal life, that they
know thee the only true God, and Jesus Christ whom thou hast
sent.' Anyone who has read Karev's articles in *Bratsky vestnik*
(*Fraternal Herald*), the magazine of the All-Union Council, will
have realized that they testified to Christ crucified and risen.

If Kargel was moving deep down into the spiritual life,
Prokhanov was moving out far and wide. In 1893 he took his
engineering examination in St. Petersburg. His rich spirit found
its faith strengthened in the congregation, but he also sought
contact and exchange of ideas with the religious philosopher
Vladimir Solovyov and Leo Tolstoy. It may have been due to the
influence of the latter that Prokhanov together with other believers
founded a settlement called Vertograd in the Crimea, taking
inspiration from the early Christian sharing of possessions. He
wanted to show the Russian intellectuals who were influenced by
socialist thought, by means of an example, that a voluntary
communism based on the gospel was not impossible. This is

reminiscent of the so-called 'brethren farms' which came into being in Germany and later abroad through Dr. Eberhard Arnold.

Prokhanov soon had to leave Russia in order to escape the persecutions of the police. In 1895 he went to Finland and from there over the 'green frontier' to the West. Here he studied theology, first with the Baptists in England, then with the Congregationalists (Free Church), and finally at Berlin University. He also attended theological lectures in Paris. Everywhere he went in the west, he drew people's attention to the plight of the stundists in Russia. Three years later he returned to southern Russia via the orient (Egypt, Palestine and Syria). He broke his journey in Cyprus, where he acted as interpreter for the Dukhobors who had been driven out of Russia. This spiritual sect had an affinity with Tolstoy. Prokhanov almost fell a prey to the dysentery epidemics in Cyprus. Because he crossed the frontier at Odessa illegally, he was taken under police guard to his home in Vladikavkaz. He managed to find his exiled father and other believers. From here he went to Riga to work with the railway administration, and at the same time he worked as a private lecturer at the Technical College (Polytechnic) there. He was soon dismissed from there on the orders of the Ministry of the Interior on the grounds that he was a 'stundist leader'. After that he obtained a very good job with the English firm of Westinghouse in St. Petersburg. This firm provided the whole railway network throughout the large empire with their 'Westinghouse brakes', as every Russian traveller could see inscribed on the railway carriages. As an employee of Westinghouse, Prokhanov had no further trouble from the authorities. He now had to make long journeys, which took him as far as America; everywhere he went he sought contact with live Christians. In the Caucasus he found a wife, Anna Ivanovna Kozakov, who shared the way of faith with him.

He had a successful, often humorous way of dealing with people. His intellectual superiority and his wide horizon were a help to him in this. He even knew how to handle his opponents. He never denied his faith, but neither did he provoke anyone, and thus even before the decree of tolerance he was able to help those who had been exiled and imprisoned.

Prokhanov had a considerable poetic talent and he gave stundism, which up to then had taken most of its songs from German and English, a good number of beautiful songs. His little hymnbook containing songs by himself and others, *Gusli*, is still known today. It was printed on the press of the Ministry of the Interior – a sign of his good connections. After the decree of tolerance he published a weekly magazine, *The Christian*, which was both evangelistic and instructive for Christians, and showed no denominational narrowness. Each issue of the magazine had as a supplement a hymn with music. Thus he provided the congregations throughout the empire, and their choirs, with a rich treasury of music.

Prokhanov was an inexhaustible source of new ideas. When the tsarist government published more and more 'ministerial clarifications' weakening the law on tolerance, he found constantly fresh ways of protecting the congregations and their members. According to the law of 13 October 1906, religious congregations outside the state churches were permitted the rights of a person at law and allowed to keep their own church records, if at least fifty people signed a request for this. For this reason Prokhanov now devoted himself to organizing the congregations, something which Pashkov and his circle had paid little attention to until that time. Since Prokhanov was the first to seek a legal basis with regard to the state, his congregation was later called 'the First Evangelical-Christian congregation in St. Petersburg'. Alongside it was the much older congregation in the Lieven household, which now organized itself in a similar fashion. It was probably due to the broad-mindedness of this older circle that the 'All-Russian Union of Evangelical Christians', despite its adherence to believers' baptism, did not become Baptist. Prokhanov gathered these Evangelical-Christian congregations throughout the empire. It may be that Prokhanov's rather erratic and enterprising nature was alien to the Baptist brethren and they therefore preferred to remain independent.

VIII   THE RUSSIAN STUDENT CHRISTIAN MOVEMENT

During these decades before the first world war, God awakened many Russian students to a living faith in the gospel. In order to understand this movement, it is necessary to know the contemporary conditions of Russian student life.

The drive for education which had arisen among the people since the liberation of the peasants in 1861 was further awakened and strengthened by revolutionary propaganda, which was carried on mainly by the students. Most Russians were still illiterate. But the revolutionary youth promoted education among the lower classes.

In the second half of the last century and into the beginning of the twentieth century, the universities were particular centres of dissatisfaction and rebellion. The reactionary policies in education, the great shortage of places of higher education for the growing population, the lack of grants and state subsidies for study, and social need – all this brought about a radical political swing in the academic world. Sometimes the universities were completely closed down because of unrest, professors were censured and students arrested. But this was the worst method imaginable for dealing with these problems. As in so many cases, here too it was the symptoms of the disease which were being fought, instead of its causes being established and removed.

There were only nine universities in this gigantic empire. Many new plans were indeed being made for additional schools. The *zemstva*, the rural organs of self-government, which had been in existence since 1864, were setting up their own primary schools. But it is reckoned that at the time of the first world war there was still about sixty per cent illiteracy. Many students had tried to prepare themselves for university through taking private courses. But they found themselves in dire need. We have already seen how Pashkov and his friends tried to meet these needs in St. Petersburg. But the believers soon realized that the external need was surpassed by an inner one. The propaganda of unbelief was bearing evil fruit, and the scepticism of the so-called intelligentsia was shaking all religious foundations. The Orthodox Church had few priests who were in a position to answer the questions of those who doubted.

At that time God called a man who for thousands of students would be the one who called them to Christ. This was the Finnish nobleman, Baron Paul Nicolay (died 1919). One of his young friends said of him: 'Paul Nicolayevich was an outstanding preacher and also an unusually gifted preacher for the student intelligentsia.' His biographer, Hedwig von Redern, who was acquainted with the Nicolay family, describes him thus: 'A gentle man, often frail, by nature rather turned in upon himself, and yet leading a life of dedication and self-sacrifice.' She emphasizes his humility, purity of heart and conscientiousness, which fitted him particularly well for his ministry among the students.

Nicolay came from a Swedish family which had emigrated first to Lübeck and then to Alsace. His ancestors had been created nobility for diplomatic service in Austria and Russia. His grand-father had been tutor to Tsar Paul. He bought from the Duke of Württemberg the estate of Monrepos near Vyborg, where the family then settled. His father was a Minister for some time. His devout mother, born Baroness Meyendorff, made a deep impression upon Paul Nicolay, who lost his father early in life. From childhood he was accustomed to pray and to read the bible. He attended secondary school in St. Petersburg. At the age of nineteen – very late according to the custom of that time – he was confirmed in St. Anne's in St. Petersburg, an event which he took very seriously. He studied law in St. Petersburg, and lived there with his uncle, who was Minister for Cults at that time. His weak health forced him to forego many things, and hindered his participation in social life. His closest friend became Count Konstantin Konstantinovich von der Pahlen, son of the Minister of Justice, one of the noblest figures in St. Petersburg before the first world war. Through him, while still a student, he found his way into the Lieven household and the Christian circle there. Pahlen later married Nicolay's youngest sister. Young Nicolay's passion was sailing. In his yacht 'Lady' he sailed the sea between the countless rocky islets and cliffs of his Finnish homeland.

It was at the meetings in the Lieven palace that Nicolay was first asked to speak. In Finland he often visited the family of Baron Wrede and together with the famous Mathilde Wrede he visited Finnish prisons. In a Finnish bible study circle, someone let fall the expression 'semi-Christians'. This expression disturbed Nicolay. His drive for independence from other people led him to make personal decisions for himself. Alexandra von Peucker of the Lieven circle made a strong spiritual impression upon him. In 1888 he decided to live his life totally for Christ.

With his yacht – and his friend Baron Henrik Wrede on board – Nicolay began a missionary work among the fishermen on Finland's thousand islands, where a pastor rarely came. Here he learned to conduct pastoral conversations with simple people. He was soon to have them with very complicated people. But before he received the commission concerning the students, he visited Russian prisons with Dr. Baedeker. In 1898 he was able to write in his diary: 'I feel so refreshed after my prison visiting, as if I had taken some deep breaths of beautiful, pure air, and I cannot thank God enough for the privilege of being able to carry on this ministry at all.' These words are characteristic of Nicolay's inner attitude. Once he found that a cab-driver in Siberia was more grateful for the New Testament he gave him than for the fare – this showed again the hunger of the Russian people even at the turn of the century.

In 1899 Nicolay left state service in order to be completely free for the service of his heavenly king. For the door was now opening to his real life's work. During this year he met the American Secretary-General of the world Student Christian Movement, Dr. John Mott. With him he discussed the question of bringing into being a Russian student Christian movement. Nicolay wrote that 'the low moral condition of the Russian student world, as well as its spiritual need, makes such a work urgently necessary'. He accompanied Mott to St. Petersburg. Here, as in Dorpat and Riga, Mott spoke to small student groups. In a meeting at the Lieven home, it became clear to Nicolay that this was God's call for him.

Nicolay had no doubt that for him, a spoilt aristocrat, contact with the hundreds of embittered students would not be easy. 'For them, to be religious is to be a reactionary.' But he set about the work in faith. He called Witt, the young secretary of the German Student Christian Movement from Germany to St. Petersburg. Witt later became missionary superintendent for the Liebenzeller Mission in Changcha, China. With him, Nicolay hoped to reach the German students first.

The Russian Student Christian Movement (RSCM) was founded on 18 November 1899 in St. Petersburg in the home of the book-dealer Grote. Apart from Nicolay, Grote and Witt, there were four German students present. There were many prejudices to be overcome, even among the Lutheran pastors. Thus in the beginning it had to work as a branch of the German YMCA. In 1900 Nicolay took part in the German student Christian conference at Eisenach. He met Jasper von Oertzen and Eduard Count Pückler. He met Hudson Taylor at the Blankenburg Alliance conference.* It was encouraging that in Finland there were already 150 students who wanted to put into practice a missionary Christianity. Finland had been a place of spiritual life since the time of Gossner. This was another mustard seed falling into the Russian earth.

For two years the circle failed to grow. It was a spiritual struggle over each individual. When fifty students appeared on one occasion, they spoke of this as victory and success. It was not until 1902 that the situation began to improve. A group of Russian Orthodox students now joined, so that the bible studies were soon being held in Russian. Outsiders were reached through discussion evenings. During all this preparatory work, the end goal was never lost from sight. 'Our purpose in all the meetings is to lead souls to Christ and a thorough conversion,' wrote Nicolay. Because of his frailty, he was only able to exercise his ministry by dint of tremendous self-denial. He was adept at pastoral work with the individual. What joy it was when one student was able to testify: 'I lived without God. Existence had lost all purpose for me and I wanted to throw it away. But now I have found God.' Nicolay wrote of this gifted, energetic man:

* A conference of the German Evangelical Alliance, similar to the Keswick Convention in England. Blankenburg is now in East Germany.

' – and this life was almost thrown away. What a joy to see him saved and happy!'

The work grew again in 1903 when the women students, for whom there were special college courses, were also invited. The *kursistki* were a well-known phenomenon in St. Petersburg.

Soon the work was bearing good fruit. In 1905 the RSCM adopted its basis of faith. Fifteen students in St. Petersburg signed this confession of faith: 'On the basis of the gospel, I believe in the Lord Jesus Christ as the Son of God, I have experienced an inner renewal, I have given myself to the Lord and I know that he has accepted me.' Thus there came into being at the centre of the work an 'active membership' which continued to form its mainstay.

In 1907 Nicolay received a severe blow. One of his most faithful friends, who took an active part in the work, was Alexander Maximovsky. Because he had an influential post in penal work, a revolutionary student decided that he was a representative of the hated tsarist regime, and shot him in his office. The dying man prayed for his murderer. For Nicolay, this sacrifice was a new spur to dedicated labour.

After the revolution and the tolerance edict of 1905, in the era of the liberal policies of Witte, foreign evangelists and preachers were able to speak in student meetings, and Nicolay served as interpreter, since he could speak not only German but also French, English and Swedish fluently. In 1903 Karl Heim – later the unforgettable professor of theology and student pastor in Münster and Tübingen – visited the student circles in St. Petersburg, Dorpat and Riga, as travelling secretary of the German Student Christian Movement. Nicolay had come to know him at the Paris world conference of Christian students in 1900. Nicolay also took Heim to meetings in the Lieven household. He called these evenings 'a quite unexpected encounter with a piece of New Testament Christian life'. 'It was the greatest experience of my time in Russia that through Baron Nicolay and Princess Lieven I came into contact with this New Testament Christian movement.' Heim testified to his lasting memories of Nicolay's brotherly love.*

* *Ich gedenke der vorigen Zeiten*, Wuppertal 1964 R. Brockhaus Taschenbücher, Vol. 76/77, pp. 53–62.

In 1906 Nicolay published a little booklet on the Gospel of Mark, a fruit of his work in the student bible groups, where he usually started with this gospel. This simple introduction, with questions for beginners, shows how foreign the bible was to the students. But now they were getting to know it.

In 1907 he began a work among the students in Moscow. Here he found a co-worker for the women students – it was said of her that she fought like a lioness for Christ! In 1910 the work began at Kiev University. Nicolay spoke twice here, each time before 500 students, on the themes 'The divinity of Christ' and 'How does Christ become a practical reality in our lives?' Three student groups were the result of this early pioneering work. The next place was Odessa: 'an unparalleled mixture of peoples and religions' wrote Nicolay. 'The Lord prepared the way, opened the door and removed obstacles; I saw with my own eyes how He went ahead and accomplished the work with his own hand.'

The influence of Pobedonostsev was felt when confirmation of the RSCM statutes was witheld. One Kiev professor wrote in a church paper: 'If anyone wanted to destroy state and Church, the student Christian movement would be extremely useful!' This was the old Russia of the tsars.

In Moscow, too, the work was hindered by the Church, despite the tolerance manifesto of 1905. 'The work is seriously threatened in Moscow,' wrote Nicolay, 'because the clergy there have more power than in other places. We wanted to distribute ten thousand invitations among the students. But the police would not allow it. It's so boring to be in constant uncertainty, arguing with all kinds of officials. But then I remember that I don't need to worry at all, for the Lord will certainly not leave his cause undefended, but will carry it victorious through everything. I am very thankful for the intercession of my friends, which is my support' (Hedwig von Redern, p. 96).

The decade before the first world war may be described as the decade of revival among Russian students. The war then virtually put an end to this work as well. But Nicolay saw what lay ahead: 'I am afraid that the social upheavals after this war will bring something worse than the war itself.'

When the revolution broke out in 1917, the active Christians experienced it at first as a liberation. 'Our students have gone through the streets selling New Testaments and giving out eight thousand tracts, which were accepted gladly.'

But Nicolay's time was soon to be over. In a final letter before his death (1919), he wrote to John Mott: 'The present situation of total anarchy makes all addresses unreliable ... There have been so many massacres in Kiev that I do not know which of our friends are still alive ... But we do know that a religious revival is going on in various parts of Russia, and that our scattered members are holding packed meetings in different towns.'

Already in 1907 Nicolay, who was in frequent pain, lay seriously ill at his estate Monrepos. At that time, he wrote in his diary: 'If it is God's will, I am happy to leave this earth and go to him. I would also be happy to go on living, if I could work at full strength.'

During the days of revolution, which were very violent in Finland – almost thirty Russian officers were killed near Monrepos – Nicolay only escaped death when one of his Russian workers intervened and emphatically praised his master's goodness. In the spring of 1919, Nicolay suffered a heart attack; the doctor forbade him to speak in churches; in August he caught paratyphoid fever, and at the beginning of October his weakened body collapsed. The Lord took his servant home on the morning of 6 October 1919.

At his funeral. Miss Brechet, one of his most faithful co-workers, said:

'Through him, hundreds of desperate, lost, seeking souls found the way to a living faith in God. They have become happy people, who found in the RSCM the realization of the ideal and the strength to lead a better life. Baron Nicolay is the instigator of a new era in Russia's religious life. The student movement has given Russia teachers who are able to give young people answers to their forbidden questions, doctors who have a remedy for the diseases of the soul, educated workers from various walks of life who have learned to do their job faithfully and honestly.'

One of these teachers, whom Nicolay won for the Lord, was

Vladimir Filimonovich Martsinkovsky, who became Nicolay's spiritual successor. Martsinkovsky's path is typical of this student generation. He has given us a precise account of Nicolay's pastoral work with him.

In 1903 Martsinkovsky was invited to Nicolay's group by a fellow-student. He relates: 'The meeting had not yet begun. The students were drinking tea. Some were standing around, others were conducting a lively argument. There were university students, students of commerce, students from the technical college and the polytechnic. Someone clapped their hands: we were asked to finish our tea. We went into the next room. The students – about thirty of them – sat in a circle. In the middle stood the leader, Paul Nicolayevich, a man of about forty, medium height, lean, beardless but with side-whiskers. He had such a simple and engaging face.

"Let's begin with a short prayer, friends!"

Everyone stood up.

It was the first time I had heard such a simple, free prayer to God, that he would bless us all and illuminate us by his word! I felt that this was no formal prayer, but something natural, like breathing, and at the same time I felt the invisible presence of a person . . . We sat down. After a short introduction, he read the parable of the prodigal son. He read with such fervour, and explained it in such a lively way, so freshly – I felt that he was talking about me, about each one of us. It's me that is wandering far away from the Father, feeding on husks and about to starve. And most important: I discovered a new side to the gospel. Until then I had understood it as the inexorable preaching of a duty which I could not fulfil: you must! you must! Now from the depths came the Father's friendly, encouraging voice: "You may! Come as you are! I'll give you a white robe and a ring of shining beauty. I love you – I came for your sake."

It was as if a door had opened out of the dark and cold into a lofty room, where it was pleasing and light . . . I went home full of new thoughts and hopes.'

This is how Professor Martsinkovsky described his first encounter with Baron Nicolay. He goes on: 'I am happy to have met him. He is associated in my mind with the best side of my time as a student, he brought the most important influence of my life, the greatest joy, which still fills my life today . . .'

'Our movement is on the offensive, not the defensive' – this was a slogan that Nicolay tossed among the students. His favourite sayings included such expressions as: 'Every Christian is a missionary.' 'If we don't go forwards, then we're going back.' 'If there's no growth, then there's decay.' 'Still waters become brackish.'

It was a small student conference in Kiev with about twenty-five participants which gave Martsinkovsky that first incentive to take a decision about his life's direction. The helpful pastoral conversation which Nicolay had with him is so typical of his simple approach that we will give it as Martsinkovsky described it from memory:

On a quiet path through the park, Nicolay said to the young student: ' "Tell me, my friend, what conclusion have you come to at the end of the year?"

"Oh, I haven't got that far . . . Sometimes it seems that I don't believe in anything."

"Tell me," replied Nicolay, "are you prepared to turn to God? Christ said: Anyone who comes to me, I will not cast out."

"Yes, but how can I do that with all my doubts? I'm not even sure that Christ was a historical person."

"Doubts needn't stop you. If he is there and he calls you, are you prepared to follow him? Let's turn to him directly, instead of concentrating on doubts and eternal self-analysis."

And then we prayed together. I felt that I was experiencing a unique moment, which would never return: it was now or never! I appealed to the Father in the name of the Son, admitting my need of a saviour and expressing my desire to follow him, with the help of his strength . . . a deep, inexplicable peace and an unspeakable joy filled my soul. Paul Nicolayevich had led me over the threshold of faith.'

After Martsinkovsky had spent six years as a secondary school teacher in the provinces, where he sought to testify to his pupils about the living Lord, he obeyed a call from Nicolay to serve the student movement full-time. With this, he gave up his official position, which was so sought after in old Russia. This was in 1913.

For the next decade, as Secretary-General of the RSCM, Martsinkovsky was Nicolay's spiritual successor. What he also experienced as professor of ethics at Samara University on the Volga (today Kuibyshev) and as a confessor of Jesus Christ in the troubled years of revolution after the war, he has described in his formerly much-read book *Gotterleben in Sowjetrussland*.

Martsinkovsky was called to be professor in Samara in 1919, the year that Nicolay died, two years after the outbreak of the revolution. During these years he found many outlets for his powerful and deep testimony to Christ. Finally he was imprisoned by the *cheka*, the Bolshevik state police at that time. He was not silent even in prison. It was about 1923 when Martsinkovsky was sent into exile by the government, because he was disturbing the students in their ideological direction. He went first to Prague, where other members of the RSCM had also taken refuge. After some years he emigrated to Palestine, where he built himself a small house on Mount Carmel. This gifted linguist learned Arabic and Ivrit, modern Hebrew, so well that he could hold lectures and bible studies in both languages. When increasing age made it impossible for him to hold large meetings, he became a literature missionary. He stood on the street corner with a tray of tracts. A quick judge of persons, he could tell with amazing assurance whether a passer-by spoke Arabic or Russian, Ivrit or German, and would give him a leaflet in his own language. He found a courageous companion in the former head of the institute for Arab girls in Jerusalem, 'Talitha cumi', founded by the Kaiserswerth deaconess house.

We have described this in such detail in order to show the kind of material of which these Russian and Ukrainian witnesses of Christ were made. 'Every Christian is a missionary!' Baron Nicolay had said. This was true not only of the peasants, but also the intellectuals. It was not a question of human dignity and career, but of Jesus and his kingdom. Martsinkovsky was not the only one among the academics who has given us sleepy Christians in the west an example. Many students in Marburg are indebted to the old mathematics professor, Th. Schlarb, who spent the last years of his life here, for his full testimony to the gospel. Week by week for many years he gathered students and also older academics in his flat to study the bible. He too was a spiritual son of Nicolay. In Geneva and Alsace, too, we find Nicolay's pupils leaving their mark. Alongside the movement in the villages, this branch of the stundist movement too, after rich sowing, led to a harvest which brought glory to Christ.

IX   HELP FROM THE WEST

It is regrettable that, apart from the above-mentioned protests by the Evangelical Alliance and Oncken's attempt to help, world christendom took so little interest in the fate of the stundists. It may have been political or economic considerations which made other countries hold back in this respect; even from circles that were interested in mission there was little or nothing to be heard.

The fact that the Baptist World Alliance was always ready to help is largely due to Pavlov. He sent the appeal for help from Rumania, and he also attended the conferences of the Alliance.

Dr. Baedeker and his famous friend George Müller, both of whom visited St. Petersburg repeatedly, were not the only members of the 'Open Brethren' to show an active interest. F. W. Baedeker (1823–1906), a tireless visitor of Russian prisons right into Siberia, took part, together with General G. von Viebahn, in the founding of the Wiedenest Bible school in Germany (previously in Berlin on the Hohenstauffenstrasse); this was a work of the Open Brethren, where many Russian Christians were trained. Those who worked there had recognized that sound biblical teaching is a decisive help in any revival movement. Excessive enthusiasm and legalism, the two childhood diseases of almost every new convert, are a particular danger in the slavic lands, since they lacked the biblical-theological tradition and seminaries. In this land of many sects, it was difficult to guard against false doctrines among the new congregations. That is why bible schools were a great necessity.

This fact was also recognized by the previously-mentioned Dr. Johannes Lepsius, a friend of the Orient Mission and helper of the persecuted Armenians in Turkey. This son of a leading German egyptologist was one of the few who tried to make the west aware of the stundists' need. In his missionary periodical *Der christliche Orient* Lepsius published frequent news of stundism and of the problems experienced by its followers. According to Gutsche (*op. cit*, p. 52), Lepsius was also the author of the pamphlets which appeared under the pseudonym 'Christophilos', some of which were published in several editions, in other words were widely read. Although some of his research on the history of stundism is not wholly accurate, posthumous thanks are still due to him, for he felt the bond of love connecting him to these persecuted Christians.

In the year 1900 Lepsius called the Ukrainian Stefanovich into the service of the Orient Mission; after learning German, Stefanovich was ordained in Lichtenrade near Berlin in 1903. Stefanovich was primarily an evangelist in Bulgaria, but he also travelled in Russia a few times and visited the communities there. Here he observed how greatly the movement was in need of proper organization and biblical-theological training. This may have been the stimulus for Lepsius to take further steps: Pastor Jellinghaus's bible school in Lichtenrade was to undertake the training of young Russians.

When in 1905 Lepsius gave a lecture in Potsdam on the movement in Russia, and called for helpers, he was approached by Walter Jack, a theology graduate from Halberstadt. After he had come to a living faith in Jesus, Jack could not make up his mind to take a parish in the established Church. He came from an old French Huguenot family, and later he would only allow the Russians to call him Walter Ludwigovich Jacques. He was known to the stundists under this name even before he founded the mission 'Licht im Osten' together with Jakob Kroeker.

In October 1906 – eighteen months after Nicholas II's tolerance manifesto – Pastor Walter Jack travelled to Russia. We have twenty letters giving this missionary's first impressions of his journey via St. Petersburg to Moscow. He also reported on the joys and the problems in the establishment of a small bible school.

In St. Petersburg he met the book dealer Grote, the 'soul of the fellowship movement within the Lutheran Church for many years', as Jack describes him. Then he met Baron Nicolay. In both these men he found profound understanding, and received wise advice in his task. Nicolay told him: 'The people are all religious, but they are excitable, easily divided and shaken, because there are no leaders who are capable of seeing past the secondary things such as baptism, questions of the Second Coming, sabbath observance and so on, and energetically underlining the unifying aspect of faith in Jesus! That is, faith in our crucified king and the rebirth of hearts and spirits by his Spirit.'

Jack also found support from Pastor Walter of St. Peter's, the largest German Lutheran congregation in St. Petersburg, and from Pastor Findeisen, 'a deeply serious, believing man with complete sympathy for evangelism and personal conversion'. In the deaconess house of the German congregations he found a small circle which had been praying for revival in Russia for a long time, and in Senator Count K. K. Pahlen, Nicolay's brother-in-law, he found a brother and a friend who later took an active part in the founding of the mission. In St. Petersburg Jack visited a large number of stundist groups which were in fellowship with one another, although, in his opinion, endangered by certain sectarian influences. At that time there were said to be about forty of these fellowship groups in St. Petersburg.

In spite of the tolerance manifesto, conditions for the stundists were much worse in Moscow than in St. Petersburg. But Jack found a brotherly link with the leaders Yakovlev and Verbitsky. In their discussions about the needs of the community there, Jack displayed his organizational skill. This was something which the stundist brethren lacked in the early days. Because here too 'all the people were religious', the influx into the community was considerable. But at the same time, this increased the influence of immature and often unenlightened spirits. On Jack's advice, the brethren organized the community on the lines of the old YMCA: they divided active members from the rest and gave the former responsibility and eligibility to serve as elders. 'In this way we have no popes, and the word of the Lord is fulfilled: You have one master, you are all brethren.' 'This programme must be deliberated with much prayer and wisdom', Jack went on. 'I consider it to be biblical, and the best solution of the difficult question of order in the community, for on the one hand it avoids pure democracy, and on the other, the papal system.' Here we see a sound fruit of the old congregational concept among the Calvinists, from which tradition the Huguenot descendant Walter Jack came.

In Moscow he also came to know the highly-educated brother Gorenovich, the former anarchist, who had lost his eyesight through being attacked by his former comrades and who had come to faith through Pashkov's ministry in the hospital.

By this time Jack was no longer sleeping in a hotel, but on the campbed which he had brought with him, in the meeting room, and eating 'modest meals'. This spartan attitude, which particularly suited Jack for the ministry among the stundists, was one that he retained all his life. When it came to his Lord, to Jesus and his service, he put aside all personal demands.

Jack also saw to it that the leading brother in Moscow received a modest salary from the Orient Mission in Germany, so that he could be free to preach without material worries. Jack was also overjoyed to find a German Protestant fellowship group in Moscow.

Jack's real call came from the New Molokans. The venerable old brother S. D. Sakharov, whom Jack called 'the patriarch', who made great sacrifices for the cause of Jesus out of his considerable means, invited him to his estate of Sokologornoye ('falcon hills') This was in the Tauride province in south Russia; Astrakhanka was nearby, and a conference was to take place here on 7 November 1906 in order to found a preaching seminary, to be under Jack's direction.

Jack experienced the impressive brotherly hospitality of the Molokans. However, the building and establishing of the little seminary, which was to give a thorough biblical-theological training to Protestant teachers, took place only after severe difficulties had been overcome. Jack now had an opportunity to demonstrate his tough and determined character. For someone who had grown up in Germany, conditions in Russia at that time were inconceivable. To give only one example, it could happen that in winter trains were as much as forty hours delayed. His journeys by sledge through thick snowstorms, or by train to St. Petersburg, sound almost like fairy-tales to us today. Nevertheless Jack succeeded in opening a preliminary class in the spring of 1907, and in getting a Russian Christian teacher. In August of that year the regular courses began. In less than a year, Jack had learned enough Russian, a difficult language for Germans, that he could teach and preach.

This whole episode is one of the most interesting attempts to help stundism from the west. Unfortunately the reactionary government of Nicholas II brought about the closure of this important place of training. But the tireless Pastor Jack soon found a way to continue his work. From his letters we can see how his firm belief in the power and the guidance of God, and the knowledge that he was here in obedience to Jesus Christ, enabled him to overcome all opposition. On one occasion he wrote: 'Thanks be to God that we have experienced this almighty power of the saviour in our own hearts, for without his mercy we would not be any different, if we had had to grow up in the same conditions as these poor people. The fact that everything is different with us, that we were born in a nation which has been civilized by the gospel, that we grew up surrounded by the blessings and influences of that gospel, and that through personal faith we were able to appropriate it for ourselves – all this is grace and nothing but grace. It is cause for humility and deep thankfulness.'

After the closure of the school in Astrakhanka, Jack began an illegal work. Meanwhile, through his marriage to the daughter of a Mennonite landowner in south Russia, he himself had acquired a small estate, Apanlé. He invited the brethren to come here for bible study. Since almost all of them came from peasant backgrounds, they were drivers, stablemen and harvest workers, but they gathered daily for bible study. This hopeful beginning, too, was dashed by the first world war. As a German national, in other words a hostile alien, Jack was exiled with his family to the northern province of Vologda, to the little town of Kologriv, where he immediately started a work among the other exiles. When the German nationals were released towards the end of the war, he travelled with his wife and three daughters via Sweden to Germany, offered himself to the army as a field chaplain, and in this capacity came to Kiev, which was held by the Germans. Here he had close contact with the stundist brethren of the Ukraine.

Quite a different ministry was exercised by Jakob Kroeker (1872–1948), later mission director of 'Licht im Osten'. Unlike Jack, he did not need to hear the call to Russia and to learn a difficult language. His Mennonite forebears had emigrated from Germany to Russia a hundred years previously. They came originally from Holland, and under Frederick the Great had settled together with many other Mennonites in the flats of the Weichsel and the Nogat; then, when Prussia introduced universal military service before the Wars of Liberation, again with many other Mennonites they had taken up Alexander I's invitation to go to Russia.

Jakob Kroeker was born on 31 October (old style) 1872 in the colony of Gnadenthal, the eldest child of his parents. He was to follow his father on the farm, but this was made impossible by a severe leg accident when the boy ran into the blade of a scythe. The doctors did not think they could help. Then God did a miracle through the hands of a simple practitioner. The leg straightened again, but it remained weak, so that when Kroeker left school, he learned a manual trade, book-binding. Before this his parents had moved along with others to the Crimea, near Simferopol, to establish a new Mennonite village. The settlers here experienced a revival movement, which affected the young Jakob for the rest of his life; he was thirteen at the time. He wanted to become a missionary, but after his training at the Baptist seminary in Hamburg, his fiancée was pronounced unfit for the tropics. Kroeker then became a teacher at a Mennonite school in Russia. Soon he was called by the German Mennonites to be an itinerant preacher, in which capacity he travelled Russia

from the north to the deepest south – through the Caucasus right
up to the Turkish border. His work was soon supplemented by
various kinds of spiritual literature. His contact with Dr. Baedeker,
whom he met at conferences, meant a great deal to him. It was
Dr. Baedeker who also invited him to St. Petersburg to the
circle of Princess Lieven.

For a number of years Kroeker travelled every winter for six
to eight weeks to the capital on the Neva in order to serve the
many groups of believers there. Thus every Friday he was among
the German Protestant fellowship, where at the request of the
book-dealer Grote he preached the gospel. Here in St. Petersburg
he also met German visitors, mostly representatives of Blankenburg Alliance circles and fellowships like Otto Stockmayer,
Fritz Otzbach and others.

In 1910 Jakob Kroeker moved with his growing family to
Germany, and found a new home in Wernigerode in the Harz
mountains. Here there began quite a different ministry to the
stundist movement, to which we shall return.

Reading about all these witnesses whom God called forth in
these years, and about the growth of the movement after the
tolerance manifesto, one might think that the early difficulties
had been overcome. Unfortunately this was not the case. Kroeker,
well acquainted with conditions in those years, writes about many
childhood diseases in the movement: 'First there was the soulish
element. Sighs and tears belonged not only to conversion, but to
every prayer meeting. The emotional slavic soul will never let this
go completely. But the danger remained that the movements of
the soul were confused with the working of the Holy Spirit. It
was not long before the influence of the modern Pentecostal
movement was felt. Widespread lack of experience, ignorance of
church history and so on brought about many an immature
judgment. They lacked the wisdom which comes from the school
of life and a historical orientation.' It is also not surprising that
there was tremendous legalism and narrow-mindedness. This was
a fertile ground for Adventism and Sabbatarianism; but even the
strict Baptist circles were not free of legalism. In this context, the
breadth of the Lieven circle was considered suspicious.

All this shows how important was the training of responsible men in sound theology.

Unfortunately these internal dangers continued to be augmented by the threat from outside. It was the misfortune of Nicholas II's regime that it soon tried to annul any concessions which it had made. So it was with the tolerance edict. Once the danger of the revolutionary movement had apparently been crushed by the cruel field courts introduced by Prime Minister Stolypin, all the reactionary forces in officialdom again reared their head. Ministerial decrees brought about all kinds of restrictions on the freedom of belief: a strict censorship of religious literature; the obligation to seek police permission for religious gatherings, which were often forbidden without cause; limitations on youth work – all things which are still commonplace in the Soviet Union today. In St. Petersburg, under the eye of the big newspapers and a critical high society, things were still tolerable. But the further one went from the imperial capital, the more arbitrary rule took over. The Orthodox clergy watched the exodus from the Church with concern. Alongside Adventism, which was putting great energy into its work, the powerful Roman Catholic Church had also seen its opportunity and was developing a strong propaganda. Of course the stundists and the Baptists also used the freedom which they had gained. If there were no legal means to limit all these movements, there was all the greater recourse to illegal methods. This had always been the case in the huge old tsarist empire.

Johannes Warns, teacher at the Wiedenest bible school, made many trips to Russia at this time and visited the stundists. In his book *Russland und das Evangelium* (Kassel 1920) he gives a large number of letters from brethren whom he knew personally and for whose integrity he could vouch (pp. 141–54). To read these letters is a very moving experience. They speak of excited crowds storming meetings and mishandling the believers, often in the presence of fanatical priests, and with their crude encouragement. Not even women and children were spared. Even the police took part in these illegal acts. In some cases faithful confessors paid for their constancy with their lives.

Over these sufferings stand the promises of Christ: 'A servant is not greater than his master. If they persecuted me, they will persecute you' (John 15.20). The brethren in the east were learning what we in the west have largely forgotten: 'through many tribulations we must enter the kingdom of God' (Acts 14.22) and 'All who desire to live a godly life in Christ Jesus will be persecuted' (2 Tim. 3.12). One good aspect of these troubles can still be seen today: few Churches have such a small proportion of hangers-on as the stundist movement. Suffering and persecution refine the faith of the individual and purify the congregations from hypocrisy.

X   THE BEGINNINGS OF LITERATURE WORK

It is well known that the printed word is of vital importance to any revival movement. This goes first for bible distribution, then for the printing of songbooks, and lastly also for Christian magazines and writings of a revivalist nature. Although there has never – even today – been really adequate evangelical literature in Russian or Ukrainian, this has nevertheless been a continual concern.

In 1882 a revised Russian bible was published at Pashkov's expense. Part of this edition was printed in the form of a study bible, with space for personal notes. There was a further edition in 1907, part of which was in small pocket format. Pashkov also published a New Testament where those passages which in the west are printed in heavy type, were underlined. He founded a tract society which printed large quantities of evangelical leaflets. Unfortunately most of these were translated from English and thus ill-suited to the average Russian. It is difficult to understand why the 'heroes' of these stories should have been called James or John, not Yakov or Ivan. The periodical *The Russian Worker*, published by Alexandra von Peucker, found many friends. However it was soon forbidden by Pobedonostsev.

Translations were printed of John Bunyan's *Pilgrim's Progress* and his less well-known *The Holy War. Pilgrim's Progress* had already appeared in 1789, at the time of Catherine the Great, translated by Novikov. The poet Pushkin had been stimulated by reading this book to write his poem *The Pilgrim*. After Pashkov had been sent into exile abroad, the new edition was halted, especially since there were still large stocks of the old editions, which lasted for a while.

Prokhanov also recognized the importance of the printed word. During the time that he was forced by Pobedonostsev to live abroad, he published in Sweden a small magazine called *Conversation* (in Russian *Beseda*) and sent it to Russia through the post. After 1905 he succeeded in obtaining a licence for his magazine *The Christian* (in Russian *Khristianin*). Its editor was Zhidkov, later long-standing President of the All-Union Council of Evangelical Christians–Baptists in Moscow. This magazine appeared every month for nine years, up to 1914, and again from 1924–28, and became an increasingly important factor in building up the believers. The contents avoided all polemic. Zhidkov writes (*Evangelical Christians in the Soviet Union*, p. 28): 'Prokhanov and his co-workers had set themselves the goal of avoiding all criticism, but only preaching Christ crucified, striving together for the evangelical faith and in so doing providing an example for the children of God. One of the principles of the magazine was: In the first place unanimity, in the second place freedom, and above all love! These aims won for it the reputation of a truly Christian magazine which was read not only by believers of the new orientation, but also by many members of the established Church. As well as articles of spiritual content, *The Christian* also published songs with music, including choral settings.'

From 1907 onwards the Baptist Union published the magazine *The Baptist*, under the direction of its president Mazayev, later under Pavlov and Ivanov. As well as purely religious articles and sermons by famous preachers, a lot of news was given about the life of Baptist congregations around the world.

From 1909 to 1914 Prokhanov also published a weekly newspaper, *The Morning Star* (in Russian *Utrennyaya zvezda*). This was intended for more thoughtful readers, and published articles on religious thought, science and politics, but also reports on the persecution of believers in Russia. In this way Prokhanov hoped to reach a wider circle of believers.

In 1909 the Mennonites founded the Christian publishing agency *Rainbow* (in Russian *Raduga*) in Halbstadt on the Molochna, Donets region. Here too Prokhanov was the leading figure, and the main depot was in St. Petersburg. Some 200 publications show with what energy this opportunity was seized – it was as if they knew how short the time was. One of the most important of these publications was Prokhanov's *Short Study on Preaching*, which was reprinted by the mission 'Licht im Osten' in Korntal in 1960. This is an outstanding practical homiletic in personal study for brethren who preach the word. There was also a translation of sermons by Spurgeon and Bettex entitled *Song of Creation*. Songbooks will be mentioned later.

The very active Latvian preacher Fetler, who had gathered together his own very large Baptist congregation in St. Petersburg, also published two magazines from 1909 onwards: *Faith* (in Russian *Vera*) and *The Guest* (in Russian: *Gost*).

The Armenian Tarayants in Baku put out the magazine *Glad Tidings* (*Radostnaya vest*). A small magazine *The Sower* (*Seyatel*) was also founded by Prokhanov, but later taken over by Rodd.

A 'Gospel House' was established in St. Petersburg for the growing work, and it housed a 'Good Literature Publishers' (*Izdatelstvo poleznoi literatury*) which acquired considerable importance.

The Russian Student Christian Movement also printed some aids to bible study. In 1911 and 1912 there appeared Nicolay's *Aid to Understanding the Gospel of Mark* and a similar *Aid to Understanding the Epistle to the Philippians*. These are excellent, practical aids for beginners with questions and topics, which are still very usable today. Martsinkovsky later published a similar aid to study of the Gospel of John.

In Moscow there appeared Savelev's *History of the Christian Church* (*Istoria khristianskoi tserkvi*); in fact this only covered the history of the first three centuries, but it was much used by the evangelical believers.

Also very valuable were the writings of Kargel: *The Reflection* of Glories to Come (*Svet teni budushchikh blag*); *How do you Stand in Relation to the Holy Spirit?* (*V kakom ty otnoshenii k Dukhu Svyatomu?*); *The Raised Curtain* (*Podnyataya zavesa*).

In Odessa, Pavlov published a book of sermon outlines: *Leaves from the Tree of Life* (*Listya dereva zhizni*).

To these publications were added a large number of songbooks. All genuine Christian revival movements sing praise to Christ and strike up the 'new song', and this was particularly the case with the Russians and Ukrainians. This can be seen from the long list of song collections which appeared within a relatively short time. Two small songbooks had already appeared in 1874, published by Pashkov: *Beloved Verses* and *Joyful Songs of Zion*, both in large editions, like everything else that Pashkov produced. In 1877 the early stundists published a songbook with the title *Gift to Orthodox Christians* (*Prinoshcheniye pravoslavnym khristianam*) – the title shows that the tsarist censorship could not forbid and confiscate the book. Voronin, founder of the first Russian Baptist congregation in Tiflis, published a songbook in 1882 called *Voice of Faith* (*Golos very*), using Pashkov's earlier collections. At the same time there appeared in Moscow the anonymous *Collection of poems* (*Sbornik stikhotvorenii*) containing a hundred songs, and later called the 'hundred collection'.

But the widest circulation fell to Prokhanov's collection of songs *Gusli*, printed on the presses of the Ministry of the Interior in 1902. Four other parts were later added to this songbook: *Songs of the Christian, Tambourine* (*Tympanon*), *Cymbals* (*Kimvaly*) and *Dawn of Life* (*Zarya zhizni*). This large collection is still called the 'Collection of Five' today; it was the best-loved and most widely-used one.

But even these titles were not the only ones. In 1903 *Songs of Russian Christians* (*Pesni russkikh khristian*) was printed on a secret press, in other words without the permission of the all-powerful censorship. And in Yekaterinodar there appeared a collection of songs which again tried to use a title to protect itself against censorship attack: *Church Hymn Book* (*Kniga tserkovnykh gimnov*).

After the revolution this diversified activity moved towards a greater unity, which will be dealt with later. But it is a testimony to the spiritual and intellectual content of the young movement, which was able to come into the open for the first time in the decade 1905 to 1914, that it could display this manifold creativity and it represents a tremendous achievement in view of the conditions under which that creativity had to develop.

XI THE FIRST WORLD WAR 1914–18

All these hopeful beginnings were again threatened by the 1914–18 war. The war had a profound effect on the stundist and Baptist communities. If arbitrary rule was already commonplace in the old tsarist empire, it is not hard to imagine how much more the conditions of war contributed to this state of affairs. It was as if the tolerance manifesto of 1905 had never been. The general popular feeling against the Germans, which led to a pogrom against them in Moscow in the summer of 1915 now affected the stundists as well. 'You have a German religion,' it was said. 'You have the same religion as Wilhelm' – that is, the German emperor. The nationalist press, which now had the upper hand, discovered a 'secret Germany' in the large and prosperous German farming settlements in the south and east of Russia. It must be admitted that the large German peasant families had bought up a lot of land and estates, some of which had gone to ruin through Russian mismanagement and were to be had cheaply. There was no injustice involved, but it was probably unwise, because people soon became envious. Even if German farmers found sympathy and support from their immediate Russian neighbours, this did not help the beleaguered stundists, who once again, as before 1905, were being exiled to Siberia without trial by ill-disposed governors and police authorities. Since no news reached the west during the war, we can only cite a few examples. W. Gutsche, who was at that time still living in Russian Poland and who as a Baptist preacher had close contact with the revival, describes the arrests of preachers and the closure of meeting houses belonging both to the Baptists and the Evangelical Christians. The congregations in Odessa had a particularly hard time. The city chief

Tolmachov had all evangelical preachers sent 'by stages' to Narym on the Ob; this was without any legal investigation, as was unfortunately possible in the tsarist empire. The preacher Fetler in St. Petersburg was sent out of the country and went to America. Likewise the preacher Neprash, formerly a faithful co-worker of Walter Jack, latterly in St. Petersburg. In 1916 Prokhanov was brought before the court 'for founding an association hostile to the state' (presumably the Union of Evangelical Christians). But this clever and eloquent brother was able to defend himself and was acquitted. In Moscow the services were kept under surveillance by the local police and under-age Baptist children and foreign guests were put out of the meetings. These events are similar to those which took place in the Soviet Union under Khrushchev. Surprisingly, however, Baptist Sunday schools for children were still permitted. Pavlov, the Baptist president, hid in the expanses of Central Asia until the 1917 revolution.

A press that had been blinded by hatred stated categorically that Emperor Wilhelm had given the Baptists money 'in order to undermine the Russian people'. We know that slander propaganda is part of the psychological side of warfare. After Prime Minister Goremykin, who was over eighty, spoke in the Duma, the Russian parliament, about the danger of the Baptist movement, commanding general Rutsky forbade all Baptist meetings in his district out of hand. Since the war was going badly for Russia, there was a frantic search for scapegoats.

Russian press commissar Kuzmin spoke in 1918 of three million prisoners of war whom the Russian army had lost to the central powers. This figure is certainly not exaggerated. However severely his judgments may affect nations and people, God has always worked through them to show mercy. This was particularly true of the fate of these prisoners. In almost every one of the many prisoner camps, there was a group of Evangelical Christians or Baptists who from the start had moved from man to man testifying about Christ; they knew their bible and were able to answer questions and objections. Just as the Russian is a born political propagandist, so the Russian Christian is a natural missionary. This is why Walter Jack, who knew stundism well, always emphasized: 'Don't send any foreign missionaries to Russia! The Russian believer himself is the best missionary for his own people.' What he needed then, as today, was the bible and a good grounding in sound theology, in order to avoid wrong paths.

In 1916 Professor D. Schrenk, who was in charge of assistance to the prisoners, asked us why there should be such a great demand for Russian bibles in the prisoner camps. He said that he was having considerable difficulty in getting the number of copies he needed, and these were then soon gone. According to his knowledge of the Orthodox Church, it was not usual to make so much private use of the bible. It was only some years later that we discovered how many evangelical revival centres had come into being through stundist prisoners who underlined the vital importance of the word of God.

Many Christians made use of this opportunity to evangelize among people to whom the bible was largely an unknown book. The Christian tract society operated by the German Baptists in Kassel alone sent some one and a half million pieces of literature into the camps. It worked among sixty-four camps in Germany, seven in Austria and four in Hungary. As well as that, there were about fifteen work brigades. According to Warns, evangelical congregations were formed in thirty-eight of the camps.

One of Christ's messengers in the camps was David Bekker, who had been trained at the Neukirchen mission school, who himself came from south Russia and had an excellent command of the Russian language, and also understood the slavic mind well. He writes:

'In view of the many possible difficulties and hindrances that could have come against me in this work, I must confess that in the beginning I had a feeling of anxiety. After all, it was fresh territory that I was moving into. One could not assume even the most modest acquaintance with the truths of scripture among most of the prisoners. Many had never seen a New Testament, not to mention a bible, and still fewer had read the scriptures. And there were so many who could not even read! I probably counted on a certain mistrust, too, from people to whom such a manner

of preaching the gospel was after all completely foreign. But later
to my shame I saw all my fears disappear like mist before the sun.
When I entered a camp for the first time, and told the people why
I had come, their joy was tremendous. "We've been hoping for
this for a long time!" said some. Sounds of home, comfort and
God's word, the awareness that here was someone who understood them, who had sympathy and compassion for them, this
and much else drew the poor prisoners like a magnet. It was a
particularly joyful and welcome event when I was able to
distribute the first bibles and New Testaments. Thus, for example,
one man received the bible very tenderly and pressed it to his
chest, beaming, and said: "Oh how grateful I am to you for helping me to get this precious book!"' (Warns, pp. 188–9).

But the best missionaries were still the believing brethren
among the prisoners themselves. Many names have been preserved which may not mean a great deal to us today, but they are
written in God's book. There is no doubt that this book contains
the names of many witnesses and martyrs, who have never become
known to wider circles.

Under the chairmanship of mission director Schreiber a 'Committee for the Assistance of Prisoners of War' was formed in
Berlin, which not only found many ways of helping and caring
itself, but also smoothed the path for other groups to work as
well. Fetler, the preacher who had been sent into exile from St.
Petersburg, organized a large relief work from the USA. In
Germany groups within the established Church and the Free
Churches competed with missionary societies whose work abroad
had been suspended by the war. Anyone who reads the reports
and surveys of all these works must be thrilled that during the war
so much brotherly love was shown towards those who had been
captured while fighting against Germany itself. Switzerland also
took an active part, and many Russian émigrés living in Germany.

After the end of the war, the civil war in Russia delayed the
return of the millions of prisoners, so that it was possible to
continue this ministry for several years, unhindered by barbed
wire. Mention must now be made of the new mission 'Licht dem
Osten' ('Light to the East') – in response to requests from the

slavic believers, the name was soon altered to the more appropriate 'Licht im Osten' ('Light in the East').

Jakob Kroeker and Walter Jack, brethren who have already been mentioned in a different context, joined together with other East European missions to form this group. Swedish brethren who had already been active in the camps, people from the German state Church and representatives of the Free Churches, members of the Blankenburg Alliance committee, Mennonites and Baptists, Methodists and Lutherans, Open Brethren and Reformed Christians – Germans, Swiss, Dutch, Scandinavians and Americans joined hands to undertake this important task.

Particular attention was paid to establishing systematic bible courses and bible weeks in a number of camps; these eventually led to the founding of a Russian-language bible school in Wernigerode. The gospel was also preached among the émigrés, so that Russian-language Evangelical-Christian congregations arose in several parts of Germany, particularly in Berlin, where one of these congregations met regularly for several decades. A lot of faithful work was done at grassroots level by a large number of believers who could speak Russian. A work later developed also in the so-called border states: many Russians after the war lived in Finland, Estonia, Latvia, Lithuania, Poland, Czechoslovakia and Yugoslavia. The mission on principle never founded its own congregations. As Walter Jack said: 'The Slavs can do it better than we can. But wherever a few sparks start to glow, we will certainly fan the flame with the word of God and our prayers!'

The earliest back numbers of the mission's magazine *Dein Reich Komme* (*Thy Kingdom Come*) represent documents of primary importance on the God-given revival in Russia after the great revolution. At the same time they offer valuable reports on what God was doing among Russians, Ukrainians and Poles outside their own countries as well. Some of these stories are worth including in this report on stundism because they give the reader a lively picture of the spiritual hunger of that time, and also testify to the openness of the slavic people to the gospel. In all this it must be remembered that the constant rise in prices and the fateful time of inflation almost crippled the economic capacity of the German Christians. Without faithful help from abroad, especially from Sweden, Holland and Switzerland, the ministry would soon have had to be abandoned.

The bible courses which Kroeker and Jack introduced in the camps were gratefully received. But the hunger of the listeners was too great to be met in the matter of a few weeks. They wanted a thorough introduction to the world of the bible, and training to minister among their own people. This need was to be met by the bible school which was established in Wernigerode with the help of friends abroad. No other bible school in the west had such a good command of the Russian language as this one. Since the guest-houses and hotels of Wernigerode were standing empty in this time of inflation, there was no shortage of space. Kroeker visited the landlady of a guest-house with whom he was acquainted, and asked her what she would say if he were to fill every room in her house. 'Oh, Mr. Kroeker, how grateful I'd be to you!' was her reply. But when she heard that it was a question of Russian soldiers who had been in prison camps for years, she wanted to change her mind. Only Kroeker's persuasion, and the words of these men whom God had called, strengthened her resolve again. Some years later, as she took leave of the men who had been in her care, she wept like a mother taking leave of her own sons.

These Christians in the east are still examples to us in the west. We often find difficulty in putting our faith into practice in daily life. Dogmatics and ethics – faith and morals – often represent for us a work in two volumes. We read the former book first, and because it causes our ponderous understanding so much trouble, often we do not get to studying the second volume. In the east, things are different. Anyone who comes to Jesus finds new life. The gospel among the stundists had an amazing effect in terms of sanctification. Although the understanding may be limited, the love and thankfulness are great. Although there may be an element of legalism, the most important thing to these brethren is that they should glorify their Lord through a new life. One example of this is their abstinence. The alcoholic tendency among Russian peasants is well known. But among the Evangelical Christians and Baptists there is not an alcoholic to be found. The believers avoid all alcohol, also tobacco. The decisive thing is always ministering, sacrificial, self-denying love.

The selection of a limited number of pupils for the bible school was not easy, for there were revival movements in many of the camps and the new converts were pressing to get in. The events in Salzwedel camp in Altmark offer a particularly impressive example.

This camp had been almost completely cleared, because they were expecting some sections of the Red Army which had been forced over the East Prussian frontier in 1920 and here disarmed by the Germans. But a small group of believers had remained behind out of the former camp population, with the aim of ministering to their newly-arriving fellow countrymen and testifying about Christ. They were all from peasant backgrounds, without any of the problems of the 'intelligentsia'. In a few weeks with their simple testimony they had brought about a situation in which a mighty forward move of the gospel could take place. They had obtained permission from the 'tovarishch general' for a religious meeting. The response of that camp leader was typical of the early Bolshevik era: 'Yes, we have freedom of religion now. Everybody can believe what he likes. But the condition for such a religious gathering is that everyone has the right to speak.' This last condition was just what the brethren wanted.

They wrote to Wernigerode asking for two brethren to come for some meetings. Two of the most gifted bible students set off. The meetings were prepared with much prayer. The canteen was made available for the occasion. The brethren watched the situation develop with anxious hearts – this was the first attempt to bring the message of Jesus to Bolshevik Red Army soldiers. When the brethren entered the canteen after fervent prayer together, all places were taken. The men had their caps on and cigarettes in their mouths – it was a lively, noisy, expectant group.

The first of the brethren who had come from Wernigerode stood up and addressed the meeting briefly: 'Comrades, we've

come to bring you a joyful message. But it's our normal practice
to pray first.' With that he put his hands together and prayed
briefly and freely, as the stundists are accustomed to do. This was
something new for Russian soldiers. They were used to the sign
of the cross, appeals to the saints and the mother of God, the
liturgical prayer of their own Orthodox Church and kneeling in
front of the icon at home. Free prayer in someone's own words,
in the natural manner of a man who has been redeemed, was
something unfamiliar to them. Cigarettes were stubbed out and
many of the caps disappeared.

Then the brother began with John 15.13: 'Greater love has no
man than this, that a man lay down his life for his friends.' It
may be that these young Red Guards had not yet been plunged
too deeply into the doctrines of atheism – in any case, every
Russian understands the meaning of sacrificial love. The one
speaking to them made no secret of the fact that he too was
nothing more than a helpless prisoner of war. He spoke in the
language of the people, without the solemn terminology in
which Orthodoxy is so rich. The men listened to this brother
without a sound. Then the other one stood up and read the word
of Paul in 2 Cor. 5.20: 'We are ambassadors for Christ, God
making his appeal through us. We beseech you on behalf of
Christ, be reconciled to God.' Again this was a brother speaking
to brethren: 'We were no different from you! We lived like you,
swearing and drinking and breaking God's commandments. But
we have been reconciled to God through Christ. Now we come
to you and ask you: be reconciled to God too!'

The effect of these two addresses was unique. When the brother
closed with the words: 'Now let us pray!', all caps had long since
disappeared, many fell to their knees, and tears flowed down
many sunburnt cheeks into the soldiers' beards. The Spirit of God
was moving through the meeting. When the brethren indicated
that there was a table at the front with New Testaments and
bibles, which could be taken free of charge, there was a rush to
the literature table and it was soon empty. Several more deliveries
had to be requested from Wernigerode during the next few
days.

The two messengers from the bible school remained a few more days. They were besieged from morning to evening by those with all sorts of questions, wanting to know more. Later there was established here in the camp a congregation of believers, which only accepted new members after very detailed examination, and yet soon reached well over a hundred members.

When the president of the Russian Baptist Union visited the mission 'Licht im Osten' in the 1920's, and told of the great revivals in those years, he was asked when this new movement had begun. 'After the prisoners of war returned from the west,' he replied. In this way God used the terrible time of judgment during the war to prepare new mission tools for the wide expanses of Russia.

C. Under the Atheist Regime

I THE GREAT RUSSIAN REVOLUTION

On 15 March 1917, after pressure from the imperial Duma, Nicholas II abdicated. This was the end of the tsarist empire, and the Romanov rule which had lasted for more than three hundred years. The democratic government tried, particularly under the influence of the 'moderate' socialist Kerensky, to continue the war. But the people and the army were tired of war, the crumbling state order dissolved, and on 9 November that same year the Bolsheviks, led by Lenin, seized power.

This change of government is important for our history of stundism. Along with tsarism fell the state Church; in the succeeding years of civil war the Church suffered terrible losses among its clergy and members. For the revolutionaries, the Church was a prop of tsarism and a pillar of reaction. Now the Church, which had been in alliance with absolute monarchy for centuries, was exposed to a revenge that was wreaked mainly against innocent people. The slogan 'autocracy, Orthodoxy and nationalism' unleashed its own fateful consequences. On the other hand the 'heteredox', as they were officially called, breathed a sigh of relief because they were no longer subject to the governors and their whims. Many Orthodox too, both priests and lay people, welcomed the liberation of their Church from the shackles of state protection and lack of rights. They hoped for a new blossoming of mature piety on the soil of the Orthodox faith. Leading stundists – once again Prokhanov must be mentioned here particularly – hoped for a great reformation of the Church on the basis of the gospel, as had happened at the time of Luther in Germany.

On 15 August 1917 an All-Russian Council opened in Moscow, which elected Tikhon, Metropolitan of Moscow, as Patriarch; this took place in the midst of the growing troubles. This marked the end of Peter the Great's autocratic intrusion into church life two hundred years previously.

A further result of the revolution which is of particular interest to us at this point was that the preachers and confessors who had been sentenced and exiled were now able to return home, just as in 1905 after the tolerance manifesto. Pavlov too returned from Turkestan to Moscow, where the Baptist Union was now able to unfold a new activity. His son headed the large Baptist congregation in Moscow which, on the initiative of the new government, reverted to capital of the empire. This was another corrective to the policies of Peter the Great who had opened 'the window on the west' at the estuary of the Neva. 'Mother Moscow' was once again 'the navel of the world'. Usurpers are always good at passing new decrees pandering to the taste of the people until such time as they have become strong enough to act in an 'unpopular' manner and to have their way.

Prokhanov had been able to remain in St. Petersburg throughout the war. He is supposed to have defended himself before the court against the accusation of having a 'German religion' by pointing to English influences (Lord Radstock, George Müller in Bristol, Baedeker in London). It is clear that he had friends in high circles in the capital who protected him. It comes as no surprise to see how energetically he exploited the new freedom.

On 23 January 1918 the Soviet government passed a decree on the separation of church and state, a resolution that was to be expected and one which was welcomed by all believers. They had suffered enough. Even devout Orthodox were glad to see this separation. The fact that the promised freedoms were withdrawn over the next decades – especially under the dictator Stalin – simply shows that the Soviets are still heirs of the tsars. 'Religion' or personal philosophy was still regulated by the state.

The Constitution of July 1918 stated in its thirteenth paragraph: 'In order to ensure for the workers true freedom of conscience, the church is separated from the state and the school from the church, and freedom of religious and anti-religious propaganda is recognized for all citizens.' It is sad to look back to paragraphs like this one, which disappeared so swiftly into the wastepaper basket.

In the decree, the Church lost its corporate rights and all church property was declared 'the property of the people'. This formulation was a clever one from the propagandistic point of view. But it soon became clear that the real power of disposal was in the hands of the Party, not the people. The Party never had the majority of the people on its side. In practice it was the Party officials, the *apparatchiki*, who came out on top. In this way there arose a state capitalism which is much more difficult to combat than private capitalism; thus in the course of time the people came out of one bondage and into another. The new one seemed even more hopeless. The fact that the Church, too, was not free but economically dependent upon the state, is illuminating. Since the churches belonged to the state, even the use of the buildings was dependent on state approval. Before long excessive rents were being charged, and popular meetings staged which 'desired' the closure of the churches. The majority of church buildings were turned into museums, cinemas, barns, storerooms and so on.

At first, however, the Bolsheviks wooed the evangelical circles. The revolution had given them the freedom which the tsarist state and Orthodoxy had denied. It was to be some time before the Orthodox and the evangelical Free Churches would form a kind of united front against militant atheism in the time of Stalin. First the situation had to clarify. We can only give a few episodes as examples from that early period after the upheaval. They show clearly how the evangelical congregations, with an optimism that later proved to be groundless, sought to use this moment of generally changing conditions to spread the gospel.

The People's Commissar for Education, Lunacharsky, had a secretary who was interested in the Christian anarchist teaching of Count Leo Tolstoy, who died in 1910. His name was Bonch-Bruevich. As a man of pacifist sympathies, he persuaded Lenin and Trotsky to allow conscientious objectors, of whom there were a good number among the stundists, to serve instead in medical work. This did not happen until five young evangelicals had been tried by a military court for refusing to carry arms, sentenced to death and shot. A 'United Council of Religious Congregations and Groups' was even set up, to which Tolstoyans, Dukhobors Evangelical Christians, Baptists, Mennonites and Adventists belonged. One very active worker on this was Tolstoy's former secretary Chertkov, son of the general's widow whom we met as a member of the revival under Radstock.

Waldemar Gutsche relates a well-attested incident from that time: 'In the summer of 1920, two young Baptists from the Urals were called up to the Red Army, but they refused to carry arms. After that they disappeared. Since they had been put on a train for Aktyubinsk, the seat of local administration, the responsible expert on questions of conscience set off there to look for them. It was not easy to find them. They were not in the prison for criminal offenders, nor in the prisons of the *cheka* or the wartime revolutionary tribunal. Finally it turned out that the drafting officer had locked them up without doing anything more about their case. When the expert asked why he had taken such drastic measures, the officer replied that the older of the two objectors had been a junior officer in the tsarist army, and so there was reason to doubt the genuineness of his convictions. He had made a snap decision to let them both sit in prison until they were willing to take weapons. The expert then asked the officer whether he too had not had a good position in the tsarist army. "Yes," came the reply, "you couldn't do anything else then." When the expert replied: "All right then, let other people have as much tolerance as you claim for yourself," the officer's assistants began to laugh. Upon which he said: "Then at least I'm going to hand them over to the wartime revolutionary council, because the so-called people's courts are far too soft."

A decree of the people's commissars had entrusted judgment in such cases to the people's courts, which corresponded to the former courts of the peace, i.e., courts of the first instance. The officer did not trust these. Nothing could be done about it. However, the expert was called when the two came before the tribunal. The red court, which had powers of life and death over every citizen, consisted of three young men in uniform, the so-called *troika*, one chairman and two assistants, who took their places at the table. The chairman was a Jew, the others Russian. Soon the case began. The atmosphere was bad. The circumstance that the elder one had been a junior officer in the tsarist army, but now did not want to carry weapons, had aroused suspicion. What could be said? It was the expert's first case. He sighed to God and began:

"There is something which we call conversion. There was an Orthodox priest in Moscow, who told this story. During the war he was a chaplain at the front. One evening after the battle, as he was giving the dying soldiers the last rites of his religion, he heard the soft call of a dying man: 'Father, my father,' he said. 'What do you want, my son?' he asked. 'I must make confession, I've committed a mortal sin.' 'What have you done?' 'I took the oath that I would kill the enemy, and I couldn't do it. I shot over their heads.' 'In that moment,' the priest went on, 'I realized that it was a saint lying before me, and I was the guilty one who needed to confess.'"

The expert tried to continue, but he was unable to do so. All three judges had jumped to their feet. Something had hit home to them. They could scarcely conceal their emotion, and they went outside to confer. Before long they reappeared, and those present had to stand to hear the judgment of the court: "In the name of the Russian Socialist Federal Republic! Both men are to be set free and put to work usefully at home." This was the rough content of the sentence.

From that time on, comrade Spiegel, the chairman, was a friend to the believers. He said: "I will never harm one of your people, if he is genuine." He kept his word.' (Gutsche, *Religion und Evangelium in Sowjetrussland*, pp. 27–8).

These early post-revolutionary years, which unfortunately passed too quickly, gave the evangelicals frequent opportunity to testify to the biblical gospel in discussion with the atheists. Anyone who reads Professor Martsinkovsky's book *Gotterleben in Sowjet-russland* will soon realize that crude atheism was not equipped to meet the testimony of the spirit. For this reason, discussions of this kind were later forbidden. But the fact that even now atheism has still not achieved the success which the Party expected from its propaganda is evident in that today, after almost sixty years of the unrestricted teaching of godlessness in schools, universities, meetings and courses, the press is still recommending new and more energetic measures in this propaganda. The expectation of strict Marxists that with communism 'religioùs prejudices', as the official terminology goes, would disappear of themselves, has been revealed as a gross error.

For an example of how such discussions went, we quote a report by Martsinkovsky:

'At about this time large posters appeared in the streets of Moscow, advertising a lecture by A. V. Lunacharsky, People's Commissar for Education, on the subject "Why man should not believe in God". I went to this lecture. It took place in the large hall of the polytechnic museum and was so crowded that many were unable to get in. I managed with great difficulty to push my way in, and I actually found a place on the stage, opposite the audience. So I had a good view of everything, and especially of the speaker, who stood near me.

He explained that everyone was permitted to believe what he wanted, but a thinking man simply could not believe in God. He listed the various eras in religious history: animism, fetishism, etc. Very decisively he said: 'With us marches the vanguard of human thought.' His address was full of telling points and quotations from literature; sometimes these were put over with tremendous pathos, as if he was trying to hypnotize his listeners. Although he rejected God, he still looked to a bright future since, according to his words, men would form "a fraternal union of gods in nature".

I could not stay quiet any longer. I took a piece of paper out of my pocket and wrote on it: "I would like to speak! Martsinkovsky." The speaker read the paper and said that this was a lecture, not a discussion. But he put it to the audience whether I should be allowed to speak or not. In that case he suggested that I be given ten minutes.

A clamour arose, some crying "Yes!" and some "No!" There were at least three thousand people present. By raising of hands, it was established that the majority were in favour of allowing me to speak. As I came forward, I sensed a silent tension. I had to use the short time given to make as clear a testimony as possible for the faith. "Citizens!" I cried, "it is not true what the

speaker has just said, that reason and science do not permit a man
to believe in God. The previous speaker has stated that religion
belongs to the bourgeois class. But I say that the materialism which
he proclaims is a bourgeois, in fact a petty bourgeois faith, for he
only believes what he can touch. But that is quite natural, for
according to his own theory, he has a bourgeois soul, because he is
from the bourgeois class – excuse me for this personal remark.

The speaker also referred to fetishism and heathen religions.
Why did he not mention Christianity? It's true that fetishism
does not agree with science, but the greatest scientists of all times
have been men who believed in Christ. Jesus said: 'Let not your
heart be troubled, you believe in God, believe also in me.'
Choose now, friends, whom you want to believe, Christ or
modern teachers? Our life itself, so full of suffering, testifies
against godlessness. Without God we cannot work or achieve
anything, we can only destroy. Without faith we are ruined and
we only confirm the words of Christ: 'Without me you can do
nothing'." Long and deafening applause followed my words'
(pp. 86–7.)

When we think of what happened later, this account sounds
almost like a fairy-tale. But fortunately it took several years
before the central regime in Moscow managed to impose its
ideas and organization upon the whole empire.

Among the Baptists, Timoshenko was a powerful speaker. Later
he went to be with his Lord as a martyr bearing witness to his
faith. This man, who had been in the service of Christ for many
years, knew how to get through to the ordinary Russian, but he also
knew how to give convincing answers to the atheists. Thus the
public meetings and discussions closed all too often with a defeat
for atheism. On one occasion, one of the godless lecturers shouted
angrily at the meeting: 'You Baptists are worse than twenty
Orthodox! Once you've made a fanatic out of a man, there's
nothing more that can be done with him.'

Since intellectual weapons did not seem to be adequate, the
struggle against the Christian faith was subsequently carried on
with prohibitions and state power. But by that time the Christians
had made good use of the opportunities.

During the first world war the German Baptist preacher Karl Füllbrandt was exiled to Siberia. He tells of the great revivals that took place around the Siberian town of Omsk. The former millionaire Mazayev was preaching here; he was one of the leaders of the Russian Baptist Union. As a result of the expropriations he had lost all his tremendous wealth, and now he was completely given over to the service of the gospel. There were many conversions. But this ministry was threatened not only by Bolshevism and its hatred of God, but also by the anarchy reigning in the empire. The land was devastated by civil war and marauding bands, and later also by a famine such as had never before been seen in Russia, which is such a rich agricultural country.

Meanwhile I. S. Prokhanov had founded the 'All-Russian Union of Evangelical Christians', which stood independently alongside the Baptist Union; as its president, he was able with his tremendous energy to exploit all possible opportunities given by the freedom obtained through the revolution. He indicated his attitude to the revolution in a report dated 6 April 1924:

'Inasmuch as we saw social and economic reforms in the revolution, we welcomed it. To some extent we saw in it God's judgment on the guilty. Or else we considered it as a purification, out of which Russia must come forth renewed' (Gutsche, *op cit.*, p. 102).

Nevertheless, Prokhanov emphasized, political and economic reforms do not solve the religious question. 'All of this is outward, it does not feed the soul. The soul, not the body, is what shapes the life. That is why a spiritual foundation must be laid in order to build up a man's life.'

Prokhanov still believed that it was not too late for a spiritual reform within the Orthodox Church too. He hoped to find a ready ear for the reformed gospel among a group of dissident priests. He had particular hopes of Metropolitan Antonin. He appealed to these reformist priests with a 'gospel call', in which first of all he promised forgiveness for all that representatives of Orthodoxy had done in the times of persecution against the stundists. But then he called on them to carry out genuine evangelical reforms, using the holy scriptures as a basis for this. He promised the intercession of all the believers and suggested that combined prayer meetings be held in Leningrad and in Moscow.

This appeal was distributed in a hundred thousand copies. Prokhanov was invited to speak in one of Moscow's oldest churches. Here he said, among other things:

'Behold, brothers and sisters, today a miracle has happened before my eyes! More than thirty years ago, I said in St. Petersburg that we would have the chance to preach the gospel in the Orthodox Church. No-one believed me at that time – and today it has come to pass!'

Prokhanov also visited Metropolitan Antonin of Moscow at that time, and rejoiced over his agreement with the appeal; his joy was increased when the high churchman went to his bookcase and took out a hymnbook, *Gusli*, which Prokhanov himself had published. 'From this book I draw daily food for my soul,' he said. The metropolitan was also present at the prayer meeting in Moscow, and he gave an address.

In the spring of 1923 these opponents of Patriarch Tikhon held a council in Moscow. Because this council sent a letter of loyalty to Lenin, recognizing the revolutionary government – five years after the revolution – as the divinely appointed government, it is termed by conservative circles among Orthodoxy the 'red council'. Prokhanov was also invited, and he had the opportunity to give an hour-long speech, setting out the necessity for a true evangelical reformation.

But Antonin and his followers never gained the upper hand. It has been demonstrated repeatedly in church history how dubious it is to mix political and religious motives. This has harmed many a 'confessing' movement. They lacked that resoluteness with which Luther was prepared to shake off all social and political hangers-on for the sake of the pure gospel, even though it brought him many enemies. One need only think of his withdrawal from the Peasant War.

On his deathbed, Antonin made his collaborators promise to put the Church of SS Peter and Paul, where he had served, at the disposal of the stundists for their meetings. Prokhanov preached here frequently in the following years. But although a number of priests are believed to have joined themselves to the stundists, the reformation that Prokhanov hoped for did not take place. He had much more success in building up the Union of Evangelical Christians. Despite the great troubles of the civil war and the famine, many missions and bible courses were held. This was particularly true from the year 1923 onwards, as conditions in Russia began to settle down. Prokhanov made appeal to article 13 of the Constitution, which guaranteed freedom of 'propaganda' to believers as well as atheists. No citizen of the USSR was supposed to suffer any disadvantages as a result of his attitude to religion. There was even a decree saying that up to fifty persons could meet for worship even in private homes. The law also provided for penalties against anyone who disturbed services. The stundists had good reason to rejoice! At the same time the local authorities continued to act in an arbitrary fashion, as in the tsarist time – Prokhanov was to experience this personally.

The sixth youth congress of the Evangelical Christians was scheduled to take place in 1921 in Tver (now Kalinin). It had official permission. Since food supplies in the capital had broken down – 1921 was a famine year – everybody travelled in high spirits to the provincial town. Prokhanov writes: 'Everything went wonderfully, until the third day, when a mob appeared, armed with revolvers. There was an investigation, and forty-three participants were marched along the streets under military guard. We were taken to a cellar in the executive committee building, but we were in the best of spirits and sang the whole time. The head of the prison cried in amazement: "I've never had prisoners like this before!" Soon there was a dispute between the prison superintendent and the young people who were singing. The superintendent told them to stop singing, but the young people resisted. Finally he had to give in: "All right, sing! But be quiet when I'm working." The young people agreed to this, but in the intervals they never stopped singing. All the groups took turns: when one stopped, the next one started. The singing filled every-one with joy and gladness. Even the soldiers started to join in. This hastened the committee's decision. Ten day later most of us were released, with a written injunction to await trial. Twelve men were sentenced to forced labour. Three older brethren were condemned to three years' forced labour in Vladimir province. We were taken to camps where we held meetings in the evenings, and even opened a bible school. The first meeting had already taken place in the executive committee building! The whole experience was very profitable for us spiritually. It also served a missionary purpose. Everybody was interested to know more about the evangelical movement, and many were later converted. Thus it was a spiritual as well as a civil victory. The All-Russian Executive Committee held that our arrest was unjustified. A delegation was sent over to investigate our case. Kalinin, the president of the Soviet Republic, became interested in us. The investigation disclosed that the whole thing had happened on the initiative of two people: Spitzberg, a fanatical atheist, and the priest Vinogradov, who was also a fanatic, and besides his ecclesiastical office held a post in the red authorities. When it came out that our arrest was illegal, because we had permission for the congress, we were released, Spitzberg was dismissed and Vinogradov arrested. He was held in Moscow for six months while it was discussed whether a man could be a priest and at the same time an official in the *cheka*. The decision was negative, and Vinogradov was dismissed from his government post. Similar arrests and persecutions on the part of local authorities persisted. But they were exceptional cases, which took place as a result of ignorance of the laws' (Gutsche, *op. cit.*, pp. 103–4).

Prokhanov was accustomed to see God's hand in incidents like this. This was the strength of these Christians: they knew that their very hairs were numbered by God, and in his name they walked even into trouble and death.

Gerhard Fast, a Mennonite teacher, was placed by the *cheka* in the dreaded Butyrka prison in Moscow. During his difficult time of imprisonment there, two Evangelical-Christian preachers also arrived. The first thing they said was: 'God has sent us here to testify to the good news of Jesus Christ.' This they did day after day, strengthening their fellow-prisoners who had been discouraged by their long, hard imprisonment. When one of the brethren was transferred to another section of the prison because of this activity, the one who remained declared: 'They probably need the gospel over there. That's why God has sent my brother there.' It was difficult to come against a spirit like this.

Prokhanov knew that no amount of apologetical labour, or good organization, in which he had tremendous ability, could create faith and renew lives. Through studying and travelling in the west, he saw even more clearly that faith comes only through the word and through preaching. He wrote a long ode to Martin Luther, whom he praised for recognizing the power of the word of God and making it accessible to men again. He once remarked to us in a personal conversation: 'You Lutherans don't really know what you owe Luther.' Because he too placed all his expectation in the power of the bible word, he did everything in his power to spread this word and to teach it; he also placed his poetic ability at the service of the word.

Since the printing work in St. Petersburg had been halted by the civil war and the synodal press had also stopped printing bibles, Prokhanov tried to get bibles from the west. Until 1924 the mission 'Licht im Osten', in collaboration with the British and Foreign Bible Society in London, was able to send large consignments of bibles to Russia; these reached their goal. In the mission's magazine *Dein Reich Komme*, the representative of the Bible Society in Reval, capital of the still free republic of Estonia, wrote after the bible deliveries had seemed to be delayed: 'Permission has now been received to deliver the following to Russia: 5,000 New Testaments, 5,000 bibles, 1,000 copies of *Gusli* (songbooks), 1,000 *Spiritual Songs*.' Unfortunately this door closed for good in 1924. Prokhanov then put all the more effort into trying to print the word in the country itself and to distribute it.

According to Zhidkov senior, President of the 'All-Russian Union of Evangelical Christians', there were two editions of *Selected Evangelical Songs* in 1918 and 1920. Then Prokhanov put together his great collection *Spiritual Songs* with 1,237 songs – 'the most complete songbook at that time'; many of these songs had been written by Prokhanov himself. This was the 'collection of ten' (*Desyatisbornik*) because it brought together ten collections that had previously been available. The book was printed in 1924 in Lódz by the society *Compass*. There was a second edition (25,000) in Leningrad in 1927, published by Prokhanov and Zhidkov. Prokhanov wrote in the foreword:

'This edition is intended to meet all the demands of the Christian churches with respect to spiritual songs. Up to now there have been few songs for the young believers. May this gap be filled by the songs in the collection *David's Flute*. There were no songs at all for our sisters. The demand for such songs has been growing constantly. This has been met by the collection *Songs of Hannah*. The collection *Songs of the First Christians* was put together in such a way as to take the believers back to the first centuries of Christianity. This is not even necessary, because the evangelical movement in Russia today is a revival of original Christianity, that is, Christianity at the time of the apostles. Finally there is the collection *Songs from the Depths* on the serious problems of Christian faith and life. These will win the love of those who go through deep religious experience. The brothers and sisters will find in these collections songs for all events in their lives.

Looking back, we can see what a powerful means the spiritual song has been in spreading the evangelical movement in Russia. We are firmly convinced that in the days to come it will again be the evangelical spiritual song that will fire the hearts of believers to deeds of love and heroic deeds of faith.

So sing, brothers and sisters, so that all living things around you may join to sing praise to him who alone is worthy.'

But this was not the end of music publishing. In 1926 a small collection of 549 songs appeared under the title *Voice of Faith* (*Golos very*), in an edition of 15,000. In Kharkov the 'All-Ukrainian Baptist Union' published the Ukrainian songbook *The Harp* (*Arfa*) in two editions (1924 and 1928). In 1927 there was a music edition in three volumes for the 'collection of ten'. There were a few other small collections as well.

From all this we can see that the congregations took seriously the apostle's command: 'addressing one another in psalms and hymns and spiritual songs, singing and making melody to the Lord with all your heart'.

With American gifts, a Christian calendar called 'The Christian Adviser' was printed for 1927 in 15,000 copies. The magazine *The Christian* (*Khristianin*) appeared monthly in an edition of 15,000. In Leningrad – the new name for St. Petersburg which, ten years previously in 1914, had become Petrograd – seventy brethren were trained each year through bible courses. The number of applicants rose three times over. The demand and the need were so great that Prokhanov limited the training to one year. Unfortunately, plans to extend this preaching school were never fulfilled.

It was not only their own people that these workers had in mind. In the northern parts of Siberia there were still heathen who had never heard the gospel. On the other hand, there were already small evangelical congregations among many peoples of the empire. This was the case for example with the Mordvinians, the Cheremiss and the Chuvash on this side of the Urals and among the Yakuts and Votyaks of Siberia, and certainly among Armenians, Georgians and Osetians in the Caucasus. The harvest field was immeasurable.

Prokhanov himself told how one day a young Christian girl, not yet twenty years old – probably a servant girl in his own house – came to him and said she felt the call to Siberia, to the Yakuts, whose capital Yakutsk lay 1,500 kilometres north of the Siberian railway. Although many sensible people tried to talk the girl out of her plan, Prokhanov gave her his blessing for this missionary work. 'I cannot stand in the way of anyone who has received the command of Christ,' he told us. So the young girl set off through the *taiga* (primeval forest) and the tundra, the northern marshes of Siberia. Nothing was heard of her for years. Then she wrote to say that the number of those who had believed and who were spiritually touched had become so large that she did not feel herself capable of carrying out the number of baptisms that were necessary. She asked for a brother to come, so that a proper congregation could be formed. Prokhanov writes: 'Thanks to her exemplary life and her selfless work of love, which did not shun the meanest service in the Yakut huts, she soon won the love of the people.' A brother was sent out and a congregation of believers was formed.

A few brothers were working among the Ostyaks, a wild Samoyed tribe in the far north of Siberia; they attempted with some success to make these nomadic tribes settle. These brethren had gone out in 1913 and they worked there for fourteen years, cut off from all culture. When they came back to Tomsk, the railway station, for the first time in 1927, it turned out that they had heard nothing about the war or the revolution. However, a number of disciples had been won for Jesus among the wild Ostyaks.

In Wernigerode we got to know a noble representative of the Osetian people. a mountain race in the Caucasus, part Muslim and part Orthodox, who offered strong resistance to the Russian conquest in the nineteenth century. His name was Kapo-Bayev, a cultured Osetian, who had been mayor of the large town of Vladikavkaz. He had been driven out of his country by the revolution. On his departure, he said to representatives of his people; 'I am going away, but I will do all in my power to send you the most precious thing on earth – the word of God.' And now he sat in the Harz mountains, like Luther on the Wartburg, translating the bible into his mother tongue. Up to that time there had only been the four gospels in Osetian. Later he moved to Berlin-Friedenau and lived in the Gossner Mission house. It was here that he died during the second world war. At his funeral, the leaders of the mission house described him as the friendly genius of the house, whom everyone loved like a father.

Even in these years of relatively free activity, the brethren – especially those in leadership – lived under constant threat. Prokhanov also experienced this. It was probably in the year 1922, although this is not quite certain. There was much insecurity among the people, particularly since the *cheka*, the political police, had almost a free hand. Although the Bolshevik takeover in 1917 had occurred almost without bloodshed, the number of those who were shot often on barely substantiated charges soon reached tens, even hundreds of thousands.

Thus Prokhanov too, and his secretary Dubrovsky, found themselves in the dreaded Butyrka prison in Moscow. He wrote at that time:

'It was a wonderful field for spreading the gospel. For example: we would go into a cell where the atmosphere was terrible, with a constant stream of the most varied curses. Inside a week the atmosphere in the cell would have changed so much that there was not an angry word to be heard. The men would begin to display a tremendous consideration and purity. Instead of playing cards, they started holding religious conversations. We always paid the greatest attention to those who swore, we appealed to their feelings of human dignity, we reminded them of their childhood and youth. Once their conscience had been awakened, they began to listen to the word of God. Almost all of them promised not to swear any more. We tried to get books for them. In one cell there were fifteen counter-revolutionaries. They became interested in us and asked me to give a lecture, which I did. They were gripped by it, and started a discussion, and some of them became my disciples. I told them that the greatest social problems could be solved only by means of the moral rebirth of the individual. Almost all of them promised to go to evangelical meetings, and some of them began to pray.'

Prokhanov was then forced by the state police to recognize the Soviet government on behalf of the Evangelical Christians. Today this step no longer seems so significant. But anyone who has experienced years of revolution will know what conflicts arise at such times. Which government is the legal one? In the last century there was a movement of so-called legitimists who rejected every revolutionary government as ungodly. Ludwig von Gerlach, a courageous fighter for the gospel, reproached Bismarck for dealing with Napoleon III, who, he said, was an illegal revolutionary; Bismarck replied that in that case there could be no contact with Sweden either, since the Bernadotte family was not the legitimate dynasty in Sweden either. One must give credit to the practical politician Bismarck. Because Prokhanov made peace with the revolutionary government, we in the west at that time felt that the same reproach should be made against him.

Because this is an important question of principle, we quote Prokhanov's notes, as Gutsche records them (*op. cit.*, pp. 113 ff.):

'I explained my attitude to the red government, pointed to Romans 13 and said that the ideals of the Soviet government were close to Christianity, because the ideas of pure communism corresponded to the second chapter of Acts, and that the apostle Paul called for respect for the workers when he said: 'Whoever will not work, let him not eat.' In Christ himself we see love for the weary and heavy-laden. But the investigating judge was not satisfied with an oral statement, but demanded a written one, to be handed in within five days. Finally, he told me something which horrified me: five representatives of the Union of Evangelical Christians were supposed to have called on the representative of the All-Russian Executive Committee, Smidovich, and to have stated that they completely disagreed with what I had said in the *Voice of the East*; in fact, they were so amazed at what I had said that they did not even want to visit me. I could scarcely believe these words and said: "That can't be true. I won't believe it unless I see them." "That's impossible, they don't want to see you," came the answer. We were driven back in a closed black van, which prisoners call the "black Maria". I drafted a written statement and returned five days later. As I went in, I saw brother Andreyev and the representative for civil affairs in Moscow. Andreyev told me that he had been called to the GPU (*cheka*) and asked whether the Evangelical Christians could make a public statement concerning their attitude to the Soviet government. He and other brethren in St. Petersburg had discussed it and had agreed on principle to declare themselves in favour of the soviets and of military service.

The investigating judge read out what I had written and said sharply that it was unsatisfactory. I replied that I could not write any more. I was taken back to prison. My mind was fresh and I even wrote two spiritual songs there. But physically I was very run down and my nerves were on edge. I fainted twice, but I did not pay much attention to my weakness. Then I was put in solitary confinement in the interior of the prison. Solitude had its advantages, but it affects a man's emotions. Sleep, which is a prisoner's consolation, left me completely. My nerves were stretched to breaking point, and nothing brought me any peace. The investigating judge visited me two or three times and said that a clarification of our attitude to the government was absolutely necessary, and that the brethren were in agreement about this. On one occasion he brought a written appeal, addressed to the Evangelical Christians, but I rejected it. But when he replied that the others agreed to it, I began to pray. Had the brethren really declared themselves in agreement? If that was true, then it must be all right. Some time after this, I saw several brethren who told me that they were ready to agree if the appeal addressed to us could be regarded, not as a declaration, but as an invitation to a conference. I was in a very depressed state and could only agree, in the hope that this was all that was involved, but that the question would only be finally settled at an All-Russian congress. One reason for signing was that there was disunity among the Evangelical Christian sthemselves on this question. I also thought that the brethren who were free could come to a better decision than I in prison' (Gutsche, *op. cit.*, pp. 11 ff.)

This account by Prokhanov contains many unclear points, which may be due in part to a poor translation. But behind it can be sensed the sharp reproach which was made by Christians in the west, even in the Baltic lands, that he had made peace with the Bolsheviks. In those years many people hoped that the Bolshevik regime would soon disappear. The Evangelical Christians obviously had a clearer insight. Prokhanov was certainly no friend of Bolshevism. On the other hand, for the sake of the gospel he had also come in conflict with the absolute rule of the old tsarist empire. He had been in Western Europe and America too long not to know what a democratic government could mean. One can see from his hard bargaining that even he had not yet recognized the dictatorial character of Bolshevism. Thanks to the underhand methods of investigation which, as so often, made use of statements by people not present to influence a man in prison, Prokhanov felt himself forced to make some kind of recognition of the government. These questions, including the burning question of participation in military service, which was not easy for the stundists influenced as they were by Tolstoy, were then debated publicly at the Stockholm Baptist Congress. Prokhanov reported:

'At that time the Baptist Congress took place in Stockholm. Here it was resolved to recognize military service in all its forms, but to leave power of decision to the individual and his conscience. After returning from the congress, I went back to the investigating judge and told him that before making our position known publicly, we intended to make a few essential alterations. The investigating judged seemed to be forthcoming. It was promised that a meeting would be called on Monday, to make the necessary alterations. But the appeal was already printed on Sunday, and it was rather unclear. Important phrases had been left out, and other undesirable ones added. We decided to join together in prayer that God would clarify everything at our congress and give us the opportunity to put everything right. This congress was fixed for 1–10 September in St. Petersburg. There were almost 340 participants. We explained everything in detail and assured those present that the appeal was not a declaration, but only an invitation to this conference and a pointer to the questions we wanted to discuss.

We judged all questions from the point of view of the word of God. The question of our relationship to the government was solved very simply, on the basis of Romans 13. Paul wrote these words with reference to a heathen power and the cruel emperors. The concept of power comes from God and he appoints the various governments to carry out certain purposes. Clearly the Soviet government also has its purpose. The congress accepted this point unanimously.

Secondly, the congress discussed the question of military service and here too it came to almost immediate unity. The resolution read: "We regard military duty, according to the laws in force, as an obligation, but we leave it to the individual Christian to act according to his conscience. This formula is based on our doctrine of faith. We regard military service as our duty, but we have brotherly fellowship with those who think differently about this." With this formula, we also protected those who cannot reconcile the carrying of weapons with their conscience. The phrase "according to the laws in force" refers to those articles of the law under which men can be released from military service for reasons of religious conviction. Some gave a positive opinion on this, others were negative. Kargel was for full recognition of military service. The resolution was adopted by a significant majority.

What was the attitude of the Soviet government? It understood the decision perfectly, and in many cases brothers who found carrying weapons impossible were completely freed from service. Before I went abroad, I heard that a brother in Minsk had been freed from service on the basis of this protocol.

These decisions produced unexpected successes. In the first place, up to that time the government was still unclear about our attitude towards it. In the second place, however, Orthodox circles suspected us of political unreliability. Now everything was made clear. Previously when preachers were arrested, they found it difficult to make their biblical viewpoint clear. Now anyone can show interrogators our resolution, and everything will be settled very simply. No gospel worker is experiencing any problems at the moment.

The Baptists have done the same thing. Their congress took place in Moscow, and their decisions correspond to ours.

The government wanted to see what the attitude of the Evangelical Christians and Baptists to it was. Now it is satisfied and thanks to this, there are unlimited opportunities for evangelism. Now for the first time there is real religious freedom. There is no more oppression; we can have meetings wherever and whenever we like. We can found fellowships and unions without difficulty.'

In this mood of optimism about the situation, Prokhanov went to the west to draw the attention of the Christians there to their responsibility for the evangelistic activity of the stundists and to secure their aid. It was a bitter disappointment for him that he was not permitted to return to the Soviet Union. He travelled to America, Bulgaria and through Germany, and he died on 6 October 1935 in Berlin. We carried him to his grave like a king.

II AFTER LENIN'S DEATH

If one compares the father of the Russian revolution Vladimir Ilich Ulyanov, called Lenin, with his Georgian successor Joseph Vissarionovich Dzhugashvili, called Stalin, the man of steel, one must recognize that Lenin pushed for order and the rule of law among the people and tried to put an end to the time of civil war with its anarchy. Although Lenin had great dictatorial powers, it was left to his successor Stalin (1879–1953) to rule with absolutely arbitrary force. Lenin died on 21 January 1924, but he had been seriously ill since the previous year and could no longer carry on government business. Although he was deeply concerned about who would succeed him in the leadership of the Union, he could not prevent Stalin from becoming sole ruler of the USSR a few years after his death. With this began a new time of severe suffering for all the stundists.

It is not our task here to depict the character of this sinister figure, who was not bound by any ethical principles. We are interested in Stalin's policies only insofar as they affected freedom of religion. And their effect was terrible, even though Stalin's policies were not immediately recognizable as anti-Christian.

Stalin had already been Secretary-General of the Central Committee of the Party since 1922; in 1929 his opponent Trotsky had to leave Russia. Stalin then removed the other Party chiefs through show trials, until in practice he had acquired total control over the Soviet Union. By the year 1928, the new time of suffering had begun for the believers.

Stalin's Five Year Plans were the instrument he used to bring the whole people into line with his ideological thinking. The enforced collectivization led to the extirpation of the independent peasants. During the 1917 revolution Lenin had won over the majority of the people to his programme with the slogan 'All land to the peasants'. Now the peasant population was uprooted insofar as it clung to farms and property. The 'kulaks', as the free farmers were called, were said to be the obstacle in the way of the people finding happiness through a socialist agrarian policy.

Stalin brought about 'a radicalization of the revolution such as the world had never seen up to that time' (Gutsche). Up to 1928 the Party was still engaged in internal struggles. That is why until that time the believers were largely free to build the congregations and to evangelize. But the Party still had as one of its goals the struggle against all religions. Alongside Martsinkovsky, the leading Tolstoyans Bulgakov and Chertkov were also exiled. The latter actually died in Moscow before he could leave. Prokhanov exploited his good contacts with the west to bring in large sums of money for bible printing. The government was in need of this hard currency from the west, so he was not hindered. In 1926 he printed 25,000 bibles in Leningrad; in 1927, 10,000 Ukrainian bibles in Kiev, 25,000 New Testaments in Leningrad and 10,000 bible concordances. He also printed 40,000 calendars. Of course these figures were quite inadequate in view of the size of the country, nevertheless they testify to Prokhanov's tireless energy. Also, large quantities of bibles were brought in by the western bible societies at that time. Together with the German Mennonites who were constantly active, a missionary society was established called *Mayak* ('Lighthouse'). Understandably, not much information has been preserved about its quiet activity. At that time the elderly Baptist brother Vasili G. Pavlov travelled to Baku as a missionary to the Muslim Tatars.

In the beginning the government tried to carry on the anti-religious struggle on a 'private' basis. It supported the 'League of Militant Godless' founded by Yaroslavsky. The comic and crude methods of this league were unable to make any impression on the stundist front. They even experienced severe defeats, until Stalin made this propaganda and the struggle against all religious belief into a state matter. In July 1928 Odintsov, president of the Russian Baptist Union, was able to attend the Baptist World Congress in Toronto (Canada), where Prokhanov was also present. At a Russian missionary conference, which followed on from this in New York, Odintsov gave a report on the situation of the evangelicals in Russia, which still sounded very optimistic.

'The gospel movement is growing against a background of Orthodox feeling among a spiritually lively population of 114 million. There is a quiet struggle going on for the soul of the people and People's Commissar Lunarcharsky puts the question in his lectures: Who is going to win, the Baptists or the communists? The number of Baptist members is not large, about 200,000; that of the Evangelical Christians is even less, certainly not above that of the Baptists. On the other hand, both movements exercise a mighty influence. Millions of people attend our meetings. The godless are trembling. The struggle with the godless is under way on all fronts. They organize themselves along the same lines as us. When their cells accept members, they oblige them not to drink or smoke, and not to play cards. They are put out for bad behaviour. They say; we'll prove that we can live the same way without God as the Baptists with their God! But the influence of the godless is declining. The editions of their literature have dropped from 400,000 to 70,000. Anti-religious demonstrations and debates have already stopped in many places. Who will conquer? Nobody but the Nazarene!' (Gutsche, *op. cit.*, pp. 61-2).

If optimism is a sign of youthfulness, the stundists may be forgiven for indulging in it. At that time the Russian Baptists had about 3,200 congregations, 3,700 preachers and 1,100 meeting houses. The Union of Evangelical Christians was about the same size.

Before leaving Russia, Prokhanov had made serious plans for a model settlement on Christian communal lines, which he wanted to call 'sun city' or 'Yevangelsk' – 'gospel city'. With his excellent knowledge of Russia, he had found a suitable site in western Siberia and he made his plan public at the tenth Congress of Evangelical Christians in 1927. But he did not get permission from the government since they already had the plans ready for the enforced collectivization of the whole peasant population.

Stalin's iron hand put a terrible end to all these hopeful beginnings.

The beginning of Stalin's first Five Year Plan was set for 1 October 1928. The Bolsheviks with justification call this date the beginning of a second revolution. But in the dictator's words, it was the building of socialism. As well as socialization of agriculture, there was to be a build-up of heavy industry. There was to be a concentration on armaments and economic independence from the west. But there was another goal: the unification of the thinking of all Soviet citizens. Those who had formerly lived a private life were to become people of the collective. This was called the overcoming of capitalist thought. In reality, it was the enslaving of men's consciences. This had the most serious consequences for the evangelical believers. Waldemar Gutsche, who was well acquainted with these events, called it the 'cause of a sea of suffering and tears'. Since wood export to the west was to supply the necessary foreign currency, the great forced labour camps sprang up in the northern forests. The state acquired free labour forces by declaring millions of Soviet citizens suspect of capitalist inclinations, and sentencing them to forced labour. This included the independent farmers and peasants. These 'kulaks' alone are estimated to have numbered five million. Also among these 'suspect' persons were all who still held to a religion. It is true that Karl Marx taught that 'religious needs' would die a natural death in a socialist society, for there would then be no more longing for a 'better world beyond', since the workers' paradise had been set up on earth. But Stalin was not a very faithful disciple of his master. He obviously did not put his trust in this automatic process, and therefore helped it along with the most cruel measures. Thus this former pupil of an Orthodox seminary created a hell on earth.

Paragraph 124 of the new Constitution read: 'In order to ensure to citizens freedom of conscience, the church in the USSR is separated from the state, and the school from the church. Freedom of religious worship and freedom of anti-religious propaganda are recognized for all citizens.'

The first sentence in this paragraph is similar to some in western democracies. But the second sentence makes it clear that only anti-religious propaganda is permitted. The concept of religious worship restricts the congregations to the church buildings. At a pinch, the Orthodox Church with its liturgy could be satisfied with this. But for the Evangelical Christians and Baptists, it meant a significant limitation.

This became even clearer when on 8 April 1929 the following

regulation came into force: 'Religious associations may not: (a) create mutual credit societies, cooperative or commercial undertakings, or in general, use property at their disposal for other than religious purposes; (b) give material help to their members.'

In this way, the mutual service of love which had been binding since the foundation of the Church was forbidden.

Also forbidden was: '(c) to organize for children, young people, and women special prayer or other meetings, circles, groups, departments for biblical or literary study, sewing, working or the teaching of religion, etc., excursions, children's playgrounds, libraries, reading rooms, sanatoria, or medical care. Only books necessary for the purpose of the cult may be kept in the prayer buildings and premises.'

Another paragraph stated that: 'Any kind of teaching of the religious cult in schools, boarding schools, or pre-school establishments maintained by the state, public institutions or private persons is prohibited.'

These regulations and prohibitions hit the work of the stundists very hard. Since the state quickly realized that biblical-evangelical faith was immeasurably more dangerous to its own world-view than Orthodoxy piety, many of these prohibitions were aimed directly against stundism. Evangelical faith trains people for maturity and the independent formation of conscience. It prevents a passive attitude. It was against the above-mentioned paragraphs of Stalin's law that the well-known *initsiativniki* Baptists were later to protest. Since the 1960's these groups have been making appeal to the paragraphs concerning religious freedom, and do not wish to recognize those regulations which restrict it. We shall come back to this.

Preaching was more of a threat to those in power than a liturgy which never changed. For this reason, too, bible printing was prohibited. An edition of 50,000 bibles was confiscated in Moscow. In Odessa, the Baptists had received printing blocks for German bibles and songbooks from the German Baptist Oncken Publishing House in Kassel. Despite permission to print already having been received, everything was confiscated. The brethren were also imprisoned. This took place in 1929.

The rent for church buildings, which were now state property, was arbitrarily increased until it could no longer be met, so that the rooms could be put to 'more profitable uses'.

First, all the active Christians, in other words preachers and elders, were put on the black list. Religion was to lose its leaders. They were counted as *lishentsy*, that is, those who had no electoral rights because they were not engaged in productive work. They did not get ration cards, so that they had to rely on support from the believers, or else pay the high prices of the black market. If they managed to get flats, it would only be on the edge of the towns. As well as this there were crippling taxes which the congregations had to pay for their preachers – often many times higher than their salaries.

Before long all the leaders were in the labour camps. Even house meetings were prohibited, and those who made their flats available for this purpose were imprisoned and carried off. Children were questioned about their parents' religious activity; bibles and songbooks had to be hidden, even buried.

The climax of these repressions seems to have been reached in the years 1935–36. The aim was to put an end to 'all religious prejudices'. Even at that time, an attempt was made to divide the congregations. The authorities tried by means of threats and force to obtain written denials of the faith. The torments that were endured at that time will probably never be known; there is only one who sees all that is hidden.

There was also an indescribable mockery of everything sacred through caricatures, films and so-called 'scientific lectures' on the part of the League of the Godless. Enforced statements requesting the closure of the churches camouflaged Party measures as 'the will of the people'. Seldom have so many lies been told. 'One really had the impression that the struggle with religion was over and all interest in it had vanished,' writes Gutsche.

Nevertheless, at the eighth extraordinary Congress of the soviets in December 1936, Stalin rejected an express prohibition of religious cults; this did not correspond to the 'spirit of our Constitution', he said. But this was nothing more than a show-window for the west. There was no need to prohibit what seemed already dead. Also, National Socialism, in which Stalin recognized a dangerous enemy, had come to power in Germany.

Much of what happened in individual cases can no longer be definitely established. The Russian Baptist Union seems to have been harder hit than Prokhanov's Union of Evangelical Christians. This may have had to do with the links between the Baptists and the Baptist World Alliance. It is well known that dictators do not like international alliances of this kind. (Prokhanov did not establish his world alliance of Evangelical Christians until he found himself permanently in the west.) The Baptist meeting halls were soon requisitioned. The theological seminary which had been founded in Moscow was closed. The Baptist Union was dissolved in 1929 (other sources say March 1935). In 1936 the Baptist congregation in Moscow was itself dissolved. In the Ukraine, everything happened a few years later.

The Secretary-General of the Union of Evangelical Christians, Alexander V. Karev (died 1972), moved to Moscow in 1930, because the government wanted all headquarters to be located in the capital. This office still seems to have been in existence at the outbreak of the war. It is not known how many of the congregations were able to survive.

While the great persecution under Pobedonostsev, which was equally harsh, took place unambiguously 'for the faith', the Bolshevik GPU continually levelled political accusations, made slanders and denunciations which could not be checked, held secret trials or took open police measures, all of which created a general insecurity and mutual suspicion. This was the most damaging thing during that period. People never knew who had been suborned to act as an informer. Thus false denunciations were used to play one group off against another. As in the persecution of Christians under the old Roman emperors, now too there were *lapsi* – apostates. The trials and massive threats caused many to grow weak. We cannot judge them. On the other hand, a great number of people suffered in camps, prisons and exile and kept the faith.

On 22 June 1941 Hitler broke the treaty which had been made a few years before and his armies attacked the Soviet Union without cause and without a declaration of war. This was the beginning of the most terrible war Russia had ever experienced.

Stalin now made a certain change of policy direction, at least at official level. As early as 1938 *Izvestia* published an article which caused quite a stir; to the great surprise of readers, it evaluated the introduction of Christianity by Prince Vladimir of Kiev as a 'progressive event'! One professor had the job of holding lectures in the Academy of Sciences and even in the League of Godless to the effect that 'The Christianity of the New Testament actually played an important role in the development of social and national justice and introduced better family relationships and morals among the people'. One can imagine the amazement on the faces of the comrades from the ranks of the Militant Godless at this news coming from a competent source, not even from a church pulpit! Nothing changed in the treatment of the oppressed believers. The only difference was that the magazines of the godless now also disappeared due to 'paper shortage', just like the Christian magazines under Hitler. But Stalin had to take into account his western allies, for England under Churchill and the USA under Roosevelt were concerned about tolerance in religious policy.

But there was another side to it. Hitler's unqualified attack upon the Soviet Union awakened in the whole people a new national feeling. It was with justification that the government called this the 'fatherland war'. Stalin naturally protected every movement that could prop up his shaky throne. But the wave of national feeling was by no means invented in the Kremlin; this would be a short-sighted conclusion. In fact the people were waging a war of liberation against a foreign conqueror, just as they had done 150 years previously.

In the Russian Orthodox Church too, which had always been a bulwark of nationalism, the old patriotism now sprang into new life. It was Alexi, Bishop of Leningrad, later successor to Patriarch Sergi, who led the Church into battle. Sergi had previously demonstrated his loyalty to the Soviet state and expressly re-buffed the attacks of the so-called Karlovtsy Synod, the conserva-tive forces of Orthodoxy in the emigration. It can come as no surprise to find him, as representative of the Orthodox Church, at the side of the government in the beginning of the war. Nor can it be made into a reproach against him. At the same time, during the first months of the war Stalin's government was in extreme danger, and if Hitler and his Party had not been so blind, they could have used this probably unique opportunity to put an end to the Bolshevik rule. But Hitler had no idea how to win friends in the lands he conquered. Although at first the Orthodox churches were re-opened in the area occupied by the Germans, and baptisms took place, this was soon prohibited by the short-sighted Nazis. The stupid and often cruel treatment of the population created countless partisans who later, during the German retreat, only hastened the defeat of Hitler's army.

Stalin knew how to exploit the repression of the people; he strengthened the enthusiasm for the war and accepted the help offered by the Church which he was persecuting. It may seem regrettable to us that the Church should have raised eight million roubles to form a tank division which then took the name of Saint Dmitri Donskoi, the sacrificial and courageous opponent of the Mongols. But even this we have no right to judge. For Russia it was a question of life or death. Bishop Alexi's conduct during the years of siege in Leningrad, in which the need was indescribable, was exemplary, and it was only fair that Stalin should have recognized this. So a milder policy was put into effect with regard to the Church. In September 1943 Sergi, Metropolitan Alexi of Leningrad and Metropolitan Nikolai of Krutitsy were received in audience by Stalin and Molotov. Nikolai later became the head of the Foreign Department of the Orthodox Church for many years. The Church was now permitted to hold a *sobor*, a council, which has always been the supreme church gathering in the Eastern Church, to which even patriarchs must defer. It is true that this was only a modest gathering, which elected Sergi as patriarch; still it was done according to the proper form.

This alliance, loose though it may have been, between the Bolshevik government and the Orthodox Church also benefited the evangelical movement, both the Evangelical Christians and the Baptists. Since there was no such obvious patriotic movement in these communities – although the evangelical Christians maintained complete loyalty to their native land and state – it took somewhat longer before they felt the 'thaw'. Many of those who had survived returned from the labour camps, although unfortunately a large number of believers had perished from the hardships and probably also mistreatment they had suffered, including leading men such as Odintsov and Timoshenko, who had given tremendous service to the Baptist movement. It is not possible to estimate with certainty the number of those who perished.

In October 1944 there was a combined conference of Evangelical Christians and Baptists in Moscow. Those present from the Evangelical Christians were Yakov Ivanovich Zhidkov senior, Alexander V. Karev, Andreyev and Orlov. The Baptist side was led by Levindanto. There was also an affirmatory telegram from Golyayev, the last president of the Baptist Union, for it was on this occasion that the long-sought-for union of the two alliances took place – unfortunately, only under pressure of circumstances. There were 28 Evangelical Christians and 19 Baptists present when the 'All-Union Council of Evangelical Christians-Baptists' was formed, which still brings together the great majority of stundists in the Soviet Union today. The new union was given the former German Reformed church in Moscow (Maly Vuzovsky pereulok No. 3). This is still the well-known stundist church in Moscow, where services lasting about two hours are held three times on Sunday and on three weekday evenings.

The union was soon joined by a number of Pentecostal congregations, the so-called 'mild Pentecostals', who had to promise not to interrupt the services by speaking in tongues. As far as we know, they have kept to this promise.

III   SINCE THE LAST WAR AND TODAY

With this, our historical review of the birth and development of stundism is really at an end. With the obvious lack of authentic sources, our description is only an attempt to cover the subject and we welcome corrections from those who have access to more precise sources. Not even the leaders in Moscow have a complete grasp of the details involved in the rise of stundism. When President Zhidkov and Secretary-General Karev wanted to celebrate the centenary of stundism in 1960, they asked us for historical material on early stundism. Thus there is little grounds to hope that we may learn any important new information about that time from Russia itself.

However, some data on the years after 1945 may be established. We must also attempt some basic observations. On the whole the Soviet Union has perpetuated the custom of Tsar Nicholas II: under political pressure, some freedoms are granted, but these are again restricted over a period of time. In our press, these strange twists and turns are called 'thaw' and 'freeze'. Often the changes are quite unexpected, like alterations in the weather. However, one cannot on these grounds call Soviet religious policy 'unpredictable'. Its goal always remains the 'eradication of religious prejudices', even though the methods used to this end may vary. In this respect, Bolshevism since Lenin has been very changeable. But the dialectical materialism of the east is dogmatically conservative and thus inexorable. Here and there the realization seems to have dawned that religious attitudes have not disappeared of their own accord with the introduction of socialist economic reforms, as was expected by early Marxism. It is not only the old *babushki*, the grandmothers, who keep the meetings going, but there are also many young people; in many places, despite atheist schools and the lack of any church work among children and young people, there are just as many young people as in the west. This ought to give any serious observer food for thought. After more than half a century of Bolshevik education and propaganda, 'religious prejudices' have grown rather than diminished, not to mention disappeared. Thus, either the Soviet Union is not truly Marxist – and in the Soviet Union this charge is worse than *lèse-majesté* in the time of the tsars! – or else the doctrine that religion can only exist in feudal or capitalist states is wrong! These are the only two possibilities.

Just eight years after the end of the war, Stalin died. The Georgian from the Caucasus was a sinister figure, whose death was welcomed even by his comrades in the Party. Eight years after that his corpse was removed from the mausoleum beside Lenin, where like Lenin he was to receive an almost religious worship. The significance of Stalin for history is that he transformed the Soviet Union into an industrial state. But he 'achieved this only by creating a totalitarian rule of force, the inhuman consequences of which were the complete opposite of the end goal originally set by Marx. Stalin was a dictator who even changed the Party into an 'apparatus' over which he, as a master of the unscrupulous use of organized power, had complete control' (*Biographisches Lexikon zur Weltgeschichte*).

It was to be expected that Stalin's death should have brought about a period of thaw. But Khrushchev too, who succeeded Stalin after a brief interregnum, introduced new repressions. This man with his marked peasant cunning, made a somewhat more sympathetic impression than Stalin (whom he put down at the Party Congress) because of his coarseness, but also his peasant humour. But his hatred of the Church and the faith was barely less than Stalin's. It is difficult to follow the ins and outs of the treatment of believers in individual cases. He also took severe action against the Orthodox Church, closing monasteries and seminaries and countless churches. He too was a dictator and held to the principle that the whole people must come into ideological line. Since the state was atheist on principle, he mistrusted all religious attitudes. There was occasional recognition that Christians were honest and often indispensable because of their conscientiousness and loyalty. Many Christians were valued and protected in their jobs because of their hard work. There are many rumours, which cannot be verified, that Christians handled the money in government trade and finance bodies, because there was then no danger of embezzlement.

For more than fifty years, we in the west have been subjected to an anti-Soviet propaganda which also has its freezes and thaws. For this reason it is almost impossible for us to form an objective picture. The Russians have always been gifted actors and they know how to build Potëmkin villages, that is, to give visitors the best possible impression. Thus a certain degree of mistrust is justified. The judgment then is: 'It's all propaganda'. But this is still not an objective picture.

The fact is that the All-Union Council of Evangelical Christians-Baptists brings together more than 5,000 larger or smaller congregations. The biblical gospel, pure and undefiled, is preached in these churches both on Sundays and on weekdays. Undoubtedly spiritual life does not stand at the same level in all places. And if the Moscow church is filled every Sunday with one to two thousand worshippers, and the services on three weekday evenings, for those who have to work on Sunday, have a similar attendance, one must remember that this meeting room is simply not large enough for the evangelicals in Moscow, a city of eight million inhabitants. The fact that there are more women and old people than young worshippers should not surprise us in the west. It is no different with us. In fact, visitors constantly emphasize the striking number of young people among church attenders. We have countless examples of this. We have read repeated complaints in Russian communist papers that the offices of the *komsomol* (communist youth league) in one place or another were hardly being used because young people were 'allowing sectarians to clog up their minds'. Such complaints in the Party press carry greater weight than observations by individual visitors. Besides, the elderly today have been exposed to atheist propaganda for almost sixty years, and they too were young when that began. Thus it is certainly not a question of a few surviving religious attitudes from the monarchist time, which in any case did little to help the stundists.

Believers' baptism is carried out after a period of examination which often lasts for some time. Many candidates must wait up to two years. And since the ones baptized cannot expect any outward gain, rather numerous unpleasantnesses and difficulties, if not actual threats, this means that congregations are growing with very few hangers-on. Most congregations certainly have to reckon with informers and are closely watched.

But it would be very unfair to devalue the registered congregations as 'government-pleasers' or even 'traitors'. Here we touch on a delicate contemporary question. It is well known that since the 1960's a group of believers – albeit considerably fewer in number – have split away from the Moscow leadership of the All-Union Council. Sometimes called the *initsiativniki*, they are also often referred to as the reform Baptists. They protest against the police methods which since Stalin have restricted the religious liberty which is guaranteed in the Constitution. They are particularly concerned at the prohibition of religious education of children by the congregations. Here they appeal to the apostle's word: 'We must obey God rather than men'. Thus they seek to gather children secretly in meetings – in summer in the forests, in winter in private homes – and to instruct them. They have also protested on many occasions against the prohibition on evangelism through public meetings and through books and tracts, by engaging in precisely these activities. They have celebrated baptisms quite openly and here and there distributed tracts on the streets. All this is considered a violation of the law. Religious propaganda is severely punished. 'You can preach what you like in your church buildings, but you're not to do anything outside,' it is said. Since the printing of bibles and songbooks is very restricted and has only been permitted a few times in insufficient editions – not to mention other Christian literature – these groups try to fill the gap with secret printing presses. For the word of God is the vital bread of life. With incredible courage and submission young people, and even fathers of families, risk their freedom and often their health to spread the testimony of Jesus Christ among young and old. Many have gone underground for years, sought by the state police, living without identity papers and constantly on the move, ministering among young people or working with literature.

It is probably also true that many of these groups have applied for registration, but in vain, and so going underground is the only answer, unless they are willing to give themselves up. This new wave of testimony among the stundists deserves our highest regard. What causes us concern is the discord between brethren. These 'illegal' believers consider the 'registered' as traitors, because they give way to the restrictive police regulations. The latter, on the other hand, appeal to Paul's word, writing to the

Romans at the time of the Emperor Nero, the prototype of the anti-christ: 'Let every person be subject to the governing authorities. For there is no authority except from God, and those that exist have been instituted by God. Therefore he who resists the authorities resists what God has appointed, and those who resist will incur judgment' (Romans 13.1,2). See also I Peter 2.13 ff. Thus the leaders in Moscow feel themselves bound in conscience to obey even an anti-christian government in its regulations. God sets such governments as a judgment over the nations. Any revolutionary protest seems to them disobedience before God. They are strengthened in their attitude – most of them having themselves spent years in the labour camps – by the fact that for decades they have been able to preach the gospel and there are also many young people in their meetings.

Religious statistics in the Soviet Union are very dubious. It would appear that the government has set a figure of between 500,000 and 550,000 church members as acceptable. This figure has now been repeated for twenty years, even though the movement is constantly spreading and the losses through the death of members cannot be that large. It is certainly no longer accurate. In any case it is only referring to those who have been baptized as believers, who are the only ones that can be counted as full members. Obviously the number of those who listen to the preaching is many times greater. It is reckoned that there are four to five million people who hear the gospel more or less regularly. The brethren in Moscow do not wish to jeopardize this tremendous opportunity for preaching the gospel.

The German Mennonites have also joined the All-Union Council of Evangelical Christians-Baptists. It is difficult to name a figure here.

It is likely that in many places, the Germans Lutherans also attend these services. It is reckoned that there are some two million Germans in the Soviet Union. A large number of them may have yielded to communist propaganda. Nevertheless there are a number of registered German Lutheran congregations in Siberia and Turkestan, notably in Tselinograd where the last recognized German pastor, Eugen Bachmann, laboured for some decades with blessing. There are also supposed to be registered German Lutheran congregations in Frunze, Omsk, Tomsk, Chelyabinsk, Karangada and Alma-Ata. People also speak of 'hundreds of German house fellowships' which gather for bible study without official registration.

The fact that the all-powerful Party tries to infiltrate the registered congregations will come as no surprise to those who have lived under dictatorships. This cannot be laid as a charge against the believers and their leaders. The use of informers and spies is certainly not a Bolshevik invention. It was commonplace in the empire of Napoleon I, the old Habsburg monarchy, and under the tsars. Usually one member can be forced under pressure to betray detailed information of meetings and private conversations to the state police. These poor creatures are often well known. People avoid them, but it is difficult to get rid of them. This easily creates an atmosphere of mistrust which can only be overcome by complete openness. Many lies are told in the Soviet Union. The fact that the believers make every effort to be truthful is one of their outstanding qualities. Nevertheless there are secrets and silences and other things which come close to untruthfulness. But let us be careful of judging even here. Everyone knows the conflicts that can rise between truth and love – one might think of the situation with those who are critically ill – and thus none of us is justified in throwing stones, especially from the grandstand of the 'free west'.

Even the unregistered believers, who live in complete freedom and without the protection of law, have to camouflage their actions and hide themselves. Even when they bear courageous and public testimony – especially at trials – they do not easily betray their friends and followers.

It remains a matter of much sorrow that a reconciliation between the registered and unregistered believers has still not been possible. Individuals cross from one camp to the other. The radical unregistered believers demand from the Moscow All-Union Council a surrender and admission of guilt. The Moscow brethren on the other hand demand that the others give up their illegal activity. It is conscience against conscience. As Luther declared before the Emperor and the Diet in Worms: 'It is not good to do anything contrary to one's conscience.'

The fact that groups of unregistered believers have repeatedly asked for registration by the government authorities, and been refused, gives rise to the suspicion that the split is welcomed by the Party. It permits the state both courses of action: the ruthless persecution of some Christians as lawbreakers, and the demonstration of its own tolerance, by pointing to others who are registered.

Not long ago, a former soldier in the Bolshevik army told us about a conversation he had with an officer. The young Christian complained that he had no freedom to believe. The officer on the other hand tried to convince him about the freedom guaranteed to him. In so doing, he pointed to the barracks library, holding several thousand books. The soldier was not satisfied.

'But there's *one* book that I'm not allowed to read – the bible.'

'Yes, that's forbidden.'

'You see! What kind of freedom is that, which forbids me to read the bible!'

This question is writ large over the gigantic Russian empire. Their fear of the bible is perhaps the strongest possible apologetic for this book. It might endanger this powerful state!

'His word runs swiftly,' it says in Psalm 147. This has been true for more than 160 years in the great land of Russia and among the peoples whom it has subjected and ruled. The stundist movement is still today one of the greatest proofs of the truth of this word; its enemies can cause much suffering for those who accept it – they have done so, and are still doing it today. But in the end they will come to grief on this word.

'Is not my word like fire, says the Lord, and like a hammer which breaks the rock in pieces?' (Jer. 23.29).

The Christian congregation testifies:

'Thy words were found, and I ate them, and thy words became to me a joy and the delight of my heart' (Jer. 15.16).

Epilogue

Finally, it is worth asking the question: What is special about this revival and bible movement, one of the greatest in church history?

We are not concerned with the particular pre-conditions of a historical, sociological, psychological and ethnological kind. We know, too, that all living movements of faith arise from hidden spiritual workings, which escape the mind that tries to calculate and draw conclusions. In the end, there remains a mystery.

Twice in its hundred years history, stundism has been threatened by a systematic attempt to exterminate it: in the last decade of the previous century through Pobedonostsev, and in the fourth decade of the present century through Stalin. But today it remains, stronger than ever. What has given it its power to endure and to spread?

The first thing that must be emphasized is that the faith movement among the stundists brings together in a healthy manner the objective and the subjective aspects of faith. That is, it has always been a *bible movement*. The bible is read; people know that it is God's word, and feed on it, the yardstick of all actions.

At the same time, stundism has not fallen prey to an 'orthodox' attitude to doctrine. It knows how necessary is the subjective appropriation of the biblical message. Personal repentance and thus *personal conversion* are expected. Yet stundism, as far as we can tell, is not an 'experience' movement. People speak of Christ, of the love of God, of his faithfulness and his will. Despite some incursions of over-enthusiastic circles, the movement as a whole has remained a sober one.

In the second place, stundism is and has always been a *missionary movement*. For this reason, it could never rest content with the atheist suggestion: 'you can preach and believe what you like within your own services'. 'We cannot but speak of what we have seen and heard.' This apostolic word is also true of the stundists. Although one branch may be more militant, and another more reserved, they both train their members for genuine, existential testimony. There are many examples of this.

In the third place, this testimony is upheld by a profound *belief in the truth of the message of Jesus*. All the fanatical efforts of the militant leagues of the godless and atheists, with their lame intellectualism, have made no impression on the actual realm of personal conviction. 'We stand for truth' – the stundists are sure of this. They may succeed in drawing away young and immature people! Again and again, the atheist propagandists trained by the state have to admit their lack of success. Seen as a whole, the stundists stand rock-firm. They do not find it strange that 'the world' is unbelieving. Most of them have been like that themselves. The stundists knows the enticing power of the 'prince of this world', they know that he is the 'father of lies' and that he blinds men to the truth. But the congregation of Jesus consists of members who have been 'set free by the truth', as Jesus says. They live in this truth.

In the fourth place, the faith of the stundists is founded on *certainty concerning the omnipotence of God*. 'Nothing can touch me outside his will.' One may call this fatalism, but it is really the glad obedience of a redeemed conscience. The man who is condemned accepts his exile from God's hand. 'I shall stay here as long as my God wants me to,' the convict says to his gaolers. With the assurance that 'God has numbered my hairs!' he walks along his path of suffering. He is only concerned with God. The fact that complaints and accusations still come from the mouth of those who are being tormented is human, and should not surprise us.

In the fifth and last place, one should not forget the *great capacity for suffering among the Russian people*, who have only rarely enjoyed freedom in the course of a thousand years history. The ancestors of these stundists were serfs, i.e. slaves, for generations. And before that, the people lay for centuries under the Mongol yoke. They have truly learned the meaning of suffering. But for the disciples of Jesus, suffering becomes part of worship and the testimony of life.

These five characteristic qualities of stundism should be yardsticks for Christianity; we ought to meditate on them.

Stundism knows that Christians who allow themselves to be motivated by the bible, are missionaries in the assurance that the word of Jesus is true and God is all-powerful – their suffering is worship and testimony.

'. . . and the gates of hell shall not prevail against it,' Jesus says of his Church.

FURTHER READING on the contemporary period

Religious Ferment in Russia by Michael Bourdeaux, Macmillan, London, 1968.

Faith on Trial in Russia by Michael Bourdeaux, Hodder and Stoughton, London, 1975.

Aida of Leningrad by Michael Bourdeaux and Xenia Howard-Johnston, Mowbrays, London and Oxford, 1976.

Church State and Opposition in the U.S.S.R. by Gerhard Simon, C. Hurst and Co., London, 1974.

Christians under the Hammer and Sickle by Winrich Scheffbuch, Zondervan, Grand Rapids, 1974.

Vanya by Myrna Grant, Victory Press, Eastbourne, 1975.

Three Generations of Suffering by Georgi Vins, Hodder and Stoughton, London, 1976.

Index

207